THE VERNACULAR MUSE

Dennis Cooley was born in Estevan, Saskatchewan. He teaches Canadian and American Literature in St. John's College at the University of Manitoba. He is the editor of *Draft*, an anthology of prairie poetry, and *RePlacing*, a collection of essays on prairie writing. His books of poetry include *Leaving*, *Fielding*, *Bloody Jack* and *Soul Searching*. He has three books of poetry forthcoming: *Dedications*, *Short Circuit* and *Children of Light*.

THE VERNACULAR MUSE:

THE EYE AND EAR IN CONTEMPORARY LITERATURE

DENNIS COOLEY

TURNSTONE PRESS

Published with the assistance of the Canada Council
and the Manitoba Arts Council.

Turnstone Press
607-100 Arthur Street
Winnipeg, Manitoba
R3B 1H3

This book was printed by Hignell Printing Limited for
Turnstone Press.

Printed in Canada.

Cover design: David Morrow.

The Vernacular Muse continues a series of literary
criticism published by Turnstone Press. Other titles in
the series include *Surviving the Paraphrase: Eleven Essays
on Canadian Literature* by Frank Davey, *The Family
Romance* by Eli Mandel, and *Trace: Prairie Writers on
Writing*, edited by Birk Sproxton.

Canadian Cataloguing in Publication Data

Cooley, Dennis, 1944-

The vernacular muse

Includes bibliographical references.
ISBN 0-88801-124-5

1. Canadian literature (English) — 20th century —
History and criticism.* I. Title.

PS8071.C65 1987   C810′.9′005   C87-098141-2
PR9189.6.C65 1987

to Ken Hughes David Arnason and Wayne Tefs
who help me read

to Wayne Tefs especially
who as editor has helped me write this book

Other books by Dennis Cooley

Leaving, 1980
RePlacing, Editor, 1980
Draft: an anthology of prairie poetry, Editor, 1981
Fielding, 1983
Bloody Jack, 1984
Soul Searching, 1987

Earlier versions of some of these essays have appeared as follows:

"Antimacassared in the Wilderness: Art and Nature in *The Stone Angel*," in *Mosaic*, 11, No. 3 (Spring 1978), 29-46.

"Some Principles of Line Breaks," in Birk Sproxton, ed., *Trace: Prairie Writers on Writing* (Winnipeg: Turnstone, 1986), pp. 141-56.

"Breaking and Entering: A Workshop on Line Breaks," in *A View from the Loft*, 9, No. 4 (December 1986), 1, 8-10.

"Breaking & Entering (thoughts on line breaks)," in *Open Letter* (Spring 1987), Sixth Series, No. 7, 77-99.

"The Vernacular Muse in Prairie Poetry" (part 1), in *Prairie Fire*, 7, No. 4 (Winter 1986-87), 24-36.

"The Vernacular Muse in Prairie Poetry" (part 2), in *Prairie Fire*, 8, No. 1 (Spring 1987), 60-70.

"The Vernacular Muse in Prairie Poetry" (part 3), in *Prairie Fire*, 8, No. 2 (Summer 1987), 49-53.

" 'I Am Here on the Edge': Modern Hero / Postmodern Poetics in *The Collected Works of Billy the Kid*" in Sam Solecki, ed., *Spider Blues: Essays on Michael Ondaatje* (Montreal: Vehicule, 1985), pp. 211-39.

Patterns of discourse are regulated through the forms of corporate assembly in which they are produced. Alehouse, coffee-house, church, law court, library, drawing room of a country mansion: each place of assembly is a different site of intercourse requiring different manners and morals. Discursive space is never completely independent of social place and the formation of new kinds of speech can be traced through the emergence of new public sites of discourse and the transformation of old ones. Each 'site of assembly' constitutes a nucleus of material and cultural conditions which regulate what may and may not be said, who may speak, how people may communicate and what importance must be given to what is said. An utterance is legitimated or disregarded according to its place of production and so, in large part, the history of political struggle has been the history of the attempts made to control significant sites of assembly and spaces of discourse.

—Peter Stallybrass & Allon White, *The Politics & Poetics of Transgression* (Ithaca, N.Y.: Cornell, 1986), p. 80.

"The bastards can't keep us from talking."

—Robert Kroetsch

PREFACE

Books of essays are of three kinds—the pedestrian, the pedantic, and the polemic. We see surprising numbers of the former given the general enthusiasm for criticism now, and depressing volumes of the pedantic, stuffy things usually, barely surpassing the belles lettres of the late nineteenth century. The polemic category itself breaks down into the merely polemic on the one hand, and on the other forceful writing that treats both texts and their larger political contexts with intelligence. This book falls into the latter category. It's feisty. If you're among those who still hold with the Great Tradition or the notion of artistic genius you'll be challenged by some of Cooley's statements. Maybe even offended. Fortunately, Cooley's brought a wealth of recent scholarship to bear on his remarks, so you'll have a lot of people to be miffed at—not just him. One of the first pieces you might want to turn to is the title essay. The scope of literary knowledge evident there is matched by the acuity with which Cooley treats the entire canon of English literature. The piece on line breaks further on is, to my knowledge, unique in criticism. The studies of Dorothy Livesay's poetry and Sinclair Ross's short fiction have all the invention of the best readings plus a generosity usually abandoned in undergraduate work. As do the examinations of Robert Duncan's "Poem Beginning with a Line by Pindar," and Michael Ondaatje's *Collected Works of Billy the Kid*. All show a fine mind playing with the possibilities of texts, a gracious mind, a fair and committed mind. If you enjoy the book as much as I have, you'll read most of it a second time.

—Wayne Tefs

CONTENTS

PLACING THE VERNACULAR: THE EYE AND THE EAR IN SASKATCHEWAN POETRY

> In the end, we come to the point at which we realize that the quality of symbolic and conceptual thinking of which human beings are capable, and which is mediated by the frontal lobes which begin with little monkeys—that quality combines two extraordinary human gifts: the gift of the eye and the gift of the ear. . . . We learn most about people through the ear. We learn most about nature through the eye.
>
> —J. Bronowski, *The Visionary Eye*[1]

Since I have already written elsewhere and at length on the vernacular in prairie poetry, and since our appreciation of any writing depends on our sense of where it 'fits,' I propose here to explore a simple but, I think, useful distinction between two strains of prairie poetry.[2] The differences will not, of course, be absolute—they never are—but they will be apparent. I am, as my title implies, proposing that we can divvy up most Saskatchewan poetry under two jurisdictions—the eye and the ear. What I mean by "ear" poetry would correspond roughly to "vernacular" and what I am thinking of as "eye" poetry would compare to work commonly put in opposition to "vernacular," namely work that respects some combination of imagist, metaphoric, or expressive precepts.

Before I get into this division, let me say what I do *not* mean by "ear" poetry. The term, as I am using it, does not mean that "eye" poets lack, as we say, 'a good ear.' They may or they may not, it all depends on their play of words, the facility with which they use rhyme or rhythm or other principles of sound. But when they do use rhyme, it is often inconspicuous, in 'free' verse seldom anchoring lines by opening or closing them but distributed irregularly and lightly within the text: through assonance, consonance, alliteration, half-rhyme, visual rhyme; in short, within the phonetic resources of poetry as they have been developed and laid down in the twentieth century. By virtue of their wide practice such devices have been by now rendered familiar and therefore 'natural.' "Ear" poetry is no less concerned with sound but because it draws on speech it largely forgoes such nuance and instead abides by whatever sorts of rhymes—alliteration, emphatic repetitions in morphology, and puns (homonyms)— situate themselves in spoken language where sheer speed will not allow us to lounge or languish, or find time to adjust the text in small measures to itself. It should be apparent that what's at issue here—and I want to stress this because listeners for some reason do not always hear what I am saying—is *not* verbal or even prosodic skill. What I *am* saying is that poetry in this province arguably is being written under two very different auspicies, which it behooves us to recognize and to understand; and further, that "eye" poetry too readily enjoys, by way of its established and therefore lauded forms, some presumption of superiority.

At the risk of digression I want to take just a few minutes to make some pointed comments about that presumption. I am assuming here that ignorance is no virtue in these matters—it never is—and that to take a certain activity for granted can be downright authoritarian: my poems are 'natural,' yours are 'artificial'; my language natural as grasshoppers, yours phoney as a dictionary (or an academic's talk). Here is what Charles Bernstein has to say about this manoeuvre:

> What I want to call attention to is that there is no natural writing style; that the preference for its supposed manifestations is simply a preference for a particular look to poetry & often a particular vocabulary (usually perceived as personal themes); that this preference (essentially a procedural decision to work within a certain domain sanctified into a rite of poetry) actually obscures the understanding of the work which appears to be its honoured bases; & especially that the cant of "make it personal" & "let it flow" are avoidances—by mystification—of some very compelling problems that swirl around truthtelling, confession, bad faith, false self, authenticity, virtue, etc.[3]

We have the spectacle of literary Mounties who think their practice, recognizable as 'poetry,' needs no defence, that others must face the hard-headedness of *their* questions, their unblinking capacity to search out fraud and incompetence and other criminal acts (theorizing, for example). I would suggest to you that this is a form of tyranny and the sooner we realize that honoured forms, like any other forms, wobble through history and nationality, the better off we all will be.

Peter Berger and Thomas Luckmann have shown in *The Social Construction of Reality* how institutions get established and perpetuated. (I quote at length since this slices to the heart of what I have to say.) Once those formations have taken shape, Berger and Luckmann say, they are then

> experienced as existing over and beyond the individuals who 'happen to' embody them at the moment. In other words, the institutions are now experienced as possessing a reality of their own, a reality that confronts the individual as an external and coercive fact.
>
> As long as the nascent institutions are constructed and maintained only in the interaction of *A* and *B*, their

> objectivity remains tenuous, easily changeable, almost playful. . . . [T]he routinized background of *A*'s and *B*'s activity remains fairly accessible to deliberate intervention by *A* and *B*. Although the routines, once established, carry with them a tendency to persist, the possibility of changing them or even abolishing them remains at hand in consciousness. *A* and *B* alone are responsible for having constructed this world. *A* and *B* remain capable of changing or abolishing it. . . . They understand the world that they themselves have made [and can unmake]. All this changes in the process of transmission to the new generation. The objectivity of the institutional world 'thickens' and 'hardens,' not only for the children, but (by a mirror effect) for the parents as well. The 'There we go again' now becomes 'This is how these things are done.' A world so regarded attains a firmness in consciousness; it becomes real in an ever more massive way and it can no longer be changed so readily. For the children, especially in the early phase of their socialization into it, it becomes *the* world. For the parents, it loses its playful quality and becomes 'serious.' For the children, the parental world . . . [s]ince they had no part in shaping it . . . confronts them as a given reality. . . .[4]

This is how these things are done, my people, as I myself have done them, for some time now. Natural as the grass that breathes. At hand, immutable as marble, self-evident. As a matter of course.

I'm afraid that for want of time my remarks will have to be fairly gnomic and may therefore seem arbitrary. For those who want to examine some further basis for what I say here, I can tell you that I am drawing heavily on Walter J. Ong, whose writings have explored the impact of media on various periods of culture: oral, chirographic (writing or manuscript), typographic, and electronic culture. He further distinguishes between the orality we find early in any culture, naming that "primary orality," and the orality we develop in an electronic age which, though oral, is hugely shaped by textual awareness, calling that more recent orality "secondary orality."[5] My "ear" poetry would coincide fairly well with Ong's "secondary orality."

To return to my claim, then: in prairie poetry the (rhetorical) sense of place takes one of two major forms. The first is fairly traditional and centres on the eye. The second is more recent (in the history of poetry but less so in the history of prairie poetry) and centres on the ear. The first concentrates on landscape, the second on speech. If the one, as is often observed, uses anecdote, it is equally true to say the other depends on vignette. I will need a few minutes to outline the two categories. Before I do so, let me quote the two examples I will consider. Here is the first illustration, this one of what I am calling "eye" poetry:

> start with
> the journey back
>   the raw beginning
>   it is
> not a remembered place
> it is forgotten & imagined
>
> my father's land
>   the green hills   always
>   green
> tall kauri/rainforest
>   mists fingering
>   through trees   ghosts
>   tread softly
> the archives of leafmold
>
> my father's land
>   where sea is
>   the constant
>   tide
> moving in & out of my ear
> the trumpet shell echoing
>   the seagulls' cry
>   the drumming waves[6]

Here is the second piece we will be looking at, this an instance of my "ear" poetry:

> Scrawny's got himself this nifty sorta knob dealie
> ya clamp onto one sidea your steerin wheel
> Gotta be onea the greatest gizmos invented
> Imagine ya got your arm around some dame eh
> ya just grabaholda this here doomajig
> spin it around hard, lay it to the boards
> and no trouble at all ya got yourself a doughnut
> and the dame's smeared against ya real romantic like[7]

We will return to these two examples, but not before some general observations.

First, the poetry by eye. This poetry favours description, often of landscape, and it usually observes some correspondence between 'inside' and 'outside.' Often as not it takes its origins in Imagism and privileges vision. The poet, as observer, as person of the eye, looks out upon a world, usually but not necessarily 'nature,' to a significant degree detached from it, at least in any physical way. In many such poems, the poet observes some landscape at a middle distance, describes it in a few concrete details, and assumes that what is 'out there' stands for what is 'in here.' Set apart from what she observes, uninvolved in it other than in her capacity as isolated observer and respondent, unengaged in any dialogue, she looks out upon a world, sometimes as it exists in the mind's eye, a realm that is passive and like as not silent.

More centrally, the poet speaks in 'serious' tones and serves as originator of meaning, as one who de-scribes the world in telling images, or who in-scribes herself in it as producer of tropes—generally a flourish of fresh metaphors. This means the poet centres the poem personally, gives rise to its perceptions or conceptions, and guarantees its meaning and significance. The claim here—and I'm now getting to the centre of my thesis—extends Romantic theories of art. There are various ways of describing that aesthetic, but what I say will not surprise students of Romanticism or of the post-Romanticism which many believe has been with us ever since. "Eye" poems find their endorsement in the lyrical "I" which watches over them and in them. This "I" is for the most part contemplative, inward, emotive, sensitive, private. It is also understated. Because the speaker seeks to account for what she sees, she assumes her language largely to be referential, that is to embody, to body forth, to imitate, to show the world that is *there*. And because she operates in this economy, she migrates toward an Imagist or a referential sense of language. For such writers language ought to be brief, ought not to be 'verbose' or prolix. The thinking is consistent: if you assume words only refer or at their best refer and convey information about something there, you will grow impatient with writing that seems to repeat itself, that seems to give us the same old information all over again. In a sense all poetry is repetitive, and these "eye" poems, too, are heavily so in their modulation of theme or metaphor or scene. They certainly are in their dense reflexivity. But in "ear" poetry there is a more obvious form of repetition we're talking about. My point in raising the question of brevity will become more apparent in a moment.

I will be returning to more features of "eye" poetry, but first let's have a look at what characterizes "ear" poetry. Again, bear in mind that we're talking about differences in degree, and that we can find to some extent a few of these features in "eye" poetry. Still, we can discern important distinctions. For one thing, "ear" language tends to be anything but metaphoric, nuanced, or intricately cadenced. On the contrary, it is vernacular and, instead of speaking in soliloquy, it enacts roles, presents selves (plural rather than singular in its loyalties), rhetorically appeals to some audience, real or imagined. Imploring, scolding, teasing, begging, cajoling, exhorting, praying—it addresses someone and seeks to act on an audience. Another way of thinking about this point would be to contrast the "I" who speaks in the "eye" poem to the "I" who speaks in the "ear" poem. The "eye" "I" most often speaks to no one, to no one present at least. The "ear" speaker actively solicits some "you," and is situated always in a social occasion. This speaker not only talks to someone, he often responds to someone, engages in dialogue. In short, "The rhetorical ["ear"] self is social and playful, founded in language, while the serious ["eye"] one is 'a central self, an irreducible identity.' "[8]

In thinking about these definitions we can usefully call on Roman Jakobson's "Closing Statement: Linguistics and Poetics," where he sets up his 'communications' model (I have slightly altered the terms for clarity):[9]

CONTEXT
(referential)

SENDER	MESSAGE	RECEIVER
(emotive)	(poetic)	(pragmatic)

CONTACT
(phatic)

CODE
(metalingual)

A few words of explanation might help. Each of these elements represents only an emphasis or proportion in any verbal transaction. Jakobson stresses that all verbal acts partake of several, perhaps all, of these dimensions, but argues that we can fruitfully divide verbal acts according to their greatest or most prominent direction. But first, what do these words mean? The horizontal circuit should be plain enough: we have someone (this 'someone' could be plural or even anonymous) who originates or sends the "message" (a problematic term for literary readers), a "message" itself (what we would mean by text), and someone (again who could be plural or unknown or even merely potential) who receives the "message." The vertical terms in Jakobson's schemata are a little stranger and could bear more explanation. The "contact" is some physical or practical instrument, some tool or mechanism of delivery—tape recorder, telephone, the human body (as in body language), book, voice. The "context" is what roughly we mean by 'the world,' all those things that literature putatively gestures toward, the 'real' world and 'known' world of human experience. Finally, the "code" refers to the 'language' or system of encoding at work—Morse code, aviation signals, the English language, whatever.

Each of these parts, when emphasized, represents a verbal act different enough in degree to be thought of as different in kind. When the sender, for instance, emphasizes her actions as originator, draws attention to herself as originating and sending—"wow," "gee," "whe - EW"—she displays what we can call an emotive or an ex-pressive act. When a verbal act draws attention to the very schemata it uses—"A noun is . . . ," "Make sure you use a topic sentence . . ."—that is, when we use language to talk about language, we have a metalingual act. Hence when in literature an author speaks of making literature, we call this metaliterary—literature talking about literature. Language that emphasizes contact, Jacobson calls "phatic." By this he means words that involve or seek contact between sender and receiver, no matter how incomplete, potential, desired, or unsatisfying the contact may be. Think of what we say when we are on the receiving end of a telephone call, especially when we aren't doing much "sending": "uh-huh," "yup," "ok," "mnn-hmm," "right," "right," "I know," "sure," "hmm?" These are phatic utterances, meant to assure the sender, however faint-heartedly, that we are there. All words that point to something 'out there' function to foreground the context and therefore to privilege "referential" use of language, that is, language which conveys knowledge of something that apparently is prior and external to that language. As for the receiver, when he is especially recognized rhetorically—often in imperatives and interrogatives (Why don't you get me a beer? Make sure it's cold, eh.)—we have what, modifying Jakobson's vocabulary, we might call "affective" or "pragmatic."

Now, let's go back to our earlier discussion of "eye" and "ear" poetry. You will see immediately where we can locate either case. In instances that develop an "I" who conceives and articulates the poem, we typically have expressive language. To the degree that those poems are descriptive (and as I've argued, they often are) we also get referential language. But in poetry that's not always the case. Think of colloquial poetry. In it language, even when it refers or expresses, points much more dramatically toward the receiver and in its pragmatic features radically reorients us away from the speaker or the poet, away too from a subject to which the text points, and directs us instead toward some auditor or auditors who are *actively* invited into a relationship. I say actively because in all poetry, as we know, there is an implied relationship between speaker and reader. But in "ear" poetry, the language registers the overture in overt ways.

Let me put this to you in another way. In the meditative lyric the guiding pronoun is "I." Other pronouns do occur, of course, but they are seldom addressed *directly* by the speaker, and stand ordinarily at some remove from the "I," and in some position of dependence on the "I." This situation supposes, to pick up on claims John Stuart Mill has made, that the poet works in soliloquy and in an outpouring of emotion. Mill further proposes a separation of language into that which is eloquent and that which is poetic. You will see a close resemblance between his schemata and mine, though we value them differently:

> Poetry and eloquence are both alike the expression or utterance of feeling. But if we may be excused the antithesis, we should say that eloquence is *heard*, poetry is *over*heard. Eloquence supposes an audience; the peculiarity of poetry appears to us to lie in the poet's utter unconsciousness of a listener. Poetry is feeling, confessing itself to itself in moments of solitude, and embodying . . . the nearest possible representations of the feeling in the exact shape in which it exists in the poet's mind. Eloquence is feeling pouring itself out to other minds,

courting their sympathy, or endeavouring to influence their belief, or move them to passion or to action.

All poetry is of the nature of soliloquy. . . . What we have said to ourselves, we may tell to others afterwards; what we have said or done in solitude, we may voluntarily reproduce when we know that other eyes are upon us. But no trace of consciousness that any eyes are upon us must be visible in the work itself. . . .

Poetry, accordingly, is the natural fruit of solitude and meditation; eloquence, of intercourse with the world.[10]

It would be easy to trace in Mill the continuation of Romantic precepts that for a time ordained poets as fountains and trees, as volcanoes or lamps, and that outlawed another kind of rhetoric. In oral poetry (and we realize that it too, the poetry *itself*, is authored in solitude) the speaker behaves as if he seeks to be heard, as if he has someone beside him as he speaks and to whom he speaks, even as that audience remains in fact absent to the poet and to the reader. The rhetoric in such poems simulates public exchange. You can see how important this matter is: the one poet, in soliloquy, unengaged in a dialogic way, sings her sensitive impressions to herself—monologic; the other poet enters dialogue, acknowledges a social setting, toward which he is responsive or solicitous—dialogic.

The linguistic and literary consequences of assuming either stance can be enormous. The lyrical poet will be esteemed for her capacity to meditate, to describe, to invent, to nuance. She will proceed with a greater sense of ease and tranquillity. Alone and solemn with her inner thoughts, she can scan a landscape to find some symbolic or telling correspondence between herself or, less often, between others and the world—usually in nature, not with people—that surrounds them. Hugely dependent upon the eye as source, she will typically locate herself *in* space and outside of time, in something like a suspended present. Since she is not entangled in dialogue, that is in speech, she inhabits a world that is remarkably silent, one in which because it is unhurried, unharried, she can take the time—this is her style, is requisite to her self—to find exquisite rhythms and unusual tropes. Above all, she centres the poem and finds value in an inwardness that is personal or even private. That inwardness, Walter J. Ong tells us, derives from a print-centered culture, one that, after centuries of typography, has led us to internalize its technology and to view language not as something which connects us orally as once it did in public performance or in give-and-take, but as something under whose provisions we withdraw to organize our words along a drastically different projection, one that stresses unique personal experience.

This view of the poet we can immediately recognize as Romantic or, as I prefer to call it, post-Romantic, and it finds one of its simplest and most memorable expressions in Mill's pronouncement I mentioned a few minutes ago: "Eloquence is heard; poetry is overheard." You will notice that that eloquence, which by definition sits in an actual voicing or an oral economy, curling in our ears, is here set aside, as though it had nothing to do with poetry. Poetry becomes the preserve of the contemplative, of the lone individual, silently writing out her reflections. Here is part of what Ong has to say about this view:

> The dictum . . . prescribes poetic results to be achieved not so much by the poet as in spite of him. The poet is to function by accident, by indirection. He sits outside society—talking to no one, singing only to the moon. His mission is fulfilled only in so far as the venturesome make their way a little toward his seclusion and install themselves as eavesdroppers at his essentially private soliloquies.[11]

Later in the same essay Ong argues that

> The erection of poetry into soliloquy . . . shows in subtle fashion what was happening to the concept of language when the old oral-aural world which had nourished rhetoric, basically an art of oral communication, was abandoned for a more exclusively visualist cosmology.[12]

Ong also shows how Mill comes to think of the poet as imbued with some constitutional difference, some mark that sets her off from the rest of the species, such regard proving to be a variation on the poet-as-genius theory. And so we celebrate her innate superiority, her awareness, sensitivity, creativity. She is a real natural, a natural poet to whom vision comes fresh as rain or a well when it's clear. She is gifted, set apart, indelibly marked. In exotic forms, too extravagant for Canadians, she is inscrutable, freakish, tormented, crazed: sex-hound, drug-fiend, schizophrenic, necrophiliac. All those shibboleths of The Poet. Claims about the poet's apartness and superiority (not necessarily moral but perceptual, conceptual, or emotional superiority) can be linked to the privacy and the visionary basis of much poetry written to this day. In it the poet's eye—a *different* eye, a higher understanding—presides (again there are exceptions) over a spatialized, silenced, and therefore scarcely populated landscape. It generates out of those expectations which print culture has inscribed in us 'original' ways of reading that world.

In these poems, written under the ordinance of post-Romanticism, we ordinarily expect the speaker of the poem and the author of the poem to be brought into identity, and to offer us therefore some expression that will be 'sincere' or 'authentic.' As reassurance, she will project or declare 'herself,' and she will avoid as inappropriate exhibitions of linguistic play. She will do so in the name of all that is 'intended' and all that is 'genuine' in an enterprise jeopardized by the faked, the worked up, the disingenuous, and the clever. In so acting, she will complete an arc that began in the eighteenth century when, in order to distinguish their work and to assure its 'reliability' (its match of inner and outer), poets started to jaywalk past bold rhetorical figures which were embarrassingly available to "great poets and orators, primitive societies, and common people alike."[13] In accordance with 'honest' practice the poet usually will restrict herself to a limited range of recognized subjects, preferably love, death, art, and nature. Further, she will honour the lexical sets appropriate to her subjects. We expect the poet in her 'own' voice to speak of intimate emotions, to do so in a suspended present, to identify with what she contemplates, and to seek enlarged perception, often as climax to the poem's structure. Normally she would address no audience overtly, speak briefly but poignantly (at the limits, pungently), adopt a slightly elevated voice and a more regular rhythm than we find in speech. More generally she might structure the brief utterance by some discernible pattern of increasing density that she would round off with a firm principle of closure.[14]

I would like to go on laying out these distinctions, but if I did we would end up ignoring specifics entirely. So, knowing that my remarks are sketchy, and my proportioning lumpy, let me pick up my examples of the audible and the visual. You may have noticed, by the way, that I have often spoken of the poet in the feminine when I have discussed "eye" poetry and in the masculine when I have mentioned "ear" poetry. There is good reason for this, aside from some gesture toward the politics of gender. It seems to me that what I am calling "eye" poems tend to be written by women, and "ear" poems to be written by men. It is here, as they are named, that a lot of writers get prickly. I would hazard two other generalizations: for obvious enough reasons vernacular writing often comes from younger writers and native-born writers, iconic work from older writers and immigrant writers. Think of a quick example: Anne Szumigalski as an eye poet, Andrew Suknaski as ear poet, though neither of course is restricted to writing in one style. We could with some thought fit any number of poets into these categories, and we could of course find those—Lorna Crozier comes to mind—who hang around both yards. We could also find some important exceptions, Pat Lane, say, who though male, 'native-born,' and even relatively 'young,' has through most of his career practised a poetry that is inward and elegantly cadenced. (I once told Lane he should spray his poems with anapesticide.)

Having said that, I return to the two very brief examples we heard earlier, and I will then addend some rushed and for its consciousness, which is to say its language, to the technology of writing and of print. Look at the most obvious signs: the explicit reference to a book world (archives), the use of apostrophes and the use of the virgule (made available within the machinery of writing and of print respectively). More subtly, there are the hesitancies in the voice, set into the lines: "my father's land / where sea is / the constant / tide." This convention allows for nuance or, more precisely, delicacy of phrasing. No wonder. You don't have to raise your voice in print culture. The scrupulous pauses find their origin in a poetics of contemplation and their expressive form in words and lines distributed meaningfully on the *space* of the page, that is, within the technology of print culture, where the poet can open holes of silence in margins or within lines. This resource obviously is unavailable to a pre-literate culture and proves to be of limited use to poems which largely observe oral conventions, among them loquacity: don't stop talking! Silence is an embarrassment for the orator. Impatient, rambunctious, he requires a barrage of sounds: don't give them an opening.

There are other rhetorical marks in our example of the iconic poem—absence for one thing, its concern for the unavailable and the lost in this (very common) version. The unseen, the hidden, the inscrutable. What is not available to the eye but soon becomes available, to the inward eye. Or to memory in its migration to a source with which this author keeps faith by bringing it forward. The verbs, too, delimit conventions of inwardness. By and large they are intransitive (in spirit if not always in grammar) or simply expressive of states or definitions: "it is," "it is," "hills [are] always," "sea is," "shell [is] echoing." The copula participates in tautology, it establishes things and affixes their properties. Even the two verbs—"start" and "tread"—that seem to be active actually are not so: "start" refers to an inward action, the starting of a mental journey, and "tread" works metaphorically to express the poet's sense of a recovering in reverie. In de-scribing a relatively stable world the poet also uses present progressive tense—"is echoing," "is moving." (My argument simply strengthens, by the way, if we take the verbals, "echoing" and "moving," to be participles.) This form of the present, as opposed to simple present—echoes, moves—tends to minimize action by suggesting its suspension or its incompletion, with the consequence that the actions seem not to come with much force, seem to trail on indefinitely in some timeless present.

The audible poem, however, exists *in* time and it engages or seeks to engage some listener. It tends to be more boisterous, to ramble in loose episodic structure and in paratactic connections. Ordinarily it will use coordinate construction and normative syntax, and it will eschew the startling figure of speech. Less descriptive of setting, it will be more populated by people. So it will be less meditative and more social. It will more often use transitive verbs and action verbs and especially in its more vehement moments (our example) it will invest itself in imperatives and interrogatives (the most obvious signs, you will recall, of the pragmatic)—verbs that jostle their (would-be) recipients, that would bring them to life, into action. The "ear" poem trails quickly into the "phatic," longing for solidarity. The predicate as magic. More primitive. Less perspicacious, less judicious, this writing is never so sensitive or so serious as the "eye" poem. Or seemingly this is so, for I am arguing that poets who use vernacular like as not turn out to be more parvenu than ingenu, are more likely to be upstarts than naifs.

The "ear" poem also tends not to carry much semantic weight, and—this is what scandalizes so many readers—hence not to convey much 'significance' or 'meaning.' Upfront, it will not tantalize with hints of hidden importance. And so the cries of distress. You hear them among reviewers and among poets who play it safe and enforce given orthodoxies: this is trivial, childish, an invasion of truth, an evasion of responsibility, maturity.[17] I take these complaints to be based in a literary Puritanism which refuses to be amused or gratified, or in some species of Victorian Idealism which assumes we should be reaching to Big Thoughts, preferably in realms of eternity where words slide silently by, restored to pristine immediacy, so lexically pure they have scraped away all bumps and knocks, the hiss and slurp we hear when words are dragged through the contamination of ideolect and animal throats. You hear it in reviewers' calls for wisdom or guidance above all else. In this reckoning the ear's flutter cannot compete with the semantics, these mantics, of eye; if we abide by conventional wisdom we must prefer logos to epos, 'thought' to song, 'meaning' to play.

Here now is my example of idiomatic poetry. You will see that it is built on dramatic structure, with its sense of audience to whom the speaker addresses himself in an active way, in verbs of action, in simple present tense that points to accomplished actions, that it draws unabashedly on idiom and a refreshing vocabulary of popular inventiveness ("knob dealie," "gizmos," "doomajig," "a doughnut"), that it deliberately restricts and at the same time specializes its vocabulary, that it shows verbal redundancy ("this nifty sorta knob dealie"). You will also find that it prizes verbal speed to the point of fusing words ("Gotta," "grabaholda"), shows virtually no awareness of the poem as text—that is, as a shape laid out on a sheet of paper—and that the speech is loaded with the speaker's wholehearted commitment (recall the restraint of our eye poet) to his fantasy and his desire to win somebody over to his enthusiasms ("the nifty," "Gotta be onea the greatest gizmos invented," "ya just grabaholda," "no trouble at all," "real romantic like"), and that as a result it foregrounds the second person in contrast to the first person of the other poetry. Noisy, hyperbolic, additive. Male.

Here's the poem again. It's called "Power Steering":

> Scrawny's got himself this nifty sorta knob dealie
> ya clamp onto one sidea your steerin wheel
> Gotta be onea the greatest gizmos invented
> Imagine ya got your arm around some dame eh
> ya just grabaholda this here doomajig
> spin it around hard, lay it to the boards
> and no trouble at all ya got yourself a doughnut
> and the dame's smeared against ya real romantic like

A new music muscles in. Semantically colourful, phonetically jumpy, madly eliding and compounding (collapsing several parts of speech into one word), the poem chews on its syllables, knots them up and squeezes them, thumbs its nose at decorum. By all odds entered in a manner that flagrantly displays itself—looket me, looket *me*—the poem shouts its transgressions: shrugs inside orthography, trying to find its fit; skitters lexically ("this nifty sorta knob dealie"); beetles feverishly in search of some creature that evades its adequacy to name. Its lexical set—the car, the machine—ignores the expected vocabulary of love (nature, spirit, high art). But in its play it too nabs metaphor: "lay it to the boards" zaps us with anonymous and collective invention. Ludic, agonistic, irreverent, it dances with the snap of speech in the street. Rhetorical.

If we had world enough and time, I would venture some thoughts on where these practices might take us and what may be gained or lost in either formation. But since this paper has already gone on too long, I will only say we can cultivate *both* of them, enjoy each for what it is. I would add that one of the most exciting forms prairie poetry recently has taken, and may continue to take, lies in a combination of these practices within a single text (not *simply* in the existence of them side by side in different writers or texts). Think of Birk Sproxton. By drawing on the sort of nuance which we can generate in private lyric, and on the energy we can locate in the oral, we might well produce an even richer and fresher writing. Out of our place. Out of our minds. It will give us fits. It's being done. Already.

---

1. J. Bronowski, *The Visionary Eye: Essays in the Arts, Literature, and Science,* selected and edited by Piero E. Ariotti (Cambridge, Mass.: MIT, 1978), p. 87.

2. I was startled when I presented an abbreviated version of this paper at a writers' conference at Fort San, Saskatchewan, in June 1987, to find hostility toward my attempts at placing poems in some mode. The

resistance seemed to be based in a belief that poems are simply acts of self-expression and that attempts to identify them by kind are mistaken or impossible. That premise was precisely, I was trying to show, what was getting in the way of fair and intelligent reading of poetry, including, by the way, writing done by one of the respondents. "Clearly," I wanted to say, "attempts to see where things 'fit' [the single quotation marks were there in the original paper] do not fix them in boxes but free them from the containment of *one* box (self-expression and reference) into which they are otherwise and indiscriminately thrown." Without reflection and study we're almost certain to apply the most customary or most familiar terms as the measure of all poetry. "Poetry is not confined to an outpouring of personal experience," someone should have said, "or to a particular set of conventions—try reading Chaucer and Pope in the same way—but directed at every turn by the domain of poetry, and its shifts and lurches." None of the poets was well served by this resentment of criticism which, I am sad to say, on several occasions at the conference took the form of categorical dismissals of "the academics" and "the critics."

Pamela Banting has written an incisive critique of unreflecting "eye" poets in which she shows how they often lock themselves into a narrow theory even as they dismiss others as mere theorists: "The (Eye) or (I) Y: The Eye = E Equation as a Model for Composition," *Classmate*, 17, No. 3 (Spring 1987), 8-12. The essay has reappeared in its latest incarnation as "The (Eye) or (I) Y" in *Prairie Fire*, 8, No. 2 (Summer 1987), 33-9.

3. Charles Bernstein, "Stray Straws and Straw Men," in his *Content's Dream: Essays 1975-1984* (Los Angeles: Sun & Moon, 1986), p. 45.

4. Peter Berger and Thomas Luckmann, *The Social Construction of Reality: A Treatise in the Sociology of Knowledge* (Harmondsworth, England: Penguin, 1967), pp. 76-7.

5. See for example the following books by Walter J. Ong: *Rhetoric, Romance, and Technology: Studies in the Interaction of Expression and Culture* (Ithaca, N.Y.: Cornell, 1971); *Interfaces of the Word: Studies in the Evolution of Consciousness and Culture* (Ithaca, N.Y.: Cornell, 1977); *Fighting for Life: Contest, Sexuality, and Consciousness* (Ithaca, N.Y.: Cornell, 1981); and *Orality and Literacy: The Technologizing of the Word* (London: Methuen, 1982). Richard A. Lanham has written a superb account of orality in his *The Motives of Eloquence: Literary Rhetoric in the Renaissance* (New Haven, Conn.: Yale, 1976). The introductory chapter, "The Rhetorical Ideal of Life," pp. 1-35, is particularly valuable for the general reader.

6. Elizabeth Allen, from "transplant," in her *A Shored Up House* (Winnipeg: Turnstone, 1980), p. 48.

7. Gary Hyland, "Power Steering," in his *Just off Main* (Saskatoon: Thistledown, 1982), p. 48.

8. Anthony Easthope, *Poetry as Discourse* (London: Methuen, 1983), p. 108.

9. Roman Jakobson, "Closing Statement: Linguistics and Poetics," in Thomas A. Sebeok, ed., *Style in Language* (Cambridge, Mass.: MIT, 1960), pp. 353-7.

10. John Stuart Mill, "Thoughts on Poetry and Its Varieties," in *Collected Works of John Stuart Mill*, eds. John M. Robson and Jack Stillinger, Vol. 1 (Toronto: University of Toronto, 1981), pp. 348-9.

11. Walter J. Ong, "J.S. Mill's Pariah Poet," in his *Rhetoric, Romance, and Technology*, pp. 237-8.

12. Ong, p. 254.

13. Peter Dixon, *Rhetoric* (London: Methuen, 1971), p. 42. The book is quite readable and useful.

14. I have used David Lindley, *Lyric* (London: Methuen, 1985) as a basis for much of what I have said here about lyric.

15. "Elizabeth Allen," in Doris Hillis, *Voices & Visions: Interviews with Saskatchewan Writers* (Moose Jaw: Coteau, 1985), p. 154.

16. "Elizabeth Allen" in *Voices & Visions*, p. 150.

17. Easthope writes these thoughts on playing with words:

In describing word-play as childish, Freud's account shares the ideological assumptions of an epoch. Shakespeare's plays are vigorous evidence that Elizabethan adults did not have the same degree of inhibition about 'treating words as things.' Prejudice apart, two conclusions can be drawn from the account. . . . First, verbal repetition foregrounds the phonetic properties of language and so the materiality of the signifier. This leads to the pleasure of the joke but the same factor also is integral to poetry. . . . Second, Freud's account supposes a polarity in discourse. At one pole (identified with the infantile, the unconscious and pleasure) signifier is linked to signifier in a pleasurable repetition of sound; at the other (that of the adult, the conscious and control) signifier is lined up with signified in completed and meaningful sentences. (*Poetry as Discourse*, p. 34.)

ANTIMACASSARED IN THE WILDERNESS: ART AND NATURE IN *THE STONE ANGEL*

Margaret Laurence opens *The Stone Angel* with a long description of the Manawaka cemetery. Like many other contemporary writers she so seldom uses sustained set pieces, is in fact leery of them because she fears "over-writing," that the passage deserves full quotation, especially since its very atypicality draws attention to itself:

> In summer the cemetery was rich and thick as syrup with the funeral-parlor perfume of the planted peonies, dark crimson and wallpaper pink, the pompous blossoms hanging leadenly, too heavy for their light stems, bowed down with the weight of themselves and the weight of the rain, infested with upstart ants that sauntered through the plush petals as though to the manner born.
>
> I used to walk there often when I was a girl. There could not have been many places to walk primly in those days, on paths, where white kid boots and dangling skirts would not be torn by thistles or put in unseemly disarray.

How anxious I was to be neat and orderly, imagining life had been created only to celebrate tidiness, like prissy Pippa as she passed. But sometimes through the hot rush of disrespectful wind that shook the scrub oak and the coarse couchgrass encroaching upon the dutifully cared-for habitations of the dead, the scent of the cowslips would rise momentarily. They were tough-rooted, these wild and gaudy flowers, and although they were held back at the cemetery's edge, torn out by loving relatives determined to keep the plots clear and clearly civilized, for a second or two a person walking there could catch the faint, musky, dust-tinged smell of things that grew untended and had grown always, before the portly peonies and the angels with rigid wings, when the prairie bluffs were walked through only by Cree with enigmatic faces and greasy hair.[1]

A close look at the particulars in this passage shows how carefully Laurence has written it. Without exception, what we discover in the graveyard finds its corresponding opposite flourishing in the surrounding prairie. In the cemetery "planted," "plush," and "portly" peonies grow, in contrast to local "tough-rooted cowslips," "coarse" couchgrass, "untended" things, and rough scrub oak rooted in the land. Laurence further emphasizes the alien lushness of the peonies when she says they are "hanging leadenly, too heavy for their light stems." In colour, too, the "wild and gaudy flowers" outdo the painstakingly nurtured flowers of "wallpaper pink." The same goes for their smells. The "musky, dust-tinged" odour of the local plants rivals the "funeral-parlor perfume" of the peonies, whose fragrance clings "rich and thick as syrup." Laurence as deliberately describes the attitudes and activities of those who tend the cemetery. They, like the prissy young Hagar Currie, see native life as "encroaching," "disrespectful," and "unseemly" in its "disarray," fearful as they are that their peonies will become "infested" with "upstart" ants. Determined to cultivate the "neat and orderly" graveyard, to maintain the geometric precision of its edge, they have torn out the indigenous plants and have "held back" their tenacious irregular growth. The place they try to defend is anaemic, artificial, and imported. It is a freakish hot-house world created and maintained only with the greatest effort. It is so at odds with the surrounding life that the grounds-keepers are "determined to keep the plots clear and clearly civilized." The tensions working throughout the section find their most symbolic representation in the distinction between the dead "angels with rigid wings," sightless and unfeeling, and the "Cree with enigmatic faces and greasy hair" who once inhabited the prairie, and who imaginatively now live on as the spirit of it.

In the cemetery passage Laurence raises a series of alternatives that will figure throughout the rest of the book. She opposes what is foreign to what is native, what is imposed to what is discovered, what is artificial and refined to what is natural and forthright. In psychological terms she contrasts conscious and unconscious experience. In general, she lays out a setting in a realist style, but she so loads her description with binaries that we recognize the writing also operates on a higher level of generality, which is to say it functions symbolically to establish some equivalence between inside (of the characters, but above all, of Hagar Shipley, the protagonist) and outside (or physical setting).

From the start there is no doubt about where Laurence stands. Those things which had "grown always" are ineradicable, timeless, and essential; those things which "civilization" makes are ephemeral and relatively superficial. At the same time, they are lifeless since the "clearly civilized" spaces are "the habitations of the dead"[2] filled with "funeral-parlor" odours. In *The Stone Angel* things which are foreign, imposed, artificial, or conscious—all those things which are matters of art or "civilization"—often show a repudiation of life.

The activities meant to subdue nature are both mistaken and heroic, as Laurence indicates elsewhere, where she has paid tribute to pioneers' accomplishments in settling the West:

how mixed were my own feelings towards that whole
generation of pioneers—how difficult they were to live
with, how authoritarian, how unbending, how afraid to
show love, many of them, and how willing to show anger.
And yet—they had inhabited a wilderness and made it
fruitful. They were, in the end, great survivors, and for
that I love and value them.[3]

But mere survival is not enough. What is needed, Laurence
argues, is "the survival of some human dignity and in the end
the survival of some human warmth and ability to reach out and
touch others."[4] The failure to express such love afflicts all of
Laurence's Manawaka protagonists, none more than Hagar.

Hagar, respectable daughter of Manawaka's leading citizen,
Jason Currie, learns at an early age to walk only "on paths," set
patterns sanctioned by the civilized town. In doing so she avoids
the open spaces of the countryside. One would expect as much
of a girl raised by one of the "fledgling pharoahs in an uncouth
land" (3). Returning from her training in a young ladies'
academy in Toronto, Hagar sees herself with poetic precision as
"Pharaoh's daughter reluctantly returning to his roof, the square
brick palace so oddly antimacassared in the wilderness" (43).
Hagar's expression, strange to modern ears, needs explaining.
The word "antimacassar" once was the name for the covering
put on the arms and backs of upholstered furniture to keep it
from soiling, specifically to keep it from being stained by hair
oil, then known as macassar. The significance of the stout Currie
house, which, like other Laurencean houses, defines its oc-
cupants,[5] begins to emerge more fully when one remembers the
imaginary Indians striding through the "wilderness" with
"greasy" hair. As a very young girl, Hagar learns to keep her
hands clean from the stain of living.

Throughout most of her life she is torn between "civilization"
and the "wilderness." Herself full of life, she takes pleasure in
food, strong colours, flowers, the splattering of sparrows, and
even wine, a forbidden drink for someone raised in a strict Scots

Presbyterian family. Despite her shock, she also feels a grudging admiration for the sexual passion of her son, John, and his girlfriend, Arlene.

Hagar's fresh language further testifies to her vitality.[6] To cite only a few examples: Mrs. Reilly, a huge patient in Hagar's hospital room, is, Hagar thinks, "lethargic as a giant slug"; and Mrs. Dobereiner, on the same ward, sings "like the high thin whining of a mosquito" (281). Another woman at Silverthreads nursing home, Hagar notices, "pats at her hair with a claw yellow as a kite's foot" (101). And, during prairie thunderstorms, Hagar recalls, "the lightning would rend the sky like an angry claw at the cloak of God" (161).

Hagar speaks with special imagination in describing Doris, her dull but decent daughter-in-law. Hagar's perverse inclination to criticize her takes the form of unflattering, often humorous, animal comparisons. Doris, she thinks, "heaves and strains like a calving cow" (32), "gapes" at her husband, Marvin, "like a flounder" (95), and utters "a high hurt squawking, like an unwilling hen the rooster treads" (36), "broody hen" that she is "in her dowdy brown, dandruffed on either shoulder and down the back like molting feathers" (29).

Another kind of exuberance appears in Hagar's teens, when she revels in dances:

> Lord, how I enjoyed those dances, and can hear yet the stamping of our feet, and the fiddler scraping like a cricket. My hair, pinned on top of my head, would come undone and fall around my shoulders in a black glossiness that the boys would try to touch. (22)

On such occasions Hagar contemptuously tosses her dark hair, symbol of her budding sexuality, like a mane (46). This is before a stint at an Eastern academy almost finishes her off. Upon leaving Manawaka, she is "Hagar with the shining hair, the dark-maned colt off to the training ring" (42). Presumably that civilizing school tames the wildness in her, acting as yet another cemetery or antimacassar. The ring encircles and circumscribes her, impounds her impetuous energy, just as her upbringing earlier has instilled an affected primness in her. Appearing as a little girl at the town dump, Hagar and some of her friends, she tells us, "tiptoed, fastidiously holding the edges of our garments clear, like dainty-nosed czarinas finding themselves in sudden astonishing proximity to beggars with weeping sores" (26-7). In no time at all she learns to be "resplendent, haughty, hoity-toity" (6) in politely skirting life.

Hagar learns to check her innate energy (except for unbridled fits of pique as an old woman). Raised as a prig, she soon becomes cripplingly inhibited and private. Her appalling sense of propriety prevents her from ever being at ease with people or trusting them. She silently congratulates herself on having "manners" and avoiding "coarse" talk, readily equating acquired mannerisms with personal worth. She is so fastidious about such niceties, in fact, that when her neglected son, Marvin, faithfully writes each month from the West coast, her only response is the complaint that "his letters were always very poorly spelled" (130), placing his orthography ahead of his love. (Interestingly, Hagar is so withdrawn that she, herself, rarely writes letters or, for that matter, seldom speaks to anyone, as the striking paucity of her dialogue in The Stone Angel indicates.)

Hagar's overweening concern for respectability makes her unusually conscious of audiences. Her expressions indicate as much: "They are no tears of mine, in front of her" (31); "People are always listening" (89); "I preferred possible damnation . . . to any ordeal of peeking or pitying tears" (90); "I can scarcely nod my thanks, fearing she'll see my unseemly tears" (92); "That damned outhouse bothered me most of all. It always looked so foolish" (114). Fittingly, the taciturn Bram Shipley exposes Hagar's obsession with appearances, her vulnerability to the eye. Outraged when he pisses on the steps of her father's store, she tears into him, ever sure of her rectitude: " 'I don't disgrace myself.' " " 'No, by Christ,' " Bram answers, " 'you're respectable—I'll give you that' " (116). Later, when Hagar says " 'They'd think we were hicks' " for taking lunch onto the train,

Bram replies, " 'That would be an everlasting shame, wouldn't it?' " (142). He recognizes that, for all her strength, Hagar weakens in facing public opinion. Concern about how things look also determines Hagar's attitude toward clothes. Except for a period when she is on the farm, she forever worries about being "decently" dressed. And she is, of course, always comparing her own "lilac silk" to Doris's "brown rayon" dresses, a matter I will return to later.

First, I want to suggest that Laurence presents Hagar in strongly Jungian terms, even though she apparently has never read Carl Jung.[7] *The Stone Angel* certainly makes sense to anyone reading it as realist text, and recognition of the book's Jungian undertones will not supplant whatever insights such practices offer. The Jungian dimensions extend and deepen our understanding of the book; the method complements rather than departs from representational approaches. A word here about methodologies might help. Any Jungian reading will presume an essential, prior, and finally stable self (that is, one which will show remarkable continuity, whatever changes it might go through). This self, in Jungian psychology, precedes any cultural formation and in large part—large in comparison to the actions of a Lacanian self—resists it. Out of a belief in a pre-verbal realm Jung would in one sense reinforce realist conventions with their observance of a language that gestures, more: *points*, toward an anterior reality which it is then the business of the linguistic system, and the literary text, to deliver. In this essay, I will for the most part set aside critiques which have been forcefully levelled against essentialist thinking and proceed to treat realism and Jungianism in a spirit of their own systems.[8]

The persistent effort to keep up a good front, according to Jung, can be damaging if a person starts to rely on the disguises she assumes in presenting herself in public or if someone lives so often and so completely by masks that she confuses herself with them. Hagar doesn't lack a rich inner state, and she doesn't assume she is what she wants others to think she is. Still, she does pour a lot of herself into manufacturing costumes and roles behind which she can hide. She lives by her *persona*, the archetype Jung says we rely upon in developing a social face. The *persona*, he argues, "is a complicated system of relations between individual consciousness and society, fittingly enough a kind of mask, designed on the one hand to make a definite impression upon others, and, on the other, to conceal the true nature of the individual."[9] The description applies precisely to Hagar who plays the role for those very reasons.

She is divided between her inward and outward selves—the one natural and vital, the other acquired and stultifying. Just as her father's stiff stout house stands "antimacassared in the wilderness," so she learns to wrap herself in her sanitary *persona* and to scorn the dark Metis from "the wrong side of the tracks" (115) and the strange Ukrainians "beyond our pale" (46). So, too, she learns to turn up her "dainty" nose at the "stain and stench" of the "festering" garbage dump (26-7). For similar reasons she also draws back in fear and revulsion from farm animals, whereas Bram, uncultivated man that he is, accepts animals for what they are. Take their opposing attitudes toward bees:

> His damned bees sickened and for the most part died, looking like scattered handfuls of shriveled raisins in the hives. A few survived, and Bram kept them for years, knowing full well they frightened me. He could plunge his hairy arms among them, even when they swarmed, and they never stung. I don't know why, except he felt no fear. (57)

The degree to which Hagar has learned to hold back nature, both without and within herself, determines her response to the bees. Bram, in touch with what is local, natural, and unconscious, and never part of Hagar's genteel world, feels none of her contempt or anxiety. Hagar doesn't find Bram's unreflecting farm life altogether insignificant or unattractive, but she carefully keeps it in hand, measures it out in her mind. Hagar's view of chickens, reminiscent of her nausea when earlier she stumbles across bloodied chicks, shows as much:

> Messy things—how I detested their flutter and squawk. At first I could hardly bring myself to touch them, their soiled feathers and the way they flapped in terror to get away. I got so I could even wring their necks when I had to, but they never ceased to sicken me, live or dead, and when I'd plucked and cleaned and cooked one, I never could eat it. I'd as lief have eaten rat flesh. (126-7)

Hagar's very next thought (like her use of the archaic "lief") tells the story of her retreat into polite culture:

> I bought a gramophone with a great black cornucopia on top and a handle you had to crank incessantly, and records to go with it. *Ave Maria, The Grand March from Aida, In a Monastery Garden, Believe Me if All Those Endearing Young Charms*. They had *Beethoven's Fifth* listed in the catalogue as well, but it was too expensive. I never played them in the evenings when Bram and Marvin were there. Only in the days. (127)

The immediate attempt to displace unbecoming realities with sentimental or inspirational music shows what Hagar's upbringing has done to her. The same behaviour characterizes her view of horses: "I have kept Rosa Bohneur's *The Horse Fair* . . . and still in my room the great-flanked horses strut eternally." But "Bram never cared for that picture," she says: " 'You never gave a damn for living horses, Hagar,' he said once. 'But when you seen them put onto paper where they couldn't drop manure, then it's dandy, eh? Well, keep your bloody paper horses. I'd as soon have nothing on my walls' " (83). The key words, "living" and "paper," once more reveal Hagar's ambivalence. She's always drawn to life, especially at its most intense, though she can never quite admit its full power, almost as if she dreads being overwhelmed by it. Bram's accusations, she realizes years later, cut to the heart of her inner constraints. Her fear of horses discloses more than a fussy concern for tidiness:

> I have to laugh now, although I was livid then. He was
> quite right that I never cared for horses. I was frightened
> of them, so high and heavy they seemed, so muscular, so
> much their own masters—I never felt I could handle them.
> I didn't let Bram see I was afraid, preferring to let him
> think I merely objected to them because they were smel-
> ly. Bram was crazy about horses. (83)

A good measure of how repressed Hagar has become in bridling
the colt within her shows up in her avoidance of the powerful,
even sexual, forces embodied in horses and in Bram, who identifies with them.

'Art'—with its eternities, its removal of the body—enables
Hagar to evade or to control the dark side of life; to "handle" it,
she says, as in the above example where she reserves the day—
clear and full of light—for her escapist listening. There can be
no doubt that, given her imagination and intelligence, she
genuinely likes music and painting. Even so, the art she prefers
tends to be stylized or mawkish—the very kind that leads away
from earthy experience or that puts it in its place. It's no accident, then, that Hagar says she "thought it was a bad thing to
grow up in a house with never a framed picture to *tame* the
walls" (82, my emphasis). In seeking artificial ways of covering
up those native things she both admires and fears, she lapses
into romantic reveries about elegant and fantastic scenes:

> I always liked the gauzy ladies performing Chopin in
> concert halls, proven by photographs to exist somewhere.
> (126)

> Oh, I was the one, all right, tossing my black mane
> contemptuously . . . and seeing the plain board town and
> the shack dwellings beyond our pale as though they'd
> been the beckoning illustrations in the book of Slavic fairy
> tales given me by an aunt, the enchanted houses with eyes,
> walking on their own splayed hen's feet, the czar's sons
> playing at peasants in coarse embroidered tunics, bloused
> and belted, the ashen girls drowning attractively in meres,

crowned always with lilies, never with pigweed or slime. (46)

Love, I fancied, must consist of words and deeds delicate as lavender sachets, not like the things he did sprawled on the high white bedstead that rattled like a train. (80)

Those fancies again and again lead Hagar to distort the things that happen to her. At no time does that happen more dramatically than in her approach to Bram. Snob though she is, Hagar instantly takes an interest in him. It consists of both genuine excitement over his coarse sexuality and an evasive lacquering of him:

> I reveled in his fingernails with crescents of ingrown earth that never met a file. I fancied I heard in his laughter the bravery of battalions. I thought he looked a bearded Indian, so brown and beaked a face. The black hair thrusting from his chin was rough as thistles. The next instant, though, I imagined him rigged out in a suit of gray soft as a dove's breast-feathers. (45)

The extent to which Hagar wants to transform the man by imposing her will on him is evident in her verbs: "I fancied," "I thought he looked," and "I imagined." Bram's unrefined qualities make him desirable, but not quite so satisfying as a dark, hairy man clipped and perfumed into a perfect foreign gentleman fit for the castle which Hagar, as czarina or as "chatelaine" (51), plans to run on the farm. It wouldn't be long, she thinks, before "Brampton Shipley prospered, gentled, learned cravats and grammar" (50), the proper bounds she would enforce on dress and speech, before he became a Currie houseboy respectably and artfully antimacassared against the dirt of living. Hagar's marital expectations directly parallel her attempts to domesticate horses in her pictures and to avoid chickens in her music.

The opposition between art and nature finds its most sustained and symbolic representation in the long early section on the cemetery, as I've suggested. The Cree in the prairie landscape, we remember, are noteworthy for their hair. Now, in the section revealing Hagar's first feelings about Bram, we find that in her eyes "he looked a bearded Indian." Unseemly hairy creature, he, too, belongs 'out there,' in the dark 'lower' spaces full of animals, instincts, dreams, unsettled and unsettling energies, forbidden and forbidding thoughts—all the unconscious powers corrected by civilized good manners and good sense, dangerous yet fascinating for sheltered and well-trained people like Hagar.

Her mixed reaction to Bram's direct sexual approach when they first meet is completely in character, then. Offended though she may be, Hagar desires him, as we see in the stylized sexual embrace of their dance:

> As we went spinning like tumbleweed in a Viennese waltz, disguised and hidden by the whirling crowd, quite suddenly he pulled me to him and pressed his outheld groin against my thigh. Not by accident. There was no mistaking it. No one had ever dared in this way before. Outraged, I pushed at his shoulders, and he grinned. I, mortified beyond words, couldn't look at him except dartingly. But when he asked me for another dance, I danced with him. (47)

This same passage, not incidentally, lays out the art/nature binary in the boundaries Hagar puts between the Viennese waltz, height of elegance, and Bram's rough tumbleweed dance placed *within* the waltz, where it is held in inferior status. What we have just said about the cemetery scene will hold here, particularly when we think of the contention between the 'garden' which crops up so profusely in this book (later for instance with Elva *Jardine* and Hagar's garden smells in the hospital) and the weeds that, kept out, nevertheless threaten to infest the gardens, as in the infernal town dump they steep. Bram as thistle finds an equivalence in the cemetery thistles that might tear or disarray skirts. Weeds, *his* weeds, might pollute the entire garden with the spectre of crude sexuality, foul dissemination. Although Hagar's sexual passion soon heightens, she never can reveal herself to Bram, constrained as she has learned to be:

> It was not very long after we wed, when first I felt my blood and vitals rise to meet his. He never knew. I never let him know. I never spoke aloud, and I made certain that the trembling was all inner. He had an innocence about him, I guess, or he'd have known. How could he not have known? Didn't I betray myself in rising sap, like a heedless and compelled maple after a winter? But no. He never expected any such a thing, and so he never perceived it. I prided myself upon keeping my pride intact, like some maidenhead. (81)

"Now there is no one to speak to. It is late, late in the night," Hagar laments (81). A sense of lost life weighs upon her as, in old age, she reassesses herself. Despite her rich emotions she has never been able to let go with anyone, not even Bram.

> Twenty-four years, in all, were scoured away like sandbanks under the spate of our wrangle and bicker.
> Yet when he turned his hairy belly and his black-haired thighs toward me in the night, I would lie silent but waiting, and he could slither and swim like an eel in a pool of darkness. Sometimes, if there had been no argument between us in the day, he would say he was sorry, sorry to bother me, as though it were an affliction with him, something that set him apart, as his speech did, from educated people.
> *Bram, listen—* (116)

Hagar waits but she does not risk exposure, wanting to be impregnable in her emotional and mental garrison. Locked in her static spaces, she experiences something approaching death-in-life. The dash at the end of her mute appeal expresses as much. The incompletion of her thought, that pinch in her language, registers her inability to act, a failing she is well aware of. The simple, painful words of belated recognition appear time and again, recording the disastrous restraint that through most of Hagar's life keeps her alone and life at bay:

> I wanted to say . . . but I did not say that. (85)

> I felt I must pursue him, say it was a passing thing and not meant. But I didn't. (45)

The refrain goes on and on. The most powerful expression of how tightly Hagar has bottled up her inner self, spirit fermenting, occurs when Marvin comes to say goodbye as he's going off to war:

> I didn't know what to say to him. I wanted to beg him to look after himself, to be careful, as one warns children against snowdrifts or thin ice or the hooves of horses, feeling the flimsy words may act as some kind of charm against disaster. I wanted all at once to hold him tightly, plead with him, against all reason and reality, not to go. But I did not want to embarrass both of us, nor have him think I'd taken leave of my senses. . . .
> "Mother—"
> "Yes?" And then I realized I was waiting with a kind of anxious hope for what he would say, waiting for him to make himself known to me.
> But he was never a quick thinker, Marvin. Words would not come to his bidding, and so the moment eluded us both. He turned and put his hand on the doorknob.
> "Well, so long," he said. "I'll be seeing you." (129-30)

Laurence catches the unvoiced feelings, the eloquence of the unsaid, extremely well.

Clearly, then, the walls are up. Hagar consistently refuses closeness and openness. When her brother, Dan, dies, she "stiffened and drew away . . . wanting above all else to do the thing he asked, but unable to do it, unable to bend enough" (25). On other occasions, rigid and armoured, she jerks her hand away from her father (44) and shoves aside Marvin's "paw" (33). She keeps up her defences, fearing above all else that she might be vulnerable behind her protective *persona* of stern disapproval and respectable dress: "Aloof. Alert. Not to be taken in" (34), the firmness of her withdrawal reinforced by the tight resolve of these one-word sentences, so resolute in their brevity and their self-sufficiency, no 'and's,' 'but's' or 'if's' about it. Retracted and concealed within herself, she speaks "guardedly" (70) and steps "with a cautious foot" (105) whenever there's a chance someone might understand or touch her.

Hagar's worry over property, like her fretting over propriety (the two words tellingly relate), has a lot to do with her search for an emotional refuge. Her cranky insistence on referring to her house and her solid, heavy furniture in the first person singular, and in the possessive ("my," "mine"), doesn't derive from financial worry. The recursions encode her psychological need for a certain, immovable world. To her mind, her household fixtures "are mine. How could I leave them? They support and comfort me" (58-9). "If I am not somehow contained in them and in this house, something of all change caught and fixed here, eternal enough for my purposes, then I do not know where I am to be found at all" (36), she says to herself. "Contained," "caught," "fixed"—the language of renunciation, consciously warding off the dark flux of life. Unsullied and unsoiled, she is antimacassared in her wilderness.

Hagar likes to barricade herself behind walls, characteristically wanting to lock her bedroom as an old woman. Fearing "violation," she seeks "concealment" in the house (74). Granted, she is trying to maintain a bit of human dignity in a place of her own, but the action reveals something less flattering and more profound. Without realizing it, she is shutting out the outer world and rejecting her natural inclinations. Her repression on the inside becomes suppression on the outside.

Hagar can be at least as hard on others. Her sharp-tongued attacks, especially those she makes on Doris, are often unfair. In fact, she is opinionated—quick to think and to speak ill of people. In Jungian terms, Hagar is suffering from her *animus*, that archetype of maleness incipient in every woman which, if she allows herself to be possessed by it, will lead her to take rigid and cantankerous positions.[10] That Hagar's obstinacy may have something to do with Jung's *animus* seems even more likely when we remember that Jung linked its appearance to the impact of a girl's childhood experiences with her father. In Hagar's case, she "takes after" her father. For all her own striking speech and dislike of worn words, she speaks in cliché only when enjoining his financial catechism to her son John. On those occasions she reverts to all the stubborn triteness, the full weight of linguistic lead, her father had been able to muster in extolling the virtues of private initiative. Hagar's unusual lapse into such stupidity makes Jung's argument at least tantalizing since she is most like her father when she's most determined to have her own way.

If Hagar has been afflicted with a fierce *animus* and *persona*, in the end she tenuously manages—unexpectedly and painfully—to shake them off and to find support in a fuller life. The *persona*, a partly conscious fabrication, finds its compensating counterpart in the unconscious—in what Jung calls the *shadow*.[11] As the word implies, Jung means by it the "dark" part of the human psyche which generates all the uncivilized passions and thoughts disturbing to an ideal public figure, or *persona*, one who needs things "*clearly* civilized." But he doesn't think the *shadow* is necessarily inferior or monstrous. As a matter of fact, Jung stresses the need to unite the conscious and the unconscious minds, the light and the dark, what is "upper" and what is "lower," to bring together the very realities Hagar has separated. According to Jung, anyone who hasn't a shadow of doubt about the rightness of her aversions and preferences will suffer from psychic imbalance or dis-ease.[12]

It's therefore startling to read that when Hagar, distraught about her future, runs away to the cannery, where she experiences a personal breakthrough, she is off to "Shadow Point." The language describing Hagar's experience there is remarkably Jungian. To foreshadow and reinforce the significance of Hagar's trip to the seashore, Laurence allows her quietly to inform us that she is wearing a cotton beige dress printed with black triangles. She's never before worn such a dress, at least not so far as we know. What she does wear, day after day, as she proudly reminds herself, is a "silk" lilac dress. The black triangles offer a visual representation of Shadow Point, point to the place where Hagar will meet and start to assimilate her own lost *shadow*. And so we appreciate Hagar's acts as art critic when, sitting in the doctor's office shortly before she runs away, she dismisses "weird" paintings, "all red and black triangles and blobs that *make no sort of sense*" (82, my emphasis). For her at that point it can make no sense. Even so, Hagar's change of clothes before reaching the Point alerts us to her imminent change of heart (though she still wears vestiges of her old self—a blue cardigan and a hat with blue corn-flowers).

The switch from what Hagar likes to think is silk (though it is probably synthetic) to the common, natural fabric, cotton, is a sign of the humbleness she's about to fumble, unintentionally and reluctantly, toward. For the black and beige on the cotton dress are earth colours in contrast to the blues and purples Hagar has always preferred. Her favourite colours figure most noticeably in her lilac dresses, but the colour shows up whenever Hagar is describing things belonging to the Curries: their Limoges China, their rugs with "blue" roses, their family pitcher—a "knobbled jug of blue and milky glass" (59). Laurence deftly sets the description of this heirloom near another section where Hagar talks about a Shipley jug:

> There's the plain brown pottery pitcher, edged with anemic blue, that was Bram's mother's, brought from some village in England and very old. I'd forgotten it was here. . . . It always looked like an ordinary milk pitcher to me. Tina says it's valuable. Each to his taste, and my granddaughter, though so dear to me, has common tastes, . . . a legacy no doubt from her mother. (62)

Laurence probably intends the proximity of these passages not only to show Hagar's mind at work associating memories, but also to suggest a pattern of countering colour images, the browns belonging to the Shipleys. The distinction finds reinforcement throughout the novel. Take the selection where Hagar complains about Marvin's name:

> Whoever chose Marvin for his name? Bram, I suppose. A Shipley family name, it was, I think. Just the sort of name the Shipleys would have. They were all Mabels and Gladyses, Vernons and Marvins, squat brown names, common as bottled beer. (32)

It's no accident, then, that Doris dresses in brown as well. We see in Hagar's disdain (as well as her love of vibrance) how Hagar finds brown, beige, and (usually) gray dull and undistinguished. Her purples and blues are the traditional colours of royalty and of the sky—symbols of the social and mental ascendancy she thinks matter and she presumes to possess. In repudiating simple things she has set her eye on 'higher' matters. Now, as she approaches Shadow Point, her beige dress shows she is about to accept the shades of common night and earth. She finally will 'come down to earth' as she embraces what is "coarse" and "greasy" and as she begins to remove the antimacassars that have sanitized her mind.

In order to enter life fully, Hagar has to get off her 'high horse.' The shut bedroom she leaves in fleeing home is located on the top floor of her house, symptomatic of her mental state. Cut off as she is from the shadows deep within herself, Hagar has learned that decent ladies don't 'stoop' to such life. They're 'above' that sort of thing. Then, at the Point, she begins to descend "down and down . . . to the place I'm looking for" (148), "down the steep slopes to the sea" (150), to realities no longer beside the point. Hagar's account of the stairwell is worth quoting in full since it stresses her mythic journey into the depths and in its sustained thickness attracts our attention and takes on heft:

The stairway's beginning is almost concealed by fern and bracken, tender and brittle, green fish-spines that snap easily under my clumping feet. It's not a proper stairway, actually. The steps have been notched into the hillside and the earth bolstered at the edges with pieces of board. There's a banister of sorts, made of poles, but half of them have rotted away and fallen. I go down cautiously, feeling slightly dizzy. The ferns have overgrown the steps in some places, and salmonberry branches press their small needles against my arms as I pass. Bushes of goatsbeard brush satyr-like against me. Among the fallen leaves and brown needles of fir and balsam on the forest floor grow those white pinpoint flowers we used to call Star of Bethlehem. I can see into cool and shady places, the streaks of sun star-fished across the moist and musky earth. (151)

The descent is a *rite de passage*, an entrance into new life: "To move to a new place—that's the greatest excitement. For a while you believe you carry nothing with you—all is canceled from before, or cauterized, and you begin again and nothing will go wrong this time" (155). The hint of Hagar's approaching character change gains emphasis from the fact that the stairway is rotting away and nearly overgrown from lack of use: few have gone this way. By the same token, her dizziness on the steps indicates more than her old age and bad health. It hints of the critical confusion she will pass through in losing her conscious hold on life. Various references draw our attention to the forbidding sexuality and fertility embodied in the shadows Hagar is entering. Laurence strategically mentions fish, "satyr-like" goatsbeard, and the "moist and musky earth," and earlier Hagar's condemnation of a couple as irresponsible goats.

The risky descent is something she neither expects or welcomes. She comes to Shadow Point wanting a "fortress" (153) or a "castle" (154)—and we recall they were once the same thing, the fortress and the castle—where she can "feel somehow more barricaded, safer" (155), in "some sort of stronghold where nothing could touch me" (161). Only gradually does she start to think "Perhaps I've come here not to hide but to seek" (192). The escape then turns into a quest couched in religious terms, a painful search for her essential self, long denied.

Although Hagar, like Laurence, disapproves of the "gimcrack," "crammed," and "sequined" heaven of evangelical Christianity (120), Laurence effectively portrays her climb down the "two hundred earthen stairs" into "this pit and valley" (185) in Christian symbols. The Star of Bethlehem Hagar notices in her descent helps to open and early to establish this narrative. Numerous expressions reinforce that fact. Initially, when Hagar struggles to remember the name of the place, she suddenly recalls it with what amounts to an unwitting prayer of thanks: "It will come. Just take it easy. There, there. Oh—*Shadow Point.* Thank the Lord" (146). The expression says more than Hagar intends or recognizes. Later, on arriving at the deserted resort— which is to say a desert or a wilderness—Hagar enters one of the gray buildings (reminiscent of the gray Shipley house she scornfully rejected years before), thinking "My room has been prepared for me" (155). The words echo Christ's promise, "In my Father's house are many mansions. . . . I go to prepare a place for you."

What happens in the next few hours emphasizes the religious theme. Suffering from thirst, Hagar thinks of the line, "*Water water everywhere nor any drop to drink*" (186). Like the ancient mariner, she has offended the natural order and needs salvation. Having long ago renounced her basic self, she is lost in an inner wasteland. Hence the scattered references to her as an Egyptian wandering in the desert (pages 3, 40, 96 and 111, for example), passages meant, I think, to portray her as someone living in exile from herself. Fortunately for Hagar, like her Biblical namesake, she soon finds her "well in the wilderness" (187), in her case an old bucket that has caught the night rain. The phrase picks up the language she used upon first arriving at the Point, "What would a fortress be without a well?" (153). Once Murray Ferney Lees shows up, Hagar joins him in drinking a jug of red wine in a plastic "goblet" which Lees thoughtfully has provided for her, an action that becomes all the more meaningful when we remember that years before Hagar set aside the wine decanter Bram offered her as a wedding present.[13]

Their communal drinking releases a flood of memories which Hagar for the first time shares. Talking in the middle of the night, she opens to her own shadows. For the first time she begins to listen and to reach out. And, though she once sat rigid as a stone angel, unable to weep when her brother and her son died, now, profoundly mortified, she surrenders to her passions and cries in telling Lees what happened to her son. Hagar, who had shoved away people all her life, gives in to Lees' presence: "We sit close together for warmth, both of us. . . . And then we slip into sleep" (246). Worn down by her physical and emotional ordeal, and evidently delirious, Hagar begins to imagine she is speaking to her son John, though in her growing humanity she now learns to accept John's relationship with his girlfriend and to show her own love for him. Then, when Lees returns with Doris and Marvin and stands waiting for Hagar to pardon him, she breaks through her initial resentment and her crippling old tendency to hold back, and she impulsively touches him. Out of genuine affection and concern she actually apologizes to him. In keeping with the series of religious references prominent in this section of the book, Laurence tells us that Hagar begins to suspect "it was a kind of mercy I encountered him" (253). (Still, the growth does not come easily. The inscription, *No Cross No Crown*," which Hagar recalls having seen on a piece of petit-point sewn by Clara Shipley (193), says as much. Though it never occurs to Hagar, the adage applies to her own anguished transformation at Shadow Point.)

On a mimetic level, that is, seen as realist character, Lees, like other Laurencean characters, functions well. He appears to be an ordinary person, slightly comical, a bit pathetic, one whose job, marriage, and family life have their ups and downs. He also acts as one of many male helpers who in the Manawaka cycle assist Laurence's protagonists toward provisional growth.

There's more to him. Lees provides an instance of the archetype Jung calls the *wise old man*, a father figure who appears when the questing hero is in a difficult situation, "where insight, understanding, good advice, determination, planning, etc., are needed but cannot be mustered on one's own resources."[14] Lees certainly offers wise counsel. He speaks sanely and humanely about religion and sexuality. And, though he parodies the evangelical style, in a peculiar way, beyond his own personality or intending, he serves in the very ministerial role he mocks. Hagar's language intimates as much:

> I lean forward, attentive, ease a cramped limb with a hand, and look at this man, whose name I have suddenly forgotten but whose face, now turned to mine, says in plain and urgent silence—*Listen. You must listen.* He's sitting cross-legged, and he wavers a little and sways as he speaks in a deep loud voice. (232)

In Buddha pose, Lees speaks from his own human need in a disarming and simple honesty that wins over Hagar in spite of herself. But in turn, when she, released in her dream state, tells her own painful story, he listens and responds as spiritual comforter.

Even before Hagar exposes her secret thoughts and emotions, she has sensed the special strength he brings to her. She comes to that recognition in remarkably mythic thinking:

> If I were alone, I wouldn't find the sound [of the sea] soothing in the slightest. I'd be drawn out and out, with each receding layer of water to its beginning, a depth as alien and chill as some far frozen planet, a night sea hoarding sly-eyed serpents, killer whales, swarming phosphorescent creatures dead to the daytime, a black sea sucking everything into itself, the spent gull, the trivial garbage from boats, and men protected from eternity only by their soft and fearful flesh and their seeing eyes. *But I have a companion and so I'm safe*, and the sea is only the

sound of water slapping against the planking. (224-5, my emphasis)[15]

Without Lees' guidance through what Jungians call the night sea journey, Hagar would be unable to cope with her immersion. In mythic terms, he enables her to face and then to escape the monsters protecting the dark unconscious world and threatening to engulf her and hold her. She needs to enter the depths, but she also needs to emerge from them whole. Hence her anxiety when Lees momentarily leaves her alone in the dark:

> I dip and dart inside my skull, swooping like a sea gull. I feel ill at the sensation. I feel *I may not be able to return*, even if I open my eyes. I may be *swept outward* like a gull, blown by a wind too strong for it, forced into the rough sea, *held under* and *drawn* fathoms *down into depths* as still and cold as black glass. (235, my emphases)

Appropriately, Murray Ferney Lees works for the "Dependable Life Assurance" company. I suspect Laurence's choice of names is as deliberate as it is fortuitous.[16] She could just as easily have spoken of an "insurance" company. The point is that Lees offers Hagar reassurance in her growing acceptance of *all* life, not just her cosmetic version of it. Lees' own names work equally well. That Hagar is in the "lees" of life makes his surname appropriate. "Murray" is a Scottish name meaning "by the sea" and "Ferney," obviously enough, refers to plants found in the forest around the cannery. The Christian names indicate the "wilderness" Hagar has entered. Now, on the edges of open forest and sea,[17] Hagar is on the verge of leaving the closed, safe, and life-denying spaces she's always occupied. The sea, in particular, alerts us to the undercurrent of water images carrying Hagar toward spiritual rebirth.[18]

Several incidents at the Point anticipate the still greater maturity Hagar will find when she is dying a few days later in the hospital. The sea gull trapped in the cannery vividly denotes Hagar's situation:

> A sea gull is flying in this room. I feel the brush and
> beat of its wings as it swoops and mounts. It's frightened,
> trapped and flapping. I hate a bird inside a building. Its
> panic makes it unnatural. I can't bear to have it touch me.
> *A bird in the house means a death in the house*—that's what
> we used to say. Nonsense, of course. (217)

But in the novel the omen is not non-sense, whatever people of
'good sense' believe. When the wounded bird escapes, stray
dogs kill it. The bird's fate shows in prolepsis what is about to
happen to Hagar. Her tenuous flight from the crippling mental
prisons she has built about her barely precedes her death.

The appearance of the trapped bird does not come without
warning. Laurence skillfully slips earlier references to birds and
especially caged birds into the book, always showing Hagar's
association with them. In one instance, Hagar catches and holds
a wren in a white cage for John (69), the action revealing both
her personal repressions and the inordinate claims she makes
on her family. In another case more directly related to the appearance of the gull at Shadow Point, Hagar describes her fright
as Doris and Marvin take her to see Silverthreads Nursing
Home:

> My heart is pulsing too fast, beating like a berserk bird. I
> try to calm it. I must, I must, or it will damage itself against
> the cage of bones. But still it lurches and flutters, in a
> frenzy to get out. (95)

In the end the stricken bird within Hagar, which *is* Hagar,
frantically wanting out, does manage to break loose and
awkwardly tries to fly.[19]

As Hagar's carefully constructed garrison begins to fall, the
shadow archetype powerfully emerges, nearly displacing the *persona* and the *animus*. Hagar comes closer to what genuinely she
is when she starts to shed her acquired and her distorted selves.
Her *animus* and *persona* never wholly disappear because such
transitions are never sudden or complete, never by convention

admitted as large alterations in realist texts. Hence Hagar's many relapses into bad temper and pretense when she goes to the hospital (a place, it's worth noting, where people ideally are healed of the diseases that afflict them). Temporarily reverting to her mulish solitude there, she at first doesn't want to be in a public ward, prefers to have her bed curtained off, and turns her face away from the other patients.

The retreat doesn't last long. Soon she is relating to the others with insight and sensitivity. She comes close to Elva Jardine, the tiny woman she at first found distasteful, apologizes silently to those she offends, and tries to please others. She also expresses gratitude for almost the first time in her life, wonders what troubles a young nurse on her ward, recognizes others' points of view, develops some tact and consideration, and faces disturbing truths about herself. An indication of how far she has come can be found in her inner wish to tell a nurse about dying: "*Listen. You must listen. It's important. It's—quite an event*" (282).[20] This desire to share her inner-most thoughts, and so to enter a community (to commun-icate), is as radical for Hagar as is their source. It is a measure of Lees' tutelage that her speech directly repeats, word for word, what Lees has said to her only a few days earlier at Shadow Point (232).

The disastrous curbs she's proudly kept on herself continue falling away. As a result, she throws over what she now sees as her "absurd formality," which in the past has left her insisting on addressing people by their last names and sniffing over bad spelling and "impermissibles" in messages to the point of missing their purpose. Now she arrives at the point of using personal names and even of saying "*Okay—guy*—such slangy words. I used to tell John. They mark a person" (301). As indeed they do. Those expressions will not seem like much to a contemporary reader, but they mean a lot to Hagar and to our awareness of her. Her rigidity crumbles as she learns to respond to situations more immediately and personally, to "bash on, regardless," like the hero in Laurence's children's book, *Jason's Quest*.[21] She now enters life, instead of officiously judging it at an immunized distance. Another illustration of her greater capacity to share experiences occurs when she and her young roommate, Susan Wong, laugh over a moment: "Convulsed with our paining laughter, we bellow and wheeze. And then we peacefully sleep" (302). Hagar's love of the first person singular, with all its privacy, egotism, and possessiveness, gives way to the collective pronoun, implying her entrance into a human community and her acceptance of others into her world. Decentered, she laughs *with* someone instead of laughing at her.

For another thing, in more than generosity, Hagar of her own accord fetches a bedpan for someone, she who before has recoiled queazily at the slightest contact with "messy" things. Then in . . . camaraderie? conspiracy? . . . with her young roommate she dabs on a perfume called "Ravishing," she who had always preferred the sedately named "Lily of the Valley." Small measure, perhaps, but not so trivial when we recount Hagar's history of denying physical life, a penchant which continues into the previous scene with Lees. She is taken aback at the cannery when Lees tells her in what Hagar thinks of as plain and coarse words about his happy association of sexuality and religion. She cannot bring herself to be so direct: " 'Well, that's a mighty odd combination, I must say, prayer and *that'* " (227). True, superiority registers in the whiff of British speech, "I must say," but we can locate a certain anxiety in that "that." The grammar inscribes Hagar's residual suppression of the body. As a shifter, the word enables her to censor the topic—sex—by strategically naming what is so upsetting to her. The word "that" enables her *not* to name even as ostensibly it names, allows her to conceal what she mentions. Her style of naming amounts to a refusal to name. Since the pronoun can and does attach itself easily to other signifiers, it can be everything and hence nothing in itself. This is eminently true when as a linguistic strategy one substitutes a pronoun in order to avoid a taboo (a substantive one finds so unspeakable it is difficult to admit). The pronoun's very instability provides for Hagar a twitch of evasion.

Her use of the euphemism derives from no mystery, that is, it does not come from not knowing; it comes from scandal. It is a suppression of what Hagar knows only too well. Much the same can be said for the sorts of linguistic prejudices Hagar begins to jettison. Certain signifiers, those supercharged with error and transgression, she learns to speak. We could argue that Hagar's growth can be measured by her linguistic education, since she learns to appreciate violations of her school-marmish standards in diction, grammar, orthography, and usage. In other words *The Stone Angel* narrates Hagar's search for her lost self, swamped by the cultural taboos that have seized her very words. She needs to find and to step into a language that will allow her by setting aside her aphasias and her equivocations to ex-press the self silenced within her. We further could incorporate this shift as one instance among several progressions, including a migration from aristocratic pretensions (in an inner speech studded with references to royalty) to democratic identifications.

Perhaps the most moving indications of Hagar's recently found ability to accept and even to embrace life take place between herself and Marvin. Just before she dies, Hagar finally blesses him who, never having received his mother's love as a boy, now wrestles her as Jacob wrestled with his angel (304). Earlier her other son, John, played a sardonic Jacob to her angel, wrestling with the stone surrogate in another place of death (179); as earlier still Matt had for the only time in his life "held both my hands in his" as he unsuccessfully sought her comfort for their dying brother (25); as the dying John "put a hand on mine" (242) but found once more she could not relieve his pain nor bring him any comfort. Each plays Jacob to her petrified angel. Now, having been brought down off her pedestal and brought to life by Lees' ministering touch, she reaches out and touches, mothers one of her men. Allowing even for her white lie when, contrary to her continued preference for John, she tells Marvin what he needs to hear, that he has been the better son (as in fact he has), allowing that 'falseness,' we see Hagar at one now with Marvin, atoning for past neglect and becoming true to him as the mother she never was.

Marvin's powerfully understated goodbye duplicates in every word what as a seventeen-year-old boy on his way to the war he said ("Mother—"), solicitously calling on her in her capacity as his mother: "He turned and put his hand on the doorknob. 'Well, so long,' he said. 'I'll be seeing you' " (130). The repetition, realist text here folding inwardly like dough on itself, textually, depicts how much the partings mean to Marvin rather than how fastened to habit he is. His laconic speeches, true to prairie voice, are so charged with unspoken emotion that he expresses what he does not say.

As for Doris, Hagar does little, if anything, to show her any change of heart. Yet indirectly Laurence does reveal how much Hagar has edged toward her daughter-in-law without knowing it. Laurence carefully indicates what Doris says when, shortly before Hagar ends up in the hospital, Marvin finds it impossible to tell his mother how hard she has been on them:

> Then, frighteningly, his voice, so low and solid, goes high and seeking.
> "What will I say to her, Doris? How can I make her see?"
> Doris does not reply. She only repeats over and over the mother-word.
> "There, there. There, there." (66)

Having sown these words early in the book, Laurence brings them to fruition in the end, when Hagar is made to see. Hagar, we remember, refused as a girl to mother her dying brother (though her brother does the mothering). We also recall that when Bram sought her out in his need she "wanted to say 'There, there, it's all right,' but I did not say that" (85). However, as she herself is dying many years later, and as she is thinking her last words, we are reminded of what Doris has said in soothing her husband: "I wrest from her [the nurse whom Hagar thinks is Doris] the glass, full of water to be had for the taking. I hold it in my own hands. There. There" (308). The words circle back to earlier avoidances, her multiple failures, but turn us back too to the moment when, in textual cohesion that accords with other references, she mothers herself. Waiting for the bus that will start her on her journey to the Point, in a scene that opens that section, she tells herself "Just take it easy. There, there" (146). After all this, as her life's narrative closes, closes around her, she frames that episode in the next and final section, and gives it firmness. Departing her life, she now can speak the mothering words—simply, a little stubbornly, but as a mother, virtually for the first time.

The water she seizes picks up and closes a long series of references, all of them indicative of Hagar's spiritual drought and of her need to submerge herself in the depths. Mentally Hagar lives her last days under water. (No doubt her mind wavers there because she is heavily drugged, but literal explanations don't go far enough and therefore don't give full credit to what Laurence does.) Therefore we note that the nurse's needle slips into her "like a swimmer sliding silently into a lake" (303), her room at night is "dark and deep" while she lies "like a lump at the bottom of it" (298), and she is "hauled out of sleep, like fish in a net" (257). Hagar drifts "like kelp" (289), flowing through the shadow world she has entered. After ninety years she is getting to the bottom of things, lying there waiting for release, and, though once more she doesn't realize it, waiting for transformation and rebirth, which may come with the promised metamorphosis of the pupa Hagar sees herself as having become.

Ironically, as Hagar is dying, she is coming to life. She strays from her deliberate normal paths and static, impregnable garrisons, wandering toward the "wrong" side of life which is the deep, dark, unconscious, fluid world around her and within her—the very world she's been taught to view as subordinate or wrong. Once moved but unmoving, she now manages to surpass her fumigated version of life by flowing with it instead of resisting it.

In shaking off her fabricated masks and tenacious stranglehold on life—her self-recognition comes "shatteringly," she thinks—Hagar finally moves toward personal wholeness. Jung calls that transformation *individuation*, the realization of one's entire self, partly hidden when someone becomes fragmented as a result of taking on a "civilized" self.[22] In Jung's economy people recover authentic realities only by overcoming the false selves they have acquired. In doing so, they throw over the *persona*, the exclusive and repressive social archetype detrimental to an individual's development.[23] Hagar's process of maturation consists of abandoning specious versions of herself she has received from her society (false selves, as Bram always understood; he who all along represented Hagar's best chance, who was the only one to call her by name and thus to affirm her identity). Freed of those covers, she no longer denies what she is out of fear for what others might think.

The Stone Angel, though a piece of stunning realism, is also mythic. But it is not sentimentally or gratuitously so, certainly not in its attitude toward the Christian mythology it incorporates. *"Bless me or not, Lord, just as You please, for I'll not beg,"* Hagar says as she nears the end of her journey (307). The magnificent assertion shows how truly uncommon she has become in her common touch. She is, as Marvin confesses in the end, a Holy Terror!

---

1. *The Stone Angel*, "Introduction" by William H. New (Toronto: McClelland and Stewart, 1968), pp. 4-5. Later page references to the novel will appear in the body of the essay.

2. Laurence develops the same binaries later in the book when she describes Jason Currie's plot: "A certain sum [of his estate] went to pay for the care of the family plot, in perpetuity, so his soul need never peer down from the elegant halls of eternity and be offended by cowslips spawning on his grave" (63). The park Jason Currie provided for in his will shows the same determination to eradicate whatever is indigenous: "Within a year,

Currie Memorial Park was started beside the Wachakwa river. The scrub oak was uprooted and the couchgrass mown, and nearly circular beds of petunias proclaimed my father's immortality in mauve and pink frilled petals." (63-4).

3. "Sources," *Mosaic*, 3, No. 3 (Spring 1970), 82.

4. *Mosaic*, 83.

5. For instance, Rachel Cameron in *A Jest of God*, "Introduction" by G.D. Killam (Toronto: McClelland and Stewart, 1974), lives in the top storey of an undertaker's building, an indication of how much she has withdrawn from the "lower" things that energize life. A more obvious and more related example of a symbolic house occurs in *A Bird in the House*, "Introduction" by Robert Gibbs (Toronto: McClelland and Stewart, 1974), where Vanessa MacLeod is trapped in her grandfather's unassailable "Brick House . . . sparsely windowed as some crusader's embattled fortress in a heathen wilderness" (p. 3).

6. Laurence herself was worried about the appropriateness of assigning figurative language to Hagar. See "Gadgetry or Growing: Form and Voice in the Novel," in George Woodcock, ed., *A Place to Stand On: Essays By and About Margaret Laurence* (Edmonton: NeWest Press, 1983), pp. 83-4.

7. According to what I have heard from the novelist David Williams, who raised the question in conversation with Laurence. Of course, Laurence's inexperience with Jung's psychology doesn't mean, if Jung is to be believed, Jungian archetypes cannot appear unconsciously in her writing.

8. I am aware of the article, "Margaret Laurence, Carl Jung and the Manawaka Women," which Nancy Bailey has published in *Studies in Canadian Literature*, 2, No. 2 (Summer 1977), 306-21. However, I find her argument somewhat tangled and erroneous in its understanding of Jung. In any case, Ms. Bailey says *very* little about *The Stone Angel* in her paper, which is meant as a general statement, rather than an application of the approach to the particulars of individual novels.

9. *Two Essays on Analytical Psychology*, trans. R.F.C. Hull (New York: Meridian, 1956), p. 203.

10. Jung explains: "Animus opinions very often have the character of solid convictions that are not likely shaken, or of principles whose validity is seemingly unassailable. . . . But in reality the opinions are not thought out at all; they exist ready made. . . . The animus is rather like an assembly of fathers or dignitaries of some sort who lay down incontestable, 'rational,' *ex cathedra* judgments." *Two Essays on Analytical Psychology*, p. 218.

11. "By shadow," Jung explains, "I mean the 'negative' side of the personality, the sum of all those unpleasant qualities we like to hide, together

with the insufficiently developed functions and contents of the personal unconscious." *Two Essays*, p. 313.

12. Jung writes: "Seen from the one-sided point of view of the conscious attitude, the shadow is an inferior component of the personality and is consequently repressed through intensive resistance. But the repressed content must be made conscious so as to produce a tension of opposites, without which no forward movement is possible. The conscious mind is on top, the shadow underneath, and just as high always longs for low and hot for cold, so all consciousness, perhaps without being aware of it, seeks its unconscious opposite, lacking which it is doomed to stagnation, congestion, and ossification." *Two Essays on Analytical Psychology*, pp. 63-4.

13. It's also worth noting that Bram's decanter is unwittingly phallic, a matter emphasized in his desire to see what Hagar looks like beneath "all that rig-out" (51).

14. Jung, "The Phenomenology of the Spirit in Fairy Tales" in *Psyche & Symbol: A Selection from the Writings of C.G. Jung*, ed. Violet S. de Laszlo (New York: Anchor, 1958), p. 71.

15. The passage echoes an earlier account showing how upset Hagar becomes in the dark in contrast to Bram who finds peace and perhaps wisdom in it: "The darkness never bothered him, even as a child. It let him think he used to say. I wasn't like that, ever. For me, it teemed with phantoms, soul-parasites with feathery fingers, the voices of trolls, and pale inconstant fires like the flicker of an eye" (205).

16. In interview Laurence has said, "When I choose names I am not looking into all the possible meaning of them, but I am usually aware of reverberations." Michel Fabre, "From *The Stone Angel* to *The Diviners*: An Interview with Margaret Laurence," in *A Place to Stand On*, p. 202.

17. In "The Phenomenology of the Spirit of Fairy Tales" (*Psyche & Symbol*, p. 78), Jung connects the unconscious with wood- and water-symbols.

18. The pattern of experience Hagar passes through at Shadow Point directly follows that outlined by the Jungian critic, Joseph Campbell, in his *The Hero with a Thousand Faces* (New York: World, 1956), originally published in 1949. Campbell proposes that the passage of a mythological hero "fundamentally . . . is inward—into depths where obscure resistances are overcome, and long lost, forgotten powers are revivified" (29). The passage runs outward as well as downward, reaching into foreign regions: "the adventure . . . normally follows the pattern of . . . a separation from the world, a penetration to some source of power, and a life-enhancing return" (35). Campbell also indicates the dangers in undertaking such a journey, including the possibility that the adventurer might not be able to come back. Hagar faces that prospect in the passage quoted in the previous paragraph, when

she fears that without Lees' help she "may not be able to return" once she is drawn into the depths.

19. The symbol of the trapped bird works profoundly throughout *A Bird in the House*, where it represents Vanessa MacLeod's stifling imprisonment in her grandfather's brick house.

20. Another instance of Hagar's newly acquired wish to communicate takes place during her conversation with her grandson, Steven, while she is in hospital: "I'm choked with it now, the incommunicable years, everything that happened and was spoken or not spoken. I want to tell him. Someone should know. This is what I think. *Someone really ought to know these things*" (296).

21. *Jason's Quest* (Toronto: McClelland and Stewart, 1970), Illustrated by Staffan Torell, p. 60.

22. *Two Essays*, 121.

23. *Two Essays*, 297.

BOUNDARY WALKER: ROBERT DUNCAN IN "A POEM BEGINNING WITH A LINE BY PINDAR"

We have them with us always. They claimed, or rather jeered in Provence, remonstrated in Tuscany, wrangle today, and will wrangle tomorrow—and not without some show of reason—that poetry, especially lyric poetry, must be simple; that you must get the meaning while the man sings it.

—Ezra Pound, *The Spirit of Romance*[1]

1. Psyche

"A Poem Beginning with a Line by Pindar," anticipating in form and subject Duncan's work later in the 1960s, is the most ambitious, most experimental, and most difficult piece in *The Opening of the Field*.[2] Whether it is altogether successful cannot be easily determined, to such an extent does it depend upon density of allusion and the juxtaposition of subjects whose connections are not apparent. My comments are going to be a bit hard to follow at times because we won't have the poem before us, it being much too long to quote in its entirety, and because we will be tussling with the extreme density and reflexivity of the text, which will show in the strain of my prose.

Duncan has shown in his *H.D. Book* and elsewhere that he knows who has preceded him in the opening of the field. His literary sources have seeped into his consciousness, so deeply that they shape his poems in irregular topography and weight them with citation. They also represent a kinship beyond his own time and place, an array of what for Duncan are charged reserves. Those most prominent in the "Pindar" poem are Ezra Pound, William Carlos Williams, and Walt Whitman. But it is the Greek poet Pindar, a radiant presence, who opens the poem with his face, his step, his body movements:

> *The light foot hears you and the brightness begins*
> god-step at the margins of thought,
>> quick adulterous tread at the heart.
> Who is it that goes there?
>> Where I see your quick face
> notes of an old music pace the air,
> torso-reverberations of a Grecian lyre.

The light movement—light of foot, full of light—that brings with it the old Greek music breaks in upon the margins of Duncan's thought and heart where he is most susceptible, insinuates itself into his waking consciousness. Startled by the sudden apparition of what later in the poem he calls a boundary walker, he cries out like a sentry: "Who is it that goes there?" The lines open the field, set Duncan on a complex chain of associations, ready to receive whatever may surface. Attendant on the moment-by-moment emerging, he listens, senses, writes.

> The poet waking from waking [shaking off that first lethargy, that heaviness in coming out of sleep] takes up the challenge of the voice of the poem and wrestles against sleep, bringing all the watchful craft and learned art into the striving form in order that that much recognition and

admission enter into the event. He strives to waken to the will of the poem, even as the poem strives to waken that will.[3]

Pindar's fleeting apparition in the dance jerks Duncan to attention and releases a flood of memories and ideas which it will the poem's dance to sail.

Pindar gets things started but almost immediately the poem speeds off on another tack. According to Duncan's account of how he wrote the poem, he at once thought of a Goya painting (*Myth*, 25), the gap in the sequence indicating Duncan's improvisational method of writing. He describes the painting of Cupid and Psyche faithfully, the warm brown tones of their skin. He goes on to add literary details from the Cupid-Psyche tale as Lucius Apuleius presents it in *The Golden Ass*:[4] the two jealous sisters, Psyche's innocence, the hot oil in the lamp she is carrying.

In the first section of the poem, then, Duncan introduces the two mythic figures that he has taken over. More correctly, they would seem to have taken over him:

> Waking into the reality of the poem, so that the room where I wrote, the fact that I was writing, and the catalytic process of the works of art, passed into the process of the poem itself, dimly underlying the work, as in actual life we may be aware that dream processes are at work, the poem as I wrote forming such a powerful nexus or vehicle of this transcendent reality of Eros and Psyche and of the revelations flowing out of the myth they belonged to, *I was hard pressed to keep up with the formations as they came.* (*Myth*, 26; my emphasis)

The crucial appearances of Eros and Psyche, their story a wonder for Duncan from earliest childhood, direct the poem. Though in this essay it is not they who most interest me, I want to take a minute to establish their prominence in the poem and then at the end to return to them.

After the temporary abeyance of their story in part II, the poem reverts to it at the beginning of part III. Psyche, having already spilled oil upon Cupid's shoulder and driven him away from her, performs the arduous tasks Venus has imposed upon her. Duncan retells the story much as it occurs in Apuleius, the one exception being his omission of Psyche's third assignment which requires her to fetch water from a stream guarded by dragons. Duncan enumerates the other tasks: sorting the seeds before nightfall, gathering wool from cannibal sheep, and harrowing hell for a casket kept by Proserpine. He adds the means that enable Psyche to fulfill those three missions—an ant, a green reed, and a tower. At the end of part III, he describes how "the Beloved is lost" and how Psyche, seeking a "monster-husband,"

> travels
> life after life, my life, station
> after station,
> to be tried
>
> without break, without
> news.

Having lost Eros, she sets off diligently in search of him and thus initiates one of the major patterns in the poem—the drive for recovery and cohesion.

The first hint of what the Cupid and Psyche material means to Duncan occurs in part I when he anticipates "the soul wailing / up from blind innocence" into painful knowledge. Then in part III, Psyche, driven by doubt, burns Cupid and commits "the outrage / that conquers legend." From then on they participate almost passively in events thrust upon them. Those incidents are informed by purpose since, as we learn in part I (the repetition in predicates is Duncan's): the wind serves them, the sisters serve them, Psyche's ignorance of "what Love will be, / serves them." The dark, the oil, Fate itself serves them. Similarly in part III we read (again the repetitions are Duncan's) that the tasks *must* be impossible and that Psyche *must* obey the green reed, "must follow to the letter / freakish instructions." She must despair and she must weep, but she must not open the box she gains from Proserpine. From the start Duncan emphasizes both the necessity of events which are thrust upon the lovers and the inevitability with which they will be delivered from them. Events are for him prophecy, narratives whose unfolding lays out unavoidable misfortunes and happy resolutions—large structures which Duncan accedes to even as in his compositional methods he attends to the smallest and the most local shifts.

Psyche, we remember from Apuleius's account, feared the oracle's warning that her husband would be hideous. Her spiteful sisters actually describe him as a huge and poisonous serpent. Hence Duncan's poem refers to a Serpent-Desire and a monster-husband and in part IV mentions that Apollo's oracle says *The Gods themselves abhor his power.* Clearly this Cupid possesses powers that are dangerous or revolting to a settled order. But *she* finds a beautiful lover, "saw him fair."

Although she is apprehensive, Duncan's Psyche tries to learn more about her forbidden lover:

> Scientia
> holding the lamp, driven by doubt;
> Eros naked in foreknowledge
> smiling in his sleep; and the light
> spilld, burning his shoulder—the outrage
>   that conquers legend—

It's telling that when she drives Eros away she for the first time becomes "Scientia." Not Psyche but *Scientia* falls into what Duncan calls the "deprivations" of sight. Shocked by severance, she wanders into "dismay, longing, search." So "the Beloved is lost." The poem further underscores that loss by calling her lover "Eros" for the first time, the altered name indicating his life is changed too. The new identities accent the split that occurs between the mind and body, or the mind and heart (mentioned throughout the poem), once the human psyche is broken apart.

At the beginning of the poem Duncan establishes the couple's sensuality when he speaks of their voluptuous grace, their soft eyes flooded with rapture, their distinct eroticism:

> A bronze of yearning, a rose that burns
> the tips of their bodies, lips,
> ends of fingers, nipples. He is not wingd.
> His thighs are flesh, are clouds
> lit by the sun in its going down,
> hot luminescence at the loins of the visible.

Duncan is careful to show that the god has flesh but not wings and that the tips of the lovers' bodies are burning with heat. He stresses their sexuality because for him the sacred is always embodied in the profane, the higher in the lower—fusions which, as soon we will see, should be made.

Eros's dark world offers more than sensual delight; it harbours the life of instincts, dreams and fantasies. Yet, for all its virtues that realm lacks something. That is why, as we read in part III, Eros's existence is "Melancholy coild like a serpent / that is deadly sleep / we are not permitted / to succumb to," the figure of the snake curled upon itself representing an infantile state in which Psyche mindlessly drowses when attached to him. And so, even as she loses touch with Eros, she must move out (this is a good thing), become Scientia, the light she brings into his night world symbolizing the start of her mental journey. That trip is not easy, for her emancipation is accompanied by a fall into self-consciousness which means a distressing severance from what she was, what she needs, and what in the end she will become.

In taking this view Duncan is working firmly in the Romantic tradition with its myth of a traumatic fall into consciousness. Duncan has supposed that wholeness is ruptured by "knowledge, the contaminant," a phrase he has appropriated from Williams' *Paterson* and put to new use. Limited and abstract, that set of mind which Psyche acquires and from which she soon seeks release, shuts her off from origins. Duncan interprets that story as an allegory for our time: "The light spills," he writes. The egg shatters. "Eros is burned or betrayed. . . . It is the beginning of our era."[5] Scientia disintegrates Cupid's undifferentiated world and becomes modern.

But she must depart, since she cannot redeem herself *only* by returning to a primal state. Obviously Duncan sympathizes with her yearning to regain connection with the living flow of things. No anti-intellectual, however, he *also* approves of her struggle toward maturity. Psyche must travel "station / after station. / to be tried / without break" (like stations of the cross?), seeking her way home. Through active love, not the passive sort she has known, through the force that unites and reunifies—we will see more of this later—Psyche will discover a new and greater fusion.

In our time, Duncan finds, the established world still operates on damaging assumptions about the primacy of the upper world—mind, spirit, reason, maleness, consciousness, light, the human species, restraint. Eros, as spirit of the unmentionable and menacing depths, some sort of demon, encounters a shrivelling of sympathies that leads commonsense people to command the world within them and around them. Once the creative unconscious is discredited, forces of literalism and exclusion prevail, even to the point of organizing "marches upon disorder":

> Clovis crossed the Rhine into humanity, but his ancestor, so Gregory of Tours tells us, was a dragon or demon of the other side. The Eros within was Christ; the Mother within was a Virgin. The Eros without was "a monster Bridegroom," was Pan and then Satan; the Mother without was Nature, was Aphrodite, was a Witch, was Lilith. The Church was a bulwark against them. . . . The Nature without was lawless and false; the Church recognized a Nature within and defined what was outside her law as *contra naturam*.[6]

2. American Politics and Fraternal Artists:
William Carlos Williams and Walt Whitman

In an effort to sustain a line of the imagination, Duncan turns, as so many in our time have turned, to other artists. His writing, as "A Poem Beginning with a Line by Pindar" demonstrates, is crowded with citation. Duncan frequently speaks of this allusiveness as an attempt to create poetry by integration. He says his poetics is

> a process of participation in a reality larger than my own—
> the reality of man's experience in the terms of language
> and literature—a community of meanings and forms in
> which my work would be at once derivative and creative.
> So, I have taken Blake's "The authors are in eternity" as
> my guide. . . . I do not express meanings that are my own,
> I work in meanings which I receive or find in research. . . .
> What I experience . . . in my extreme persuasion to the
> reality of the world created by the written and read word,
> where the meaning in language has its definitions in the
> community of meanings from which I derive whatever
> meanings I can, is at times a feeling that there is no real
> me, only the process of derivations in which I have my
> existence.[7]

Intertextual to the core, Duncan enters the body of language and literature where he abides its collective enterprise even as he erodes its conventions. He does not think of himself as some intact genius who hurls things god-like into existence (though he is closest among those I have met to being what if I believed in such things I would call a genius). Rather, he sees himself—scarcely a self as many think of the self—as one who receives a language and a set of precedents that shape his work. Duncan is candid in emphasizing his acquisitiveness but he tends to play down his contributions in pulling together material, modifying it, supplementing it, and creating something out of the strands. He whimsically describes his creative borrowings when he says "I am a jackdaw in poetry. But I know when I'm coming home with a piece of colored glass that I've found that fits the design, and where to go for the fire at the center of things."[8] In the "Pindar" poem Duncan refers to at least eleven artists, all of whom influence the poem or act in it. They all inspire him. They also help to sustain him in times of trouble, as in the two middle sections of the poem (parts II and III)—it is here that my attention lies—where Duncan sets them against contemporary life.

Reflecting on the Psyche and Cupid myth, Duncan goes on at the beginning of part II to wonder "What if they grow old?" But no, *they* won't. "The gods / would not allow it." Others *do*— in our present condition in time, which is to say in history, rather than in myth. In history, the thought comes to Duncan, in the currents of his mind, it is not youth but age that is beautiful. And not merely old age but the old poets, those who in "their faltering, / their unaltering wrongness that has style, / their variable truth," shed words "like tears from / a plenitude of powers time stores." These old poets do not use traditional verse. Duncan's words and jagged lines point toward Williams (his variable foot?), Pound, and Olson, perhaps too to Whitman and Pindar.

Duncan moves from his initial account of the old poets to describe the effects of a stroke on one of the old faces:

> A stroke. These little strokes. A chill.
> The old man, feeble, does not recoil.
> Recall. A phase so minute,
> only a part of the word in- jerrd.

The sudden alteration of language at this point is dramatic and serves as a sign that new material is emerging. As it is. If it were not for the care and consistency of Duncan's references, and his adherence to certain writers, we might not suppose he has a particular person in mind. It is almost certain, however, he is referring to William Carlos Williams, who by the time the "Pindar" poem was first published in 1959 had just suffered at the age of 74 the latest and most debilitating stroke in a long series of strokes, and who in those chilling days lived in dread that they would one day drop the bomb. The lines I've just quoted show how Williams' speech has been disturbed by the lightning strokes: "only a part of the word [is] in- jerrd"; not "injured" but "in- jerrd." The damaged (misspelled) syllable isolated by means of a hyphen and a space at the end of the line visually conveys the sense of Williams' "faltering." Orthographic 'flaw' corresponds to semantic and syntactic slippage.

Following the description of the stroke and his graphic representation of the fractured word that it produces, Duncan inserts a passage—*"The Thundermakers descend"*—reminiscent of the language in what for Duncan are three major power reservoirs: H.D.'s *Trilogy*, Pound's *Cantos*, and Williams' *Paterson*. It appears Duncan is quoting some such source (most likely H.D., whose trilogy uses such diction) since that is his usual practice and since in "A Poem Beginning with a Line by Pindar" he indicates (by italics or quotation marks) expressions directly incorporated into it. The words would act then as if anchored in another text and would carry with them all the impact of that text. However, *these* words are not remembered, they are created. Duncan made up the line[9] and included it in the poem as if he had received it, plays "Finders Keepers," as he will write later in the poem. Though false citation, the passage nevertheless is activated with the authority of actual quotation, as if it were legitimate, its function in the poem being reinforced by other 'citations' similarly marked, and determined by its immediate context, which deals with Williams' aphasia:

> *The Thundermakers descend,*
>
> damerging a nuv. A nerb.
> The present dented of the U
> nighted stayd. States. The heavy clod?
> Cloud. Invades the brain.

The passage projects two different meanings. One: Zeus, classical Thundermaker (and as sky god apotheosis of established order), shames his nominal counterparts (soon to make their appearance), who are nothing but anaemic imitations of him. More likely, two: the modern warmakers who, as in a few lines we discover, are destructive presidents, mistreat Williams in some symbolic way. There is considerable evidence outside "A Poem Beginning with a Line by Pindar" for the second reading. In 1953 Williams was shocked when, following a series of bureaucratic obstructions, he was refused the chair as Poetry Consultant at the Library of Congress, partly because of his alleged communism, and partly because of the political furor caused when the Library chose, with Williams' support, Pound's *Pisan Cantos* for the Bollingen Prize in 1949. Though Williams deserved the post and needed it to help him through a time of failing health and personal crisis, his long friendship with Pound and his disgruntlement with the United States got in the way—these were Cold War days with a vengeance—and Library authorities didn't fill the position they had promised him. He—American zealot, local to the core, rooted in, snubbing his nose at Pound as he whored after foreign gods—he, Williams, had to pass a loyalty test to the satisfaction of the FBI and the Library of Congress! He had gone too far, stepped across too many bounds, spoken against official stupidity. The upshot of the sordid affair was that Williams, his nerves shot (for other reasons too), crumpled into a depression so deep he was within a few months committed to hospital for psychiatric care.[10] Duncan, familiar with what happened, depicts Williams in the "Pindar" poem as an example of artists shabbily used by a repressive society.

We are struck when we read, therefore, that the Thundermakers damage "a nuv. A nerb" in Duncan's poem. The wounds they make are in some way equated to the humiliations Williams was put through and to the lesions produced by his stroke, when he felt as if gauze had settled over his brain. Normally we would think of a poet's nervous system as something that enables him to respond and to generate meaning, as the carriage of his intelligence. It is essential for a writer, Duncan tells us in his *H.D. Book*, "that the tips of consciousness, the nervous susceptibility, be kept bare, sympathetic, ready, as a condition for reality."[11] To have that nerve, that insect sensibility. The turns and returns, fine-tuned, responsive to the tiniest oscillations, nudging to boundaries, back in broken trajectories. To keep in touch, the circuits working. Duncan's poet would seek awareness to resist military (and militant) authority. "There was an eternal conflict between . . . orders," Duncan writes of his own experience in the armed forces. "Nerves that must be kept the edges of a vulnerable everlasting consciousness, kept raw and yet fine—our nerves that must serve us if we were to be artists—strained and recoiled at each session of drill."[12] So Williams recoils in the "Pindar" poem; as he in fact in his own life sat penned up, right hand, writing hand, a maimed bird fluttering on his lap. Isolated in his personal hell, like Pound of these same years, he was brought to the point of dissolution.

Although the Thundermakers turn on Williams and jam his speech, they themselves suffer the consequences of what they do since, in struggling to speak, Williams stumbles, wounded beast, out of silence. Inadvertently, though infirm, he confirms Duncan's critique of them. Their efforts shake but cannot destroy Williams' speech. His language, as Duncan graphs it in short abrupt phrases, is spasmodic. It staggers in aphasia, speaks in "A phase," the smallest measures. For all their imprecision, the syllables are precise. The impairment does not faze Williams and in a way it does not even interfere with his basic insight or intelligibility. Though he totters through forays and self-corrections, what slips he does make become judgments on those who are attacking him. Creative mistakes, prophetic errors, the broken lines convey what we might perceive as the exactness of catachresis, truth in the slip of the tongue. The lines, "The present dented of the U / nighted stayd. States," turn on a phonetic slide that plays to us: "States," "stayed," maybe even "staid." That glide becomes, through the adjustments and readjustments it contains, a compression of something like: "You, the president(s) of the United States, have remained benighted (and dull)." Worse, the presidents, they who preside over denials, who censor the work of the word, they—not Williams—are "dented," mentally unsound, metallic and inhumane.

I hear too, in the jag which suspends "jerrd," a rhyme bobbing on the waves. Sceptics may want to put this hearing out of limits but I am encouraged by the border blur, the transgression of boundaries, the shunting of permissions Duncan himself invites. I am encouraged too by the prominence which topography accords these particular letters. Stuck out there all by themselves, the isolated letters enjoy no morphemic status, which is to say no given meaning, at least none that I can think of (homonyms in words like conjured or perjured obviously do not count for orthographic reasons). Lacking that basis, "jerrd" exists in something like a semantic vacuum, one that invites us to fill it meaningfully. One of the most ready and gratifying ways to do so—we play the poet—is to substitute according to some principle of similarity. Whatever else may come to mind, "jarred," laid in as CvC rhyme and as near assonance, presents itself as an intelligible unit—phoneme that performs as morpheme. It certainly fits: this poet is jarred, jangled by the strokes of war, insult, nervous disorder; put away in an institutional jar. Jarred, he fights back. He must speak—poet as informer—however halting the measures. He must refuse (*re*-fuse?) to comply with the authorities, must not fall into a well of silence, voice skimmed off on the cold.

It is worth reminding ourselves that Dwight D. Eisenhower was president during the 1950s when Williams was suffering from the advanced effects of his speech impediment and Duncan was writing the "Pindar" poem. A connection between Eisenhower, military hero of World War II, and the Thundermakers in the poem would be simple to make, especially with the subsequent mention of Eisenhower in the poem. President of the Cold War, presiding over the bomb, over (however inadvertently) the McCarthy brutalities, he was there for Williams, "so that," writes Williams' brilliant biographer, Paul Mariani,

> when the bomb—symbol of every form of repression—
> roared, as it had roared for Williams in 1952 and '53 . . .
> the "news" of the poet's face could outdistance the "public

print" showing the dazed, confused faces of public officials out of control.[13]

The "faces of evil," "the Devil's creatures" Duncan would call them a decade later as the American government pursued its war in Vietnam. And then, more shocking, in outrage: "Eisenhower's idiot grin, Nixon's / black jaw, the sly glare in Goldwater's eye."[14]

There may be another stitch. As Duncan pointed out to me, Eisenhower himself suffered from a speech impairment.[15] The fractured lines may refer to the president's verbal contortions as well as Williams'. Seen in that way the halting twilight talk would do double and 'contradictory' service: in drawing out Williams' statement about the president(s); and in imitating the president's own words as he trips over them and tries to correct them, wanting to "state" something but "stayed" from doing so. (There is a fine splice too for someone like Duncan who believes in the efficacy of language, in that word "state": the word of politics—the state; and the word of speech—to state.) If this were the case, we would be asked I think to view Eisenhower's speech as *public* figure, as head of state, with dismay, rather than with any sympathy and rather certainly than with admiration. It would then decode as malaise he has created rather than injury he has received. In him the spasm represents a real deficiency, a terrible impotence that afflicts his state. How seriously can we take a Thundermaker (the upper case intensifies the sense of power-mongering and self-importance) who can only sputter, and who a few lines later in the poem is called a "heavy clod"? The pathetic joves, Eisenhower among them, bungle along in verbal and mental failure. But they are harmful still—hounds at the unicorn Williams had come to be. Theirs is a deficiency that Williams himself, time closing on him like a posse, has identified in *Paterson* where he says "the language / is divorced" from such minds.[16] Because they "do not know the words / or have not / the courage to use them," Williams writes, "the language is missing them" and they die.[17] Likewise, having neglected and perhaps perverted the creative use of words, politicians in Duncan's poem waste away in a world without grace or significance, a world of their own failed making. As poor artists who rule without vision, who speak without care, the Thundermakers are directly responsible for the ruinous condition of their own country. Impotent and infantile, they lay waste their powers. Their language has become so dead, so loveless, they themselves so powerless, so contained within the maps they have defined, they can't find the words to make things any different.

The political theme in "A Poem Beginning with a Line by Pindar" is no small matter for Duncan. His concern for the state of the American *polis*, always conspicuous, becomes unusually intense at times. That happens most notably when out of its multiple guises the madness boils over into what Duncan understands to be illegitimate warfare. "The seemingly triumphant reality of the War and State disorient the poet who is partisan to a free and world-wide possibility," Duncan writes in anxiety during the American war in Vietnam, "so that his creative task becomes the more imperative. The challenge increases the insistence of the imagination to renew the reality of its own."[18]

That struggle, central to Duncan's thinking, figures conspicuously in the "Pindar" poem, beginning with the Williams section. Was it the Second World War with "the divorce in the speech for Williams" which "touched a spring of passionate feeling in the poet that was not the war but his age, his ripeness in life"? Duncan wonders. When Williams was "almost 'old'," Duncan muses, he "was able under fire to arrive at a fine distinction."[19] Duncan in part is remembering the superb section in *Paterson* that describes how mundane articles were (and by implication how Williams was) torqued into beauty and meaning by a hot fire that sweeps through them:

> An old bottle, mauled by the fire
> gets a new glaze, the glass warped
> to a new distinction, reclaiming the
> undefined.

And then:

> Hottest
> lips lifted till no shape but a vast
> molt of the news flows. Drink
> of the news, fluid to the breath.

In the end the glass is

> defowered, reflowered there by
> the flame: a second flame, surpassing
> heat   .[20]

"Scarred, fire swept," "the person / passed into the flame, becomes the flame— / the flame taking over the person," Williams writes.[21] What Duncan says in his *H.D. Book* about the transforming powers of the fire catches Williams, circuits burnt, flame in his head, as he rises into "A Poem Beginning with a Line by Pindar."

Following the few lines of fractured speech, the poem reads: "The heavy clod? / Cloud. Invades the brain." The closeness in sound between "clod" and "cloud"—and the semantic contamination they beget—sets Duncan off in another direction (as a few lines before he moved from "recoil" to "recall"). The clouds and the clods, reminders of the mean-spirited in the previous section, aggressively invade and occlude the brain, seat of language and imagination, just as earlier the war-makers short the poet's nerves (and as, to Williams' horror, in the nightmare history he inhabited, they electrocuted the Rosenbergs). The cloud points to the ever-present pall in Whitman's elegy on Lincoln (elements about to take their place in the poem) and to the fear that a cloud has fallen on Williams, injured dog in the street, and permanently damaged his speech. It may also have destroyed his capacity to recall—this is crucial to Duncan's poem and to Williams' poetry at the time—"a plenitude of powers time stores." Splintered and drifting, he may have lost touch with a past that wends through "A Poem Beginning with a Line by Pindar" as counter to subsequent wrongs.

* * *

Snap: the circuits open. With a shock of horror Duncan wonders "What / if lilacs last in *this* dooryard bloomed?," the dooryard that is Williams' mind (a flowering bottle, full of flowers, hundreds of flower poems) and the dooryard that is the American nation. Whitman and Lincoln, visionary poet and exemplary statesman, enter the poem. What if after Lincoln it were all over with America, Duncan asks himself, its finest dreams and its best people faded and forgotten? The whole dreary line of succession is paraded before us in a contemporary Duncaniad:

> Hoover, Roosevelt, Truman, Eisenhower—
> where among these did the power reside
> that moves the heart? What flower of the nation
> bride-sweet broke to the whole rapture?
> Hoover, Coolidge, Harding, Wilson
> hear the factories of human misery turning out
>   commodities.
> For whom are the holy matins of the heart ringing?
> Noble men in the quiet of morning hear
> Indians singing the continent's violent requiem.
> Harding, Wilson, Taft, Roosevelt,
> idiots fumbling at the bride's door,
> hear the cries of men in meaningless debt and war.
> Where among these did the spirit reside
> that restores the land to productive order?
> McKinley, Cleveland, Harrison, Arthur,
> Garfield, Hayes, Grant, Johnson,
> dwell in the roots of the heart's rancor.

The pitiful array prove in Poundian recitation—litany of prophetic fervour, moral outrage, counting off the names, chanting, *naming* them—not to be creative leaders in touch with their people and showing the way toward wholeness, but unmoved "idiots fumbling at the bride's door," unable—it's here we turn back to the Psyche section—to consummate a union with the female land, "the flower of the nation," and unable in their roles as Fisher Kings to make the earth fertile by restoring it to productivity. The land, as well as the language, is divorced from their minds. Their impotence and sterility, for all their political 'power,' contrasts sharply with Williams' genuine power and creativity. Williams, broken brain, right hand, pen hand, impotent in his lap, typing, typing. He has crossed over, time bomb in his brain, ticking. The authorities' separation from a land they neither speak to nor love, never speak to in love (as Williams himself makes clear in his *In the American Grain*), amounts to a division within themselves, their (permanent?) situation corresponding to Psyche's temporary divorce from her mate and her self. The public men build barriers within and walls without, barricades meant to keep irrational life in place. In their dispersals and in their containments they betray Eros, the force that builds and brings things together.

The inner sickness afflicting the heads of state—we should appreciate that metaphor: "heads"—produces disease in the nation (though the reverse is true as well). Although the politicians "hear the factories of human misery turning out commodities" and "hear the cries of men in meaningless debt and war," they cannot "hear / Indians singing the continent's violent requiem." More deterioration. They are not oblivious to the degradation, they do not care to admit its extent or to do anything about it. As Duncan sees them, the demoralized leaders have lost faith in the *polis*, the very principle they are supposed to uphold, to hold together, because they have become removed from the sources which enhance the life of a community, which actually *make* that life.

The land they are responsible for is violently dying, blighted by greed. The line about factories of human misery exemplifies Duncan's passionate dislike of modern American capitalism. He is appalled at

> the display aesthetic of packaging and advertising art to put over shoddy goods, repeated in *the display aesthetic of*

the new architecture, where a wealth of glass or cellophane, aluminum, copper, or gold paper facing takes over the city, presented in *a poverty of imagination,* housing the same old shoddy operations of whiskey, cigarette or paper companies; and back of the sell, the demand for profit and increase, *the exploitation of mind and spirit* to keep the rackets going, the economy of wage-slavery and armed forces, and over all, the threat of impending collapse or disastrous war.[22]

There is another way. Psyche and Eros, true bride and bridegroom, come together in fulfillment. Their marriage ensures new life in (pro)creative possibility, which the public men in America avoid. The Presidents, potential World Fathers or sky gods (hence their comparison to Zeus), do not rejoin the World Mother (the flower of the earth). Under their aegis things not only fall a-part, they remain apart. Duncan in disappointment asks "where among these did the power reside"? and "Where among these did the spirit reside / that restores the land to productive order?" Duncan's answer is that those in charge lack power and spirit because they possess neither the love that "moves the heart" nor the creative energy stored in time's reservoirs. Their stewardship produces a debilitating loss of energy and erosion of meaning. In their hands the plenitude of power is running down, trickling away. Dispersal, de-generation, atrophy. Entropy everywhere.

Duncan progresses through his indictments of the lapsed presidents by listing a group of them, surely as chant, in a 'big' public voice, then raising a string of charges and rhetorical questions that bring us into agreement about their incompetence. No one is slighted. The roll call is complete from Lincoln's immediate successor—aporia in the narrative—right up to the (then) current president; in chronological sequence from Hoover to Eisenhower, then backward in time from Hoover to Andrew Johnson, repeating several names (Hoover, Harding, and Wilson) more as a base in the litany (I think)—two-bit trochees lumped in their redundancies—than as instances of unusual perfidy. In view of such ineptitude Duncan despairs of America's ever being able to restore itself to its potential. There is every chance the game is over: "For whom are the holy matins of the heart ringing?" The dream has nearly dissolved like a wet blotter: belief in resolute, far-sighted leaders and in a New World that—how American Duncan is, how recent the loss is—might have been Paradise. Duncan regrets he cannot respond with anything like Whitman's love for Lincoln nor Whitman's enthusiasm for America when he considers those who have subsequently misdirected the country. The section of the "Pindar" poem dealing with politics is stuffed with disappointment. It is an elegy, angry at times, but suffused with a sense of fallen dreams and unfulfilled promise.

It keenly laments lost fellows. This thought had turned Duncan into the political part of the poem. He returns at the end of his endictment to fraternal spirits, those whose personal well-being and recognition have become more and more uncertain. Although Duncan in various ways deals with those worries, in the "Pindar" poem he concentrates mainly on the need to preserve a fellowship of imagination. Hence the appearance of still another figure in Duncan's "chrestomathy"—Walt Whitman, to whom Duncan elsewhere has paid homage.

Whitman's hopes for an illustrious America have virtually collapsed for Duncan. Whitman, in part consoled by the heart-shaped lilacs returning each spring, was able in his own elegy to carry on. Years later Duncan fears these emblems are gone: "How sad 'amid lanes and through old woods' / echoes Whitman's love for Lincoln!" The promised land betrayed and misdirected, Lincoln dead, Whitman's retreat is stripped by "fumes that injure the tender landscape." Even though Lincoln tolerated wage slavery, Duncan argues, he was able to bring and hold the nation together through its bitter Civil War,[23] something none of his successors has been able to do, their failure demonstrably registered in the topography of Duncan's poem where the one word "United [States]" becomes, broken in two across lines "U / nighted," scattered sign of a state that is not united, is anything but hale (whole) and hearty. That is why Lincoln's imagination and humanity are badly needed to bring the country through its troubles. But "There is no continuity then. Only a few / posts of the good remain."

> It is across great scars of wrong
> I reach toward the song of kindred men
> and strike again the naked string
> old Whitman sang from.   Glorious mistake!
> that cried:
>
> "The theme is creative and has vista."
> "He is the president of regulation."

Duncan reaches across the scars—his method preserves him, frees the rapid pulses in his work—toward what these ancestors have done, to touch what, later twisted and abandoned by others, they believed. Whitman had expansively predicted in his 1855 "Preface" to *Leaves of Grass* that the United States would have greater poetic spirit than any other nation, and that "Their Presidents shall not be their common referee so much as their poets shall."[24] It was in this essay that he made the statements Duncan folds into the two unidentified quotations toward the end of part II. Whitman declares himself not for the presidents of death, but for the presidents of regulation—the poets, Shelley's unacknowledged legislators. What a sad outcome when a century later those poets are neither well used nor respectfully consulted.

When Duncan tries to resurrect lilac blossoms of courage in his landscape, he discovers (Thoreau in his boots)

> I too
> that am a nation sustain the damage
> where smokes of continual ravage
> obscure the flame.

And he goes on to see "always the under side turning, / fumes that injure the tender landscape." As is his practice, Duncan conceives of the inner world as a pastoral field alive with freshness.

When it is threatened so too are the lilacs he cultivates, vestiges of what Lincoln and Whitman stood for. Icons perhaps of Williams, flower poet, blighted on the stem. The symbol consolidates the references to Duncan's fraternal order, for they all have been blasted by fire. But they do survive, as in Duncan's 'answer' to Eliot:

> Whitman was right. Our names are left
> > like leaves of grass,
> likeness and liking,   the human greenness
>
> tough as grass that survives cruelest seasons.[25]

In his portrait of the modern artist as victim Duncan closely associates himself through both language and structure with Williams. Just before the passage indicting America he describes, as we have seen, how the old man's speech was impeded. Then, following the criticism of American administrations he says he himself is damaged when smoke obscures his flames. The references to a shared predicament connect the two writers. The structural circuit reinforces the equivalence. At one stage the text dwells on Williams, moves to Whitman, and then enters its political centre. Then it moves back again to Whitman, and finally out to Duncan himself. In the symmetry of that sequence Duncan's position corresponds to Williams' and so strengthens the identification of those who persevere in a diminished world.

As I have already indicated, the poets also line up with the mythic pair we met in part I. In her desire to regain Eros, Psyche shows the way to juvenation that most Americans, supportive of their political regimes, refuse. Dispirited, dissolute, they fail to recognize their lack and as a result fail to do anything about it. What is more appalling, in their failed sympathies and segregation they oppose the generative underground by damaging nerves, invading brains, destroying the environment, endorsing greed, and conducting meaningless wars. They are much less than they have been and nowhere near what they could be, which is to say Adamic.

3. American Politics and Fraternal Artists:
Ezra Pound

In part III of the poem the paradigm of "the old man at Pisa" rises into the field, as Duncan perceives yet another tie, this to a poet he long admired and emulated.

The Pound of the "Pindar" poem is the broken, humiliated one of the *Pisan Cantos* (Cantos 74-84), not the flamboyant upstart forcing his way into the London literary scene in the 1910s, nor the literary lion of Paris in the 1920s. It certainly is not the crank of the 1930s and '40s nursing his political and economic dogma: allusive, grandiloquent, pronouncing, admonishing, summarizing, swarming with symbol and metaphor, bristling with precept and maxim. School-master, everything Williams was not. The "Pindar" Pound is the one in imminent danger of death at the Disciplinary Training Center near Pisa, where, alongside dozens of the most brutal American soldiers, he was temporarily jailed by American forces at the end of World War II, for three weeks of the time held in a poorly sheltered animal cage. Pound's thoughts of shaping a finer world, however wrongheaded, were shattered by the collapse of the Italian Fascists and, according to Duncan's account (everyone has a slightly different story), he hitchhiked to Pisa to surrender to American troops. Confined in the last small compartment in a row of ten cells holding men awaiting execution, "with the shadow of the gibbets still attendant,"[26] and afraid that in the wreckage of Europe the world would never "take up its course again" (453), Pound wrote the poems that so powerfully express his torment (the ones that won him the Bollingen prize). Pound describes himself early in those cantos, his system overloaded, "As a lone ant from a broken ant-hill" (458), one of several lines Duncan either quotes or echoes.

In prison Pound passes through dismay to lucidity, progresses beyond fatigue to clairvoyant calm—"in the condition of first things" Duncan calls it—and sustains himself through humble identification with life. He, arrogant and defiant through the war, says now a lizard upheld him, hopes "that he [may] eat of the barley corn / and move with the seed's breath" (531), watches a "brother" wasp and its new infant, startlingly green in its eye, in his eye. Ultimately, he reaches a "wisdom [that] lies next thee, / simply, past metaphor" (526); his mind swung on a grass blade, saved by the exquisite exactitude of an ant's forefoot. It is these lyrical moments Duncan diverts into his own work.

"A Poem Beginning with a Line by Pindar" soon connects Pound with the Psyche myth. Duncan's free-flowing mind takes hold of its fascinations and enables him "to draw the sorts" between Pound and Psyche in confluence of an emerging story. The couplings sometimes are hard to locate, although familiarity with Duncan makes them more visible. The helpful ant in Psyche's story (the "insect instructor") reminds Duncan of the beneficent ant in the *Pisan Cantos*. Duncan further connects Psyche, who must sort the seeds and whose spiritual progress is served by "the wind spreading the sail," and Pound, whose mind, full of mixed seeds (memories as well as potentialities), teeters (as Williams totters) on the verge of collapse, where he learns to flow with the wind and the rain.

Duncan's esteem for the *Cantos* did not in the least blind him to Pound's increasing authoritarianism in the inter-War years. In that stretch, Duncan maintains, Pound had hardened into "a pedagogue, a culture commissar,"[27] "impressed during his years as a would-be candidate for his doctorate with the concerns and ambitions of a would-be professor of literature,"[28] one of those who, in Duncan's eyes, clings to inflexible thoughts and petty ambitions. Pound, as much as the politicians he denounced, had become set in his ways, secured in his strongholds. Not until the trauma of his prison ordeal did his rigidity begin temporarily to dissolve:

> at Pisa, uprooted from his study and his idées fixes, "*a lone ant from a broken ant-hill*," Ezra Pound was to come . . . in the Summer and Fall of 1945, to a turning point, exposed,

at the heart of the matter. Mussolini had been torn to pieces. . . . *"Manes was tanned and stuffed,"* Pound remembers in the first Pisan canto. The poet had hitchhiked to Pisa and surrendered, given himself up to the army. Had he expected death? His fellow prisoners are led off to the firing squad each day. And, for the first time in the Cantos, in these Pisan cantos, some attitude of authority, some self is surrendered, so that a pose seems to have fallen apart, exposing the genuine, confused, passionate mind. *"A lizard upheld me,"* he testifies. He is in the condition of first things.[29]

With his "admission of a serious flaw, 'the six seeds of an error' " (*Myth*, 65), Pound unwillingly entered his agony, wrote in a river of fire. His whole life torn, Pound burned away his stubborn pride and with the greatest difficulty reassembled the transformed pieces of his mind.

Psyche's "sorting of the seeds," "every grain / in its right place," implies the order she derives from confusion—the precise verbal definitions and sorting of things into organic categories that Pound himself had urged in the Confucian translations he did, mind teeming with seeds, while he was writing the *Pisan Cantos*.[30] As Pound writes about "Kung" in *Confucius*, spirits or energies in the world compel people to prepare vessels for sacred grain. Meantime Pound was himself sorting things out in his own mind. Fixed ideas breaking, he rafted the debris and the currents of his mind. Pound, discomposed but mindful of his memories and dreams, found renewed vitality and direction through the organic ordering which he advocated and which Psyche in the "Pindar" poem achieved:

wheat	barley	oats	poppy	coriander
anise	beans	lentils	peas	—every grain

in its right place

Duncan's words illustrate Pound's kind of order since each word, designating a seed, has been set apart from the others: each in its right place, its own pile. The slight pauses indicated by the spaces within the lines convey the weight of the seeds being deliberately and firmly, one after the other, each in its own, put into place. In the lines, as in the act, there is a distinct hesitation for the action, line reinforcing signifier. The two words at the end of the second line ("every grain") are equally appropriate since they describe the *inclusiveness* of the (as) sorted seeds, nothing left out, everything accounted for. In the completing line ("in its right place") comprehensiveness as a concept finds its visual form and its firm affirmation, as if in summary and satisfaction, the intact phrase looking back over the careful laying out of the words/seeds, Duncan saying it is right. Duncan's task, like Psyche's and Pound's, is to ensure that all seeds are properly separated and assimilated, precisely distributed in some agricultural and cultural project. Pound's discrimination becomes in part IV Duncan's "catalyst force that renders clear / the days of a life from the surrounding medium," an act of naming (sorting) in such a way that we come to sharper and more responsible knowing.

The ants, the seeds, the wind, the mental anguish and dismay, the descent into hell, the arrival at primal condition, the organic (re)ordering—all these bring together Pound and Psyche in suffering and recovery. In showing the way back to wholeness, which is to say in collecting the golden wool and raising the dawn, Psyche induces or parallels Pound's release from his destitute state as a shipwrecked *"Man upon whom the sun has gone down!"* Her attempts to pull her world together match Pound's efforts to survive and to reconstitute himself, as they subsume, too, a broken Williams writing his way during the early '50s into a span of love and brilliance.

Pound serves as another example of the modern poet's attempts to share his dream in a deteriorating environment. "Only a few / posts of the good remain," Duncan complains, only a few of the "old faces" from the past. When "A Poem Beginning with a Line by Pindar" was published Williams and Pound were worn and old. Williams, 74, as we have seen, was suffering from bad health and disappointed hopes. Pound, 72, had finally been released from his long spell at St. Elizabeth's, where he was held as criminally insane. Even so, like H.D. who lived through the World War II bombing raids on London, Pound and Williams at the same time came under fire, caught fire, to achieve something deeper and more complex.

> In December of 1944, H.D. had finished her War Trilogy; she was 58. At Pisa, Pound was 60 when he finished the Pisan Cantos. William Carlos Williams at 62 in 1944-45 was working on *Paterson I*. For each there was to be ahead, in the last years of their lives, a major creative phase. . . .
>
> It seemed to me . . . that . . . in London, in Pisa, in Paterson, there had been phases [as Williams went through "A phase"] of a single revelation. . . . Was it that the war—the bombardment for H.D., the imprisonment and exposure to the elements for Ezra Pound, the divorce in the speech for Williams—touched a spring of passionate feeling in the poet that was not the war but was his age, his ripeness in life. They were almost "old"; *under fire to come "to a new distinction."* . . . They give, these three works out of the war, a text for the historian of our contemporary spirit. . . .
>
> In the light of these works I write today.[31]

And then there is Whitman, another in the tradition: "Once I returned to Whitman, in the course of writing *The Opening of the Field* when *Leaves of Grass* was kept as a bedside book, Williams' language of objects and Pound's ideogrammatic method were transformed in the light of Whitman's hieroglyphic of the ensemble."[32]

As Pound twines his way through the text, the wind of his own work enters to define a nation of wind, those who are used by the wind—poets and sailors. A few of the lines Duncan appropriates from the *Pisan Cantos*, particularly *"the wind is part of the process"* and *"man upon whom the sun has gone down,"* emphasize Pound's identification with Odysseus as an ill-fated wanderer.[33] In the first Pisan canto, reverberating with Homer, Pound as prisoner almost immediately sees himself as if he were

Odysseus talking to his captor Polyphemous. In those hints Pound adroitly promotes himself as Odysseus' kin, as "no man" surrounded and held by a monstrous world. The phrase "no man" is Odysseus' answer to Polyphemous. Yet it directs us too to Pound's vulnerability, barely hanging on and reduced to near non-entity in his broken house at Pisa. Debris washed ashore, he can simply say he is near the end, bottomed out. In his *H.D. Book* Duncan explicitly connects Pound with Odysseus in their precarious situations and personal offences.

Pound eventually passes, spiritually altered, through serious misfortunes, just as every one of the protagonists in "A Poem Beginning with a Line by Pindar" (Psyche, Williams, Pound) goes through personal distress and eventually finds the way home. Fittingly, the *Pisan Cantos* end with a moving expression of Pound's new humanity: "If the hoar frost grip thy tent / Thou wilt give thanks when night is spent" (540). He has eaten the flame, come like the others through fire to a new distinction.

For Pound, making restitution meant pulling down his vanity to see with clarity and affection the 'insignificant' plants, animals, and people around him. It meant too finding what in Canto 74 Pound himself called the root of the process taking place as the winds gust and veer (443)—the streaming wind and rain that upholds life and revives it, that rinses the shrine's marble white again. It breathes air fresh as chlorophyll into the face of an existence gone sour. Pound, bewildered and tormented by circumstances, in the end learned to cleave to the flux, float with the jetsam and flotsam, when he gave himself to the winds and the rain. Once he became part of nature, Pound could sort the seeds, seed them in his rocky fields. The obstructionist presidents resist, they will neither let love pass through them, nor risk the currents of life. Their evil systemic, they deteriorate into sterile, almost pathological, nay-sayers, miss the moving moment as it flies.

4. Threads

Duncan moves abruptly to, speeds through, another section so full of threads it begins to tangle. The step from Pound to the next movement is by no means certain, the gap representing (what is typical of Duncan) a drastic disjuncture in the text. "Who? / let the light into the dark? began / the many movements of the passion" the passage begins. Who indeed? One can only guess. Psyche? Psyche spilled the light of consciousness. A reversion then. Or, more distant, is it Pindar? Pindar's light foot brought brightness to the poet and introduced him to the poem.

The indeterminacies persist. Is it because people pass from the unified life of childhood to fragmented adulthood that "West / from east men push"? It may be that in their estrangement from nature modern Westerners have become oblivious to the world which we're often told Easterners know. If so, the modern American, miserable and dejected like Pound, is a *man upon whom the sun has gone down.*" Duncan uses Pound's lament, refrain in the *Pisan Cantos,* to typify the bleakness of public life in America.

It is a catastrophe for the sun to go down on man; yet an enlightened Psyche can fulfill herself only by seeking darkness. The reason is simple. Psyche's full humanity depends on incorporating both light and dark into something resembling Blake's organized innocence. To lose the darkness is to fall into rationalism; to ignore the light is to be trapped in infantilism. In order to be something more we must live in naive dream *and* in sophisticated waking. As lamp-bearer and gatherer of "the gold wool," Psyche in a sense is welcome dispeller of darkness, just as Jason in the next short section becomes a saviour by releasing the dawn. In his night sea journey, Jason must not only defeat huge armies; he must also "woo Night's daughter, / sorcery, black passionate rage," his quest coinciding with Psyche's. Like the Greek warriors seeking Helen, emblem of the fleecy sun, he must win over the engulfing powers if he is to release the "golden fleece." That fleece, the ball of light, is the light of consciousness swallowed like an egg by some snake. By overcoming the dragon, just as Psyche outgrows her monstrous husband, the hero surpasses a state that is both personal and typical of the species.

It's peculiar that Jason struggles "widdershins" to release the sun. Duncan knows the exact significations of the odd expression. He enjoys playing with it, for he writes of "my love of the eerie charm that perished words have . . . *a love supported by my perhaps special belief in the recurrence of all things and structures.*"[34] Precisely, for in the myth of restitution which girders "A Poem Beginning with a Line by Pindar" he always looks to a past, often to an archaic past. Always honouring the residual, he acts out his belief that words are not counters to be manipulated as displays of wit or startling expression, but forces full of saving resonance, "a plenitude of powers time stores," as he puts it earlier in the "Pindar" poem. "Widdershins," the *OED* tells us, means "in a direction opposite to the usual; the wrong way; in a direction contrary to the apparent course of the sun." Using the word in its specific sense, Duncan means the direction Jason travels, as opposed to the direction the sun seems to move. Most people (those upon whom the sun has set?) have travelled from East to West. So, Jason travels "widdershins" in the other sense as well: "in a direction opposite to the usual," acts as antidote to Westering and benighted mentality. In recovering the stranded light, Jason becomes prototype for those such as H.D., Pound, and Williams, who pursue "their unaltering wrongness that has style" and important meaning.

The next and last shift in this difficult section introduces American legend. In the unsettled West of the American past, and even more so in the legend that succeeded it, life was harsh. In this rugged territory, presumably Duncan's home state of California, "Snakes lurkd / guarding secrets." What connects this bit to the Jason material most superficially is the series of words describing the loneliness of outcast heroes. What more profoundly stitches them together are those snakes somewhere between myth and history, the story there too, casting its threads to take in more and more. The correspondences thicken: Cupid as serpent desire, night witch in the Argonaut story, dragon West—worlds of trapped sun. We remember now the significance of Scientia's outrage against *legend*. If those so boxed in night are ever to grow, they must give way to those who let the light in.

The poem continues to bounce between those realms in part IV. Duncan opposes the wilderness to the hostile clearing of his tame mind. The poet's domesticated mind struggles to preserve itself against a blackness, abode of the wild and the unsophisticated, threatening to overwhelm it. For a moment resisting, Duncan himself outrages legend and joins in the fall from grace. Not for long. Though the depths—Indians, sexual passion, Moon, Great Death ("Cupidinous Death"?), Night itself—give way, the garrison in his mind also falls. The emblem of collapse might be confusing. "Who is there?" the speaker asks, and excitedly replies, "O, light, the light!" And the poem turns, turns away from the rancour and pettiness, the spiritual meanness, that ate at Pound and Williams. In the transition between the Pound and Jason sections the speaker similarly has wondered "Who / let the light into the dark?" Still earlier he has asked, "Who is it that goes there?" as Pindar flashlighted his mind. Considering the way Duncan, loom among poets, jumps from one strand to another, reverting to earlier threads, then moving on, returning yet another time, the resemblance cannot be fortuitous. Each flood of light—each new revelation—opens a door in the poem, shunts us into new stanzas, induces us into related movements. In doing so, it stresses equivalences between the light passages, the disappearance and reappearance of the lines binding the tapestry until by the end of the poem Duncan, rhapsodic (stitching together, winding, ravelling, revelling in it), says "A line of Pindar / moves from the area of my lamp / toward morning," teasing one of the last ends into the face of the fabric.

From the outset Pindar and other luminous presences lurk in the corners, leak into the edges of the poet's mind, soak into his awareness, "and the brightness begins." Duncan, noticing

Goya's "sun in its going down," rises from his night vigil watching over the poem's formation, and flows through the informing myth into the dawn. Pindar and Psyche recapitulate the pattern. So does Ezra Pound. At the end of the *Pisan Cantos* he describes his release from dark night of the soul to final peace "when night is spent." He too has freed the sun that went down on him and found what in the "Pindar" poem is called—the line equates two themes and so should not be missed—"The light that is Love." And so, extratextual, has Williams: found fulfillment. Out of the disasters we have recounted, he wrote a run of poems effulgent with love, came to a new distinction. In "Of Asphodel, That Greeny Flower," Mariani tells us,

> Williams keeps weaving back and forth between memory—the memory of the race as well as the memory of his own past—and the present time in which the poem is set. But even the present—the public events drifting across Williams' consciousness in '52 and '53—float in a larger timelessness, where the threatening news about the Cold War, with its daily deaths and destructions, is contained within the larger patterns of mythic recurrence. So the swift lightning flash of the electric chair that silenced Julius and Ethel Rosenberg in June 1953, the wanton destruction of art by the forces of death—in this case the burning of priceless Goyas by Juan Peron's goons at the Jockey club in Buenos Aires—the dismal presence of witch hunters during the McCarthy Senate investigations, and the incessant pressure of instant nuclear Armageddon which Williams had feared since Hiroshima and Nagasaki are all bracketed, not by our receding distance from these events, but by Williams' measuring of these [for him] increasingly minor irritants against a world of lightbearers.[35]

Williams, over the gaps, gasps in the measure, threads his lines to love, to be loved, the beloved. He too clinches in the arms of Eros, restored. The major figures in the poem, almost interchangeable in its polysemous mythology, learn to make light of their gloom, to see things in a new light, pull things together. In rhapsody.

That is why the poem moves to the pristine vision of children dancing in the rising light, rinsing it clean:

> On the hill before the wind came
> the grass moved toward the one sea,
> blade after blade dancing in waves.
>
> There the children turn the ring to the left.
> There the children turn the ring to the right.
> Dancing . . . Dancing . . .

And then:

> In the dawn that is nowhere
> I have seen the willful children
>
> clockwise and counter-clockwise turning.

The Edenic hill, the grass billowing toward the ocean despite the stillness of wind; the children spinning, spinning in Duncan's haunting, almost hypnotic, rhythms; the clear slow-motion of dance as if perceived in trance or dream—these preternaturally intense, drawn-out details, nearly devoid of realist instance, suspend us, light as insects on a fish line or a spider's wire. "O, light the light!" Duncan exclaimed a few lines back as a radiance flooded him. The children's dance, burst of blossom, brings forth yet another illumination, its strength flowing from a vivid childhood dream Duncan has incorporated into his poem, weaving personal memory into the picture.[36]

The children's turning is a round dance, symbol of patterns taking shape, almost of their own will (if Duncan is to be believed) in the dance of the poem. The bright wheel offers a full and a fully unified life. It acts as incandescent mandala releasing, receiving, and concentrating the dazzling current pouring into the earth, shaking and kindling it. Duncan, at the centre, expresses and focuses the emanations, as he has done throughout the poem. The children's pulsing indicates a reintegration within the poem of what once was parted,[37] blazons its pattern as chief among all the recursions which typify Duncan's work, carouselling back upon itself again and again, swirling with its intertexts and its inner texts, wobbly with its sense, its register, that all things cycle through and, as they gather, find their correspondences. The children's circle enacts the harmonious and awesome cycle of life, the whirl of wind and rain Pound releases himself to, is born by, when he starts to see within himself and around himself. The power required to restore the land to productive order resides among these children, in these childlike adults, knelt in the state of first things.

5. Rhapsody

As I've tried to show, the artists' memories and visions, all corresponding to Cupid and Psyche's pro-creative act, rescue the lore badly needed in a de-generate age. The life force lies in traditional powers, as Duncan emphasizes throughout the poem. Pindar's "old music" in part I connects in part II with "the old faces," the "old poets," "the old man" William Carlos Williams, and "the old woods" of "old Whitman." Then, in part III, we find "the old man at Pisa," "the old tasks," the "old myths" of Jason, Paris, and Cupid, and the old legends of American pioneers. Finally, in part IV, we read of Indians belonging to an old way of life, the ancient myth of Isis and Osiris, the traditional folktales and games that belong to the children, and the "archaic," "obsolete" poetry of Pindar. Duncan traces his finger through these loops near the end of the poem when he suggests that "We have come so far that all the old stories / whisper once more" and that "there may have been old voices in the survival that directed the heart." Within his radical experiment Duncan works hard to keep these stories, these voices and poets, because he believes wisdom is cumulative and recursive, that poetry is rooted in the old speech, the mother tongue. As Duncan wrote me about "the question of the archetype" in his work, "there is the feel that the form of the poem presides over its coming into form—the more striking for the advance in projection in which I write."[38]

It's not surprising, then, that he would write in "A Poem Beginning with a Line by Pindar" of "passionate dispersion," of words that "shed like tears from / a plenitude of powers time stores." Perfectly in keeping with this measure of things, too, is the fact that Williams' declining ability to speak should be accompanied by his waning capacity to "recall." Duncan works here in a long tradition when he thinks of the muses as daughters of Mnemosyne. Everywhere in the text we learn that resonant language operates as psychic repository, both for an individual person and for the human race. When Williams' speech and memory begin to decay, he plainly is on the verge of losing the store of human experience.

The vision that revolves, resolves the poem ("In the dawn that is nowhere / I have seen the willful children / clockwise and counter-clockwise turning"). It climaxes a whole series of epiphanies, which we have seen. This power, Duncan tells us, is dispersion. The gods intervene in the reticulations of history to preserve Psyche, to speak to the gifted, to dance in Duncan's mind. The revelations come thick and fast, and in many forms they gather: a Greek poet of elusive footstep, a painting, an ancient tale, Williams, the flower of the land, Whitman, Pound, Jason and Medea, Paris and Helen, American legend, Charles Olson the "boundary walker / (in Maverick Road," mountains as the sites of revelation,[39] Isis, Osiris, dreams, children's games, a hymn. One must be attentive.

Openness requires more, it needs the force of love. Toward the end of the poem Duncan implies in the line *"rise to adore the mystery of Love!"*[40] that his people can find themselves through love. Appropriately, the whole constellation of characters *"directed the heart."* Pindar and the gods tread *at the heart*. There are many similar mentions. Psyche moves toward what Love will be. When Jason frees the sun "The light that is Love / rushes on toward passion." So too in reassembling "the body of her belovd / dismembered in waking," Isis gathers and reforms the light. Everywhere the gathering, the reintegrating, the coming together in marriage that defeats the divorce Williams saw and suffered. Pound, breaking through to love of nature, does not go to pieces. Duncan, like Psyche—Finders Keepers—traipses the poem, picks up the traces, rounds them up, needle and thread in hand, sparks for a new light in creative order. The drive to cohesion reveals Duncan's fascination with the residual, pungent as spruce gum on his hands. He takes hope in a past which, once snagged, could twist through swatches of history and sew together its luminous rags. For their part the estranged leaders, unrepentent and unregenerate, apotheoses of America, preside over its diminishment. Locked in "the heart's rancor," they miss the power. They have lost heart, care for no one and no thing, not even the remaining posts of the good who keep the magic and point the way to health. Rulers who cannot move the heart, and whose hearts are not moved, they cannot come together with America. They live in misconceptions, neither uniting the nation nor uniting with it.

Duncan tells us that purposive history (he might have said poetry) is "a drama in which the One is in many acts enacting Himself, in which there is an Isis in history, history itself being her robe of many colors and changes, working to restore in many parts the wholeness of What Is as Osiris."[41] By piecing together the torn fragments, Isis in effect reintegrates herself and mends the fracture. So for the most part do those Duncan approves of. They pass from ebb to purpose, dissolution to restitution, rotate on an armature of light. "A Poem Beginning with a Line by Pindar" is structured in much the same way. It begins on a high point of lyrical fluency and psychic unity in both Duncan and his counterpart, Psyche. It trails on to scenes of dispersion caused mainly by events in history: Williams' speech impediment (symbol of a larger torment), the presidents' repressions, Duncan's attempts to preserve the lilacs and woods, the severe trials Psyche and Pound are put to. Everywhere the Furies. The first signs of recovery emerge in part III with the organic ordering, the gathering of wool, the harrowing of hell, Pound's penetration to essentials, Jason's solar quest, the Greek recapturing of Helen. The drive toward reassembly builds still more in Duncan's mind following the release of the sun and Isis' search. It is then that the aging voices and the archaic stories, circulating in the text, come together in the centrifuge which the poem becomes, and focus in final light and fullness. Allowing for points of intermixture and departure characteristic of a poem that is improvisational, "A Poem Beginning with a Line by Pindar" shifts from the harmonious vision that marks its start, to diffusion and loss in the middle, then returns to the cohesion of dream vision at the end. The poem insists upon freeing and assimilating as an answer to the dissipation afflicting America.

As a result of that resolution, the poem itself, apparently fragmentary, barely holding against ruin, takes on a rough completion. There are a *lot* of loose ends, bits and pieces that resist the simplifications I am offering, but many of the most prominent elements turn out to be variations on the Psyche myth which arcs across the poem. That presiding narrative crackles in the friction of other stories, the same old stories, sparks of intelligence strung through this world. The material provides needed and inevitable form for Duncan, "a poem in the actual world" being "the fulfillment of a prophecy or story-form."[42] Even the italicized quotations in the poem struggle into form, approximate the larger amperage of decomposition and regeneration:

lyrical high point	— *"The light foot hears you and the brightness begins"*
disruption	— *"The Thundermakers descend"*
deterioration	— *"as a lone ant from a broken ant-hill"*
	— *"the wind is part of the process"* [actually the first sign of recovery]
recovery	— *"Finders Keepers"*
	— *"rise to adore the mystery of Love!"*

(inadvertent)
reversion   — *"Despair! The Gods themselves abhor*
this power."

6. Postscript

In the end, even these well-known writers—avowing, determined, sometimes (Pound) adamant, pushy—recognized as major, solidly pressed into the canon, even they are imperilled. Pound, Williams, Duncan, Whitman, H.D.: their voices are endangered in contemporary America. Outside of a fairly small readership they are set aside, ignored, ridiculed. They cry from the margins, feed on their lineage, hope to taste a preserving past, tap its reserves. For all their confidence, their sense of purpose, they are barely heard in the larger world. Quite silent, finally, for all their talking and writing. For all their brilliance.

---

1. Ezra Pound, *The Spirit of Romance* (New York: New Directions, 1952), p. 88.

2. Robert Duncan, *The Opening of the Field* (New York: Grove, 1960), pp. 62-9.

3. Robert Duncan, *The Truth & Life of Myth: An Essay in Essential Autobiography* (Fremont, Michigan: Sumac, 1968), pp. 63-4. Later references to this book will appear as *Myth* in the essay.

4. Lucien Apuleius, *The Metamorphosis or Golden Ass, and Philosophical Works of Apuleius*, trans. Thomas Taylor (London: Triphook and Rodd, 1822), p. 95. This is the edition Duncan used.

5. "Two chapters from H.D.," *TriQuarterly*, No. 12 (Spring 1968), 72.

6. *TriQuarterly*, 75.

7. *Audit / Poetry*, 4, No. 3 (1967), "Featuring Robert Duncan," 49.

8. "Preface" to Charles Olson, *Causal Mythology*, Writing 16 (San Francisco: Four Seasons, 1969), n.p.

9. Information from a conversation with Duncan in Winnipeg on April 9, 1976.

10. Reed Whittemore gives a detailed and readable account of this episode in Williams' life in his biography, *William Carlos Williams: Poet from New Jersey* (Boston: Houghton Mifflin, 1975), pp. 303-15.

11. "The H.D. Book, Part I: Chapter 2," *Coyote's Journal*, 8 (1967), 29.

12. "Beginnings: Chapter 1 of the H.D. Book, Part I," *Coyote's Journal*, 5/6 (1966), 27-8.

13. Paul Mariani, *William Carlos Williams: A New World Naked* (New York: McGraw-Hill, 1981), p. 675.

14. Robert Duncan, "The Fire," in his *Bending the Bow* (New York: New Directions, 1968), p. 43.

15. In conversation at Winnipeg on April 9, 1976.

16. *Paterson* (New York: New Directions, 1963), p. 21.

17. *Paterson*, p. 20.

18. "Robert Duncan: Rites of Participation (part II, continued from *Caterpillar* 1)," *Caterpillar*, 2 (1968), 150.

19. "Nights and Days, Chapter One, March 10, Friday. 1961. (1963)," *Sumac*, 1, No. 1 (Fall 1968), 111.

20. *Paterson*, pp. 142-3.

21. *Paterson*, p. 146.

22. *Caterpillar*, 2, 133-4, my emphasis.

23. "Man's Fulfillment in Order and Strife," *Caterpillar*, 8/9 (October 1969), 243.

24. *Complete Poetry and Selected Prose*, ed. James E. Miller, Jr. (Boston: Houghton Mifflin, 1959), p. 413.

25. "The Dance," in *The Opening of the Field*, p. 9.

26. *The Cantos of Ezra Pound* (New York: New Directions, 1970), p. 466. All other references to the *Pisan Cantos* will come from this edition and will be indicated in parentheses.

27. "March 13, Monday (1961)," *Caterpillar*, 7 (April 1969), 35.

28. "March 14, Tuesday, 1961 (1963)," *Stony Brook*, 3/4 (1969), 339.

29. *Sumac*, 1, 109.

30. *Confucius* (New York: New Directions, 1969), p. 31.

31. *Sumac*, 1, 110-1, my emphasis.

32. "Changing Perspectives in Reading Whitman" in E.H. Miller, ed., *The Artistic Legacy of Walt Whitman: A Tribute to Gay Wilson Allen* (New York: New York University Press, 1970), p. 100.

33. The two lines appear many times in the *Pisan Cantos*, as Pound struggles to survive and to find new life.

34. *As Testimony: the poem & the scene* (San Francisco: white rabbit, 1966), p. 16. My stress.

35. Mariani, *William Carlos Williams*, p. 671.

36. Here is part of what Duncan draws on:

First there was the upward rise of a hill that filled the whole horizon of what was seen. A field of grass rippled as if by the life of the grass itself, yet I was told there was no wind. When I saw that there was no wind it was a fearful thing, where blade by blade the grass so bowed of its own accord to the West. The grass moved towards the left. The seer or dreamer then was facing north. There may have been flowers—day's eyes—the grass was certainly in flower. The field was alive and, pointing that way, across the rise of the hill to the West, gave a sign.

. . . But in my dream there was no sun. The light was everywhere, and I can not be sure whether it was morning, evening or high noon.

Then, in a sudden almost blurred act of the play, there was a circle of children—sometimes they are all girls or all boys, sometimes they are boys and girls—dancing in the field.

"from the H.D. Book: Part I: Beginnings Chapter 5. Occult Matters," *Stony Brook*, 1/2 (1968), 18-9.

37. Carl Jung's work on the significance of the mandala is worth noting here. In *Mandala Symbolism*, trans. R.F.C. Hull (Princeton: Princeton University Press, 1972), he says mandalas appear at times of great personal or social stress characterized by "psychic dissociation or disorientation" (3). The mandala offers "a centre of personality, a kind of central point within which the psyche, to which everything is related, by which everything is arranged, and which is itself a source of energy" (73). As a result, a mandala often represents "very bold attempts to see and put together finally irreconcilable opposites and bridge over apparently hopeless splits. Even the mere attempt in this direction usually has a healing effect, but only when it is done spontaneously" (5). Even the direction a mandala rotates matters:

> I think I am not mistaken in regarding it as probable that, in general, a leftward movement indicates movement towards the unconscious, while a rightward (clockwise) movement goes toward consciousness. The one is "sinister," the other "right," "rightful," "correct." (36)

It is remarkable how well Jung's account applies to Duncan's poem: the critical state of conflict and anxiety, the consequent ordering or centering in a mandala, and the integrating motion of the children "clockwise and counter-clockwise turning."

38. Letter, Jan. 25, 1976.

39. The three particular mountains ("Mount Segur, Mount Victoire, Mount Tamalpais") are significant. I take it that in referring to Mount Victoire Duncan is thinking of "Cezanne working at his vision of Mont Sainte-Victoire": "Rites of Participation, *Caterpillar*, 1 (1967), 21. For "Cezanne restored the destroyd mountain" as Duncan writes in *Derivations: Selected Poems 1950-1956* (London: Fulcrum Press, 1968), p. 52. It was at Aix in his last decade of painting that Cezanne was to become preoccupied with

that mountain. In one painting after another he caught an almost hallucinatory tremor in it, his canvasses suffused with pure, intense light, the kind of radiance Duncan describes in "A Poem Beginning with a Line by Pindar" just before he mentions Mount Victoire. Cezanne, Duncan writes, was one of the painters "long exiled from the dominant taste of my day because of their false poetics": "The H.D. Book, Part 2, Chapter 3," *Io*, 6 (Summer 1969), 135. In the light of those reflections Mount Sainte-Victoire becomes a sign of resurrection in Duncan's poem. The other mountains represent similar recoveries. Duncan's reference to Mount Tamalpais, north of San Francisco, picks up earlier references to American legends and to spirits once found among the primordial rocks of the West "in my grandfathers' time" and now imaginatively regained in the poem. Mount Segur, the sacred mountain in Provence where heretical Albigensians made their last stand against the Church's crusade of extermination in the Middle Ages, towers in Duncan's mind. He views the Albigensian persecution as symptomatic of the contempt for visionary poets he has seen in his own time. Williams and Pound, he argues, have preserved in our time the *trobar clus* or ancient wisdom of the Albigensian gnosis: "From The Day Book," *Origin*, 10 (July 1963), 18. Pound, in particular, has transmitted a tradition in poetry stemming directly from heretical Provencal songs (*TriQuarterly*, 76). Duncan thinks of himself and his kin as outcast Albigensians, those who keep the storehouse of dreams and who perennially survive attempts to silence or destroy them.

40. The line comes from Charles Williams, *The Greater Trumps* (London: Faber, 1954), p. 107. First published in 1932.

41. *TriQuarterly*, 97.

42. *Origin*, 42.

BREAKING & ENTERING
(THOUGHTS ON LINE BREAKS)

1.

a poem for the other wise

they are every
where i tell you every
thing wrong with us they
wont let go
of the line wont   let you in
sist on their margins
of relief be
lief to let things wriggle
from them a kind
of bad breath

delirium—L., madness < *delirare*, to rave, lit., to turn the
furrow awry in plowing < *de*—, from + *lira*, a line furrow

they know   exactly
where   to draw
the line they insist upon

a strange sense of letters
: *she wishes*
you'd "stop   this playing
around"

this getting out
of line   this being ir
responsible foot
loose &   fancy/ free

we shld hold
our breath as long as we can
the dirty river   whats around us
we close our eyes to
log our time

the form & technique
obliterate the feeling
and the thought

when the little things
at night
shine on the bank & in
the water   at night
no one   lets
up   not even then
no one lets   go
lets you
be
not Ann   or the other Anne   they wont
give you   a break
they   deploy
their lines they are
not a
mused   they will not be caught
out   of line

not George   or Doug
certainly
not   Mark or Susan
not Brenda

<pre>
                              not even her
                  when you
                      throw things in   for good
          measure

                      they wont hesitate
              to step   in
                    in their made
              to measure lines

                              they just keep
        holding the line as long as they can long as they possibly can
                    hide in (met
                    a phor
              the hard of hereing
        when herein they take their (proper) measures

                          & you are   pretty
                    broken up about it
</pre>

2.

workshop

I've been struck for some time how much formal departure
disturbs readers. That's not surprising, I guess, since it always
generates uncertainties, but I don't think the resistance—it
varies in its outer fringes from panic to contempt—can be altogether excused. You find it everywhere: complaints about
"mannered" phrasing, fretting about "unfashionable" (or
"fashionable") lining, querulous comments about "mere" technique or "flat" writing. Above all bad writing is "artificial"—
this as a charge against art! What else can it be? The comments
are hardly confined to novices. It's been my experience that the
fiercest resistance to any straying from left margins or lines
based on simple units comes from people who should know better: editors, reviewers, and even—so help me—poets.

This is unhealthy. When sophisticated people are saying
these things, something's wrong. So, whatever I say here, there

will still be some who choose not to understand, and who will cling to their position, left margins stuck up to the axles in mud, knowing that flexible lineation is gratuitous. Those who already know that unorthodox lining is silly, if not fraudulent (pretentious distracting self-conscious academic uninspired contrived ingenious fatuous derivative—you can extend the list, you've heard it before), those who would insist on a system of power that legitimizes their operations but invalidates others', those readers ought to skip this piece. Others will know a lot of what I am going to say anyway. But I don't know of anywhere you can find a simple statement on line breaks.

I intend to outline and to illustrate several principles of line breaks and then to speculate on what has been happening to poetry that it should have been brought to such a state—past metre, past rhyme, and (here's the crux, the cause of such passion) largely past metaphor, grammatical phrasing, and (in its more radical versions) even past the image.

Once we move off & away from metre, we're in a position to rethink the line. In the first historical departures from metre what poems took the form of "free verse" were often based on grammatical phrasings, as in the case of, say, D.H. Lawrence.[1] Since then (since the 1920s, roughly) poets have tried out other possibilities, partly as they were released from romantic notions of sublime metaphor and genius.

Let me first give you a list of possible lineations as I have roughed it in. (I should say that with few exceptions my argument uses poems that have abandoned conventional punctuation. Poets need not leave punctuation behind, and most of them don't, but the shift seems a useful extension of the principles I am outlining. I would also add that using any of these devices does not in itself eliminate metaphor or simile and, further, that metered verse is quite capable of using line breaks.)[2]

In the absence of metre you can break a line in several ways.

1. *grammatical unit*

This is probably the simplest and the most common principle. It readily suggests itself since it is already in place as a unit for other forms of discourse, especially the prose we are accustomed to reading. And writing. It seems "natural," being so common. This is probably also the most popular line with readers since it asks the least of them: if we can't have metre, at least we've got grammar, *some* form. Here the line conforms to a syntactic grid, and we get limited uncertainty at lines' ends. You can see it in, say, much of Al Purdy:

> this is the moment you'll always remember
> this is the wind-blown instant of time
> that swings you into the future
> oh heavy as the heavy cellar stones of the world
> but hammering on the gates of the sun[3]

We scarcely notice the *lines* as intact units, so closely do they match grammatical units of meaning.

2. *the bardic or oracular line*

Built on chant or incantation or, more modestly, on listing, stock-piling or cataloging, this line leans heavily on repetition. It works largely by accretion, returning again and again to a base. Hence its anaphoric quality—emphatic parallels in sounds or grammatical units. Whitman pushes in:

> Voyaging to every port to dicker and adventure,
> Hurrying with the modern crowd as eager and fickle as
>   any,
> Hot toward one I hate, ready in my madness to knife him,
> Solitary at midnight in my back yard, my thoughts gone
>   from me a long while,
> Walking the old hills of Judaea with the beautiful gentle
>   God by my side,

> Seeking through space, speeding through heaven and the
>   stars,
> Speeding amid the seven satellites and the broad ring, and
>   the diameter of eighty thousand miles,
> Speeding with tail'd meteors, throwing fire-balls like the
>   rest,
> Carrying the crescent child that carries its own full mother
>   in its belly,
> Storming, enjoying, planning, loving, cautioning,
> Backing and filling, appearing and disappearing,
> I tread day and night such roads.[4]

Phyllis Webb, "On the Line," talking: "Certainties: that the long line (in English) is aggressive, with much 'voice.' Assertive, at least. It comes from assurance (or hysteria), high tide, full moon, open mouth, big-mouthed Whitman, yawp, yawp, and Ginsberg—howling. Male."[5]

A line that barges forward, almost unstoppably, builds not off nuance or hesitation, but exuberance, copia, adding on, turning on its heady fervour. Again, you will notice how the boundaries of the lines exactly coincide with the boundaries of syntax. This model is not going to cause any great problems for modern readers, either. Some might still find Whitman a bit rough, but no one is going to find these linings strange or impermissible. And why should they? They've got the sanction of the Bible behind them, and the reassurance that they are not left up in the air as the line ends. There's that comfort of having things lassooed as you come to the juncture, not having to chase any runaways.

3. Ogden Nashing

There are other versions of this sort of thing, but we all know what Nash does: the crazy distribution of (often polysyllabic and absurd) rhymes at the ends of long rambling lines that are 'prosaic' in their rhythms. The nashing of teeth. I take his practice to be representative of related twists to the traditional line.

4. Marianne Mooring

Again, there can be many other versions of this strategy, but Moore has made her lines famous. She counts out lines by syllable, each line of a stanza having its own count, which is then repeated in subsequent stanzas. Each of these lines becomes part of an intricate end-rhyme. But neither the lengths of the lines (they count out in exact syllable) nor the involved pattern of rhyme exists prior to the poem itself. Moore finds for each of her poems a pattern which, though regular, constantly surprises. The effect, as she writes, is like pulling a snake through a maze— the sentence sinuously slinks through the stanza, full of spasms and catches.

5. physical limits

This, too, enjoys a reasonable acceptance among poets and readers. I'm thinking here not simply of butting up against the typewriter bell or the furthest reaches of the right margin, of stopping only before you fall in the gutter. I may be wrongly inserting some psychological principle, but I'm also thinking of poets who will simply stop at some edge that is not defined by the printed page but possibly by some sense of an invisible vertical. Eli Mandel seems to do this in his latest books. He seems also to be defining an inner left margin by tab setting or by sliding the margin control on a typewriter.

6. arbitrariness

This may at first appear to be no principle at all, but clearly it is. If I choose to write out of randomness—and I may do so for several reasons—I have the basis for an erratic line. Not one that will please everyone, of course not. But one that can generate nimble reading. The reader can't nod over the page, confident in the linings, in any simple correspondence between the limits of the line and the limits of meaning. The lines will constantly shift under our eyes, not let them come to rest, come to an expected conclusion. Stressful, distressing. Margaret Atwood, though she lays out fairly symmetrical settings, uses something like this principle in her early poetry—setting up brittle irregular lines to reveal all those anxious figures who step warily through her poems. As if afraid of making one false move. Tense, Atwood's lines. Cracking off, bone dry, so jagged they can stab you.

7. *freeing up parts of speech*

You can see the nervousness in these lines as the grammatical units separate out and sift across lines, leaking through the containment of the single line. Working at cross purposes, purposing cross moments. You will have noticed how stretching across lines throws loose some words at the ends of lines where they lie, speak and spark in forked tongues. Doubling, dealing in duplicity. Words attaching, detaching, reattaching themselves in various configurations. As a word points back to the line it completes, or forward to the line it anticipates, it produces a hanging at the end it leaves you hanging, way out on a limb, it does double duty: a noun in this line, then by god an adjective in the next. Here intransitive, there a transitive. You don't hurry over the lines, insisting on one grammar that obliterates all others. It's not monogamy we're into—infidelity, fooling around, promiscuity all over the place. A mad series of erotic attachments and reattachments. I've grown attached to you. In so many ways. Perverse. Polymorphous. We trace several paths through the lines, *one* of them defined by its own intact standing—*this* line, entirely by itself. Self-possessed, that too. So language begins to slide, meanings to proliferate and to undermine themselves. Lines that meander & refuse to be pinned down by one grammar or one meaning. A doubling.

8. *syntactical ambiguity*

This case might be considered a larger or more extended version of 7. Whole phrases, even whole lines, can serve to complete *and* to open a unit.

> like a dog
>
> you lope off
>
> with it
>
> my love
>
> a chewed T-bone
>
> in yr jaw

Where does that "my love" fit in the sentence? Appositive to "it": with *it*, that is, with my love in your jaw? As apostrophe: you, my love, run off with it first chance you get? As opening of a new 'sentence': You lope off with it; my love [is] a chewed T-bone? You see how it goes.

It's evident that the line is freed up for overtime because none of the lines is conventionally punctuated. The insertion of markers would force us onto a more determined trajectory. This effect is most obviously and irrevocably true in the case of terminal punctuation but it also holds for internal punctuation. Both practices would hive out and insist on the integrity of designated units of syntax.

Eleanor Berry says George Oppen's recent poetry acts by

> throwing lineation out of phase with the syntactical divisions of the text and by eschewing punctuation to mark those divisions. The syntax in its relation to the lineation together with the near-complete absence of punctuation serves, further, to impede and thereby bring to consciousness syntactical interpretation and, sometimes, to invite construal of syntactical elements in more than one way, in one role in relation to preceding text, in another role in relation to what follows: *this possibility for polyvalence is not present in the technique of the rhetorical-rhythmical unit.*[6]

9. "false" or premature closure on buried idioms

> yet id be
> short with you then short
> bread shouting
> *luv me luv me*
> *i can make you*
> *feel good inside*

A variation on the power of (here sexual) idiom to alter our trajectories—the idiom that sets its expectations: "i can make you." And then the betrayal. The "you" turns out to be not so self-supporting as we have supposed and like a kite it trails a whole clause after it and into the next line. Here's another example:

> does this mean
> i am not
> a loaf of bread
> large with love
> the eyes big & liquid with it
> me gassing up for
> a shy brunette   for
> man cannot live on
> alone

When the line edges coincide with expressions that seem to stop at those same boundaries, the sense of completion is strong, especially if the rest of the poem has resisted coincidence of lining and syntax. And so the subsequent discovery, that the units do not correspond, after that first falling into place, is unusually capricious.

10. word play

If we divvy up grammatical units, why not words themselves? Chip off a syllable or two and let the pieces fall. Lay the pieces apart, carry a piece way over to the next line and see what happens. See what's cummings.

```
              yup
          getting up
       pity

                  making
                       just bare
              ly mak
                       ing
         it
                          (up)
```

Ludic. Perfectly syll able. Atwood gets a loghouse and a
houseboat simultaneously by cracking the words across the
lines:

> If he had known unstructured
> space is a deluge
> and stocked his log house-
> boat with all the animals[7]

The lines snap off like twigs broken across your knee. A lot can
be done when the right margin becomes more than a wall or a
bench to rest. Wit for one thing.

```
                  such making
          believe

                      making it
            up
                            yup
                       making it up
                              im making it
            up
                 all right
                   its hard
                       making
                 it up
                            up &
                 making
```

                              it
                        making
                                    up

Wit as it sits in syntax sidesteps the metaphor we've come to prize. Those little jags at the end, gags, they sometimes set you up—drop false clues along the trail. Aha, this is it. But the path turns, re/turns in verses / versus—betrays us to new scents, unexpected completions, false closures, to awareness of them, the inadequacies of single-minded readings. Second takes. It takes a second. We take a chance. Beware of the buried idiom, the 'complete' syntax, certain to go off on the curious, the unwary / unweary. Roger Fowler: "if the last word in a line *could* be the last word of a syntactic unit, the line-ending encourages the reader to assume that the syntax *does* end there."[8] The short line that can tip you/ through dizzy openings & closings, off quick takes, (trip you/ up) lures, springs. Exits & entrances. We stand (I can hardly stand it) en/tranced / at the entrance. In good standing, on a good footing. Where do we enter? Get off? Get on with it.

11. breath units

Time to catch your breath. I've held this one for a while because by now almost everyone's heard of it. Some think this is what line breaks *are* (and for one school they are). Like it or not, these units can be done. Have been. Has been among lines by now. We all know the argument as it originated, largely with Charles Olson (I've seen quotations from Amy Lowell that sound a lot like Olson), and that it advocates stopping a line where the poet would stop for a breath, presumably when speaking (I'm not sure the manifesto is precise on this point).[9] Contrary to common prejudices, the practice can take you in a lot of directions, since each poet will tromp a different path through the woods, pick up different tics depending on the moment/the movement and the poet's whole make-up of sounding / taking soundings.

12. *tentativeness*

The American poet, Robert Duncan, describes how William Carlos Williams came across the revolutionary phrasing of his 1920s poetry.[10] Counting out his lines to ensure he got ten syllables as some semblance of iambic pentameter, that honoured measure, he found many lines ending at odd places. Sure, there were many nouns and verbs—traditionally thought to be the proper parts of speech to announce the line is finished ("strong" endings they were called; still are, so far as I know). But what Williams was finding, often as not, were pronouns, articles, conjunctions, prepositions: all the wrong words (all the words that were disallowed—this is intriguing—at the ends of Latin verses). They could be heeled back into the line only by restructuring the syntax. What Williams discovered—the telling juncture—took him in new ways. The line, suspended on those grammatical openings, became plastic, squirming with possibilities. It opened out. Less assured than 'completed' verses, this line would not turn in, a mother putting her kid to sleep. Instead it would declare itself in all its uncertainty, stressing forward movement in the reader's expectation. A new aesthetic: not fluency. Clumsiness—an awkward turning/ on frozen feet. Clumsy, if need be, clumsy as all get out. As if for the first time, in *this* delineation. Webb, caught in her words: "—Emily—those gasps, those inarticulate dashes—those incitements—hiding what unspeakable—foul breath? But not revolting; *subversive*. Female. Hiding yourself—Emily—no, compressing yourself, even singing yourself—tinily—with compacted passion—a violet storm—."[11] A violent shading, making a dash for it.

At first this line may look like the previous one based on breath units, and often poems lined according to either principle *will* resemble one another to the point of being coincidental. That's to be expected since both of them are based in expressionist composition and ascribe to the speaker a drama of the poem's rhythm. The lines can be distinguished, however. Breath units are based in physiology, tentative lines in psychology; one outward, the other inward. Quite where that distinction takes us I'm not sure, but I do suspect it is useful.

What's the matter with you? my uncle said. *Cat got your tongue?* "Stutter," from the same base as "study"—to pay attention. Ear tuned to a new music. It would register a mind in motion, suspicious of glibness or smoothing things over. There would be a new emphasis, as Charles O. Hartman has shown in his analyses of the different lines into which for experimental purposes he lays the same words.[12] Working the edges, putting us on/ edge. The syntactical unit, opened, would hover over its moment, waiting on its yet unknown fulfillment. nervous/ nervy, uneasy. Ondaatje: a blind lover, doesn't know what he likes till he writes it out. Sends it out, casts a line, a spelling, into the stream. You don't know what the outcome will be, what you will snag, how it will all come out. Or at least you create that effect.[13] (The distinction is not so crucial as sceptics may suppose. It certainly isn't if, as I am doing, you weight the conventions not to the moment of composing—always a dubious enterprise since that moment can never be available to anyone, not even the poet— but to the moment of reading.)

Doug Barbour, walking a fine line:

> under   moon
>
> earth turns
> blue & green &
>
> terribly true
> to where its been
>
> & we turn too /
>   we do
>
> turn under its light
> white in the cold
>
> or warm night we hold
> on to / here

where   planet
still breathes in

its orbit / still
breathes[14]

The stanzas here become an active part of the punctuation. There is the apparent closure of "still breathes in" (the planet drawing in its breath), and then—its breathing in orbit.

An additional thought. Readers might wonder about that "still" at the end of the line "its orbit / still." Supposing we grant that "still" first emerges as adjective (its still orbit), slightly dislocated in its position after the noun, but no more oddly situated than we are accustomed to finding words in poetry. Supposing we grant, further, that "still" then becomes, along lines I have argued, an adverb (still breathes), attaching first to the noun and then to the verb. How is this doubling any different, we might wonder, from what Keats creates when he writes of a still unravished bride of quietness? Doesn't Keats generate the same duplicity?

We can instructively put the one case against the other. I would argue that Barbour's ambiguity is released syntactically as the lining controls it: *first* we read "still" as an adjective, by virtue of that option being the most inviting and perhaps finally inescapable. What else could it be *in that line*? Remember, we are reading off a principle of the line as a separate segment, about which I will say more under point 14. *Then* we realize "still" also carries over, through the torsions of line against syntax, into the next line and in *that* combination acts as a verb. Our recognition of the doubling comes off sequence and, I think, will in most readings follow the order I have laid out. Once we have chosen one option and feel reasonably content with it, our version tendered confidence through the line's apparent self-sufficiency, we will as if in revelation suddenly decide once we hit the next line that—"oh"—there is another option made available to us by the sequence. It becomes a matter of consequence. In Keats' poem the ambiguity is simultaneous and semantic: we could choose either or both readings on the first pass through, which does not work off suspensions and betrayals, is not subject to the principle of succession that obtains in Barbour's chain. In terms which will soon become more apparent, Keats' ambiguity enters through the paradigm, Barbour's through the syntagm.

13. *speech models*

This line works with speed. Draws on narrative, idiom, anecdote, repetition more than #12 does or can. Think of the breezy, almost smart-ass form it takes in writers like George Bowering and Robert Kroetsch, calling audibles at the line, you'll see what I mean. Check Anthony Easthope on the hegemony of iambic pentameter in the English tradition. He argues it is historically constituted in the Renaissance at the expense of an earlier accentual tradition. By promoting syllables between accented syllables, and by spacing them out fairly evenly, iambic pentameter helped to entrench the " 'Received Pronunciation' of Standard [British] English. . . . It does so because it legislates for the number of syllables in the line and therefore cancels elision, making transition at word junctures difficult."[15] It eliminates from 'serious' literature, other than for comic purposes, the radically elided voices of working people. Quickly elevated to ruling status, blank verse delivered a canon that

> asks for a clipped, precise and fastidious elocution. Such pronunciation—one thinks of Laurence Olivier—signals 'proper' speech; that is, a class dialect. Pentameter aims to preclude shouting and 'improper' excitement; it enhances the poise of a moderate yet uplifted tone of voice, an individual voice self-possessed, self-controlled, impersonally self-expressive.[16]

The argument is compelling. Once established, blank verse

> becomes a sign which includes and excludes, sanctions and denigrates, for it discriminates the 'properly' poetic

from the 'improperly' poetic, Poetry from verse. In an unbroken continuity from the Renaissance to 1900 and beyond, a poem within the metrical tradition identifies itself (in Puttenham's words) with polish and reformed manners as against poetry in another metre which can be characterized as rude, homely, and in the modern sense, vulgar.[17]

Much the same can be said for other elegant and privileged phrasings, the iamb and the anapest in particular. Pick up the argument on our end of history, in our place, and you've got big trouble. Fluent phrasings of whatever kind silence a more radical vernacular. Combine eloquence with the cache of metaphor (they stick together, in the privileged line, like expatriate English), and you leave no room for other forms and the realities they carry. All forms are historical, all are ideological—produce certain possibilities, shut down others. A simple test of how crucial these things are would be to imagine Al Purdy at his most oral wrapped and delivered in iambic pentameter. Can't be done.

So we write off speech models. And the line-ends give first that dramatic hesitation, a quick tightening, and, then, *bam!*—hitting the next word, like bumpers when you're pushing a car (or what's a metaphor?), when you run into the following line:

> you can give the
> whole damn thing away
>   far 's
> im concerned

It's *whole damn* and *im*, the stress doubly registered by the speaker's clutch at line ends—dare I say it? what is it I want to say?—after "the" and, less emphatically, after "'s," the finish coming as little bursts of determination after a hitch in speech. Since any stress we might not expect serves to emphasize the choice of *this* word, the accented one (as opposed to any others that might have fallen into place), we become all the more aware of *this* word as distinguished from all those other possible words.

So it's the *whole damn* works, not just a part of it; and it's *i*, whatever the rest of you guys think. The lineation forces us to notice what is left out, what distinctions the voice makes as it chooses one of several options.

A note: the rhapsodic line is not based on speech models, usually generates a longer line, bound & determined to observe its analogs, to return, spellbound, to home base. Go back to Whitman. Anaphoric.

14. *as a separate unit of meaning*

This condition is, for the time being, I think the least appreciated, at least among readers. The old principle of enjambement (Milton brilliant at it), which partly countered the convention of the line as a self-sustained *metric* unit, still tells us to push on, with little pause, for meaning: this next line completes what sentence I now am serving. That convention of reading leads us to blunder over contemporary lines, however troublingly set, as if they too were defined only as parts of larger grammatical units that reach across lines and swallow them. But if we are willing to entertain the line as *a unit of meaning in its own right, quite apart from whatever words precede or follow it*, we are on to new effects and to richer understanding. Try reading the second line in this as an intact unit of meaning:

> am a lantern   feeding on
> what lies below me

Forsaking all others, the line begins to offer itself in new ways, not simply as a noun clause answering to the preposition "on." It also speaks, declaratively, self-sufficiently, of discovery: "What lies below me!" I have found, where "lies" operates not as verb but noun. This second way could hardly open in enjambed poetry because the convention of enjambement would confine the subsequent line to a development of the first, even if its addition were startling or 'corrective.'

The new conventions can offer more than subversions of determined readings. They can even leave us in states of contradiction—the syntax as it strings through the lines saying one thing, the individual lines something else. Lines shuttle backwards and forwards. Make up an example: "I am certain I will never know." Now divide the line (yes, you've got it) after "certain":

> I am certain
> I will never know

We can even describe the grammatical condition that obtains: the removal of the subordinate conjunction "that" and the insertion of a negative into one of the lines so, though together the lines insist unequivocally on a claim, when the lines are read separately, that is without syntactic connections, one line asserts, the other denies. Working in uncertainties, refusals to nail things down.

15. *visual effect*

Recognizing that *printed* poems come to us *only* in a visual medium, and that they can be something more or other than a receptacle for lexia we activate, some poets have played with that opening. Not just for semantic or sonic effect (though these concerns can be closely connected). To let the eye enter, wander, enjoy the shapes, the clean empty spaces. To let the sprinklings & the saturations take shape. Loopings & threadings. *line* [ME. *line*, merging OE. *line*, a cord, with OFr. *ligne* (both <L *linea*, lit., linen thread, n. use of fem. of *lineus*, of flax < *linum*, flax)]

> inklings

> come what may

As Joseph Riddell instructs us, "Spacing suspends the semantic depth of the sign."[18]

In its most radical application the poem becomes graphic art. But in this argument I'm still thinking of poems that use recognizable words and that observe, however sub/versely, some form of syntax.

zodiac

tarnish of night

sky

dip

into the   tank

of dark

ness

emerge:

:   clean

as silver

jewelry   :

dripping cold

as memories

your memories

:

of me

The principle is fairly simple: the further the eye must travel, or the more stressfully it must move, from one word to the next (as in moving from far right to far left), the greater the silence. The holes are silent, measures of waiting. White holes in space, emitting. Admitting. Listen to them. "Blank space surrounding a word, typographical adjustments, and spatial composition in the page setting of the poetic text—all contribute to create a halo of indefiniteness and to make the text pregnant with infinite suggestive possibilities."[19]

In seeing the poem as gestalt, through whose galaxies our eyes flick, we engage in language as visually presented, as writing which, following Jacques Derrida, we might oppose to speaking. Writing *on* the page exists as its *own* transaction, with its own traction, not as some storage system for 'real' language or truths previous to the writing, even if only "discrepant by the time of a breath."[20] Writing enjoys its own conventions, enjoins us to them.

16. *lines that defy left-to-right, top-to-bottom reading*

The scheme here is to put into question, even more drastically, our presuppositions about how we negotiate our way through a text. To insist on the materiality of language, to foreground the very means by which we transact a language event.

Death

	is it
dark	
is it	black
	is it
black	is it
	dark
is it	dark?[21]

Where do you start? Where do you end? Maybe if he hadn't put that question mark in there. If only he hadn't. But you get the point.

In all these cases lineation serves as an active principle. The integrity of the line means that often it will counterpoint other trajectories and run varieties of imbalance between them, with a mixture of results.

3.

the short line

You can see how what I've been saying alerts us to the advantages of the short line. We've all read reviews that snark about the 'faddishness' of it, and that cry for sincerity; heard the call for poems that will "really touch me" or that will "sit long enough in the imagination." Poems reviewers will *recognize*. Well, there are reasons for using the short line. There are other, and perhaps better, justifications besides what I am offering here, but the short line (and we can include the ragged horizontal, or the line punched full of holes) lends itself to the sort of effects I'm enumerating here. (It also speaks of a radical shift in the sense of what literature can be in the absence of overriding structures of belief or understanding.) If you spring loose possibilities, give yourself up to them, you will open gaps and lop off lines all over the place. The more you open and break, the smaller your lines are apt to become (and as a rule the longer your stanzas will become in denying a particular reading path from one line to another). This brevity will also hold in a way for longer lines that contain horizontal holes, so the line will be broken up into smaller units. In any case, you're after (visual) suspension in smaller units so you can free up, even foreground, configurations which would otherwise be lost or less available. Within long traditional lines smaller groupings, being unsuspended to the eye, will less likely suggest themselves, as the syntax will tend to engulf them and dictate only one path through them.

I've already mentioned the wit that can be generated by the shiftiness of this form. It can also slow down the reading experience. By setting off words a poet can require us to hear every rustle in them, to hear the very silences on which the words float, bobbing here & there to the surface. Emerging out of alleged transparency and appearing—materially, prominently. To give pause / give us pause. This reading holds particularly when the words are distributed in various constellations across the page, i.e. when the left margin loses its authority, but it works always off a smallness of measure, suits itself to themes of love and loss, of unknowing—those things as they recede from us or poke into awareness. We are asked an exact attention, a minute speaking, moment by movement. To give the poem a hearing. Give it time.

> my pool of grease
> as i use it up
> do i   use you
>
> do i ever   i wonder
> crowd upon your air
> do i   take your breath away
>   even once   do i
> rub the fog off your glasses
> where your eyes hide
> does this   ever happen

To work at the joints. Articulations / to be articulate, to articulate:

> L. *articulate*, pp. of *articulare*, to separate into joints, utter distinctly [utterly distinct] <*articulus*, a joint: see ARTICLE, L *ARTICULUS*, dim. of *artus*, a joint: see ART <L, *artis*, gen. of *ars*, art, IE. base* *ar*-, to join, fit together, whence ARM [ME. & OFr. *armes*, pl. <L *arma*, implements, weapons, akin to *armus*, shoulder, upper arm <IE. base* *ar*-, to join, fit, whence ARM, ART] a call to arms, oh come into my arms, amoured. i like this joint. Goes to the nearest partner frees up another dance outside itself beside itself / with ecstasy till i consider myself / favoured in its presence in itself its own right. all right.

4.

to be carried away
from metaphor

When it comes to line breaks, we're looking at some massive delusions. Lazy or naive poets want to believe they are inside language that is natural in its origins and neutral in its use—privy to language that gestures, simply and certainly, to something beyond itself. This argument maintains that the world is already constituted and makes itself immediately available, verbally, to those who pay it proper attention. I think language points, too, but never simply and never directly, certainly not in poetry. The referential position I am doubting would hold that truths pass *through* language, and that language provides a vehicle to carry them. Hence the contempt for "jargon," which basically means words I am not accustomed to finding in certain contexts. This passenger view of poetry is so simple it continues to find favour only among reviewers, sentimental poets, and English professors. George Woodcocks all of them.

In some versions this argument takes on a moral imperative—that poems *ought* to be transport systems. Reality, or at least some superior or knowable reality—political, mythic, psychoanalytical, religious—lies outside the poem and prior to it. The poem supposedly delivers these greater truths, always from elsewhere. Meaning is previous to language, impervious to it, and therefore only conveyed (not altered) by it. There are important exemptions (the privileging of metaphor, in particular), but you see where this *a priori* position gets you. Metaphor, arguably, is a sign of essentialist thinking, since it means to bring across, to transport (a modern Greek taxi is called a metaphor), and by implication locates authority before the writing, or ahead of its verbal constitution. A bringing forward. From where, from what? On whose authority? Same applies to the continuing hunger for the image: it even more obviously puts the 'known' ahead of articulation, and leads us to value writing to the extent it re-presents the sounds, sights, smells, touch—the feel—of the 'real' world. Again, there is a place for such writing, and I myself honour and enjoy it. But we must not be simple about this and insist upon a myth of origins, the world in place, the word there/ already all ready, the poet as god/as prophet, sensitive witness who brings it to us. You grow suspicious, then, of any departures from known practices which have themselves become practically invisible through long usage. If something (God, the Unconscious, Historical Determinism, the Archetype, the Real World, Life, Whatever) is speaking to you, you don't tinker with the words. Others are mannered, susceptible to the fetish of technique. You, you simply speak truth, deliver the plain truths, the words as they are given to you untainted by thought or technique. You have your idea(l)s.

There is a terrible trap in such a theory of language. The evasions stick out: be quick to take offence at any formal departures, since such things can only be perversions of a 'natural' language referring to accessible and 'universal' truths. Above all we will not be taken/ in. Essentially at ease, occasionally puzzled, but assured in the confidence nothing untoward will happen—the reader as bourgeois consumer, poem as (sophisticated) commodity. The bad faith is appalling, when human and therefore historical *and* ideological constructs are passed off as virtual facts of nature. As if the signified always precedes the signifier, always enjoys a hierarchy over it. A metaphysics Jacques Derrida deconstructs:

> There is therefore a good and a bad writing: the good and natural is the divine inscription in the heart and the soul; the perverse and artful is technique, exiled ... within the Platonic diagram: writing of the soul and of the body, writing of the interior and of the exterior, writing of conscience and of the passions, as there is a voice of the soul and a voice of the body. . . . One must constantly go back toward the "voice of nature," the "holy voice of nature," that merges with the divine inscription and prescription; one must encounter oneself within it, enter into a dialogue

within its signs, speak and respond to oneself in its pages.[22]

Mere technique! Here is Gerard Genette, complaining about the "takeover" of metaphor in literary studies: metaphor "turns itself into the 'trope of tropes' (Sojcher), 'the figure of figures' (Deguy), the kernel, the heart, and ultimately, the essence and almost the whole of rhetoric."[23] We would have no trouble adding critics in, as they say, "Anglo-American" criticism (more narrowness: no Australian, no African, no Canadian allowed) who have elevated metaphor as the supreme measure of poetry.[24]

Among contemporaries even Roman Jakobson has done so. In his now-famous distinction between two operations in language, he has identified metaphor as the distinguishing feature of poetry.[25] But I want to put his model, slightly altered, to quite different ends. Jakobson divvies up language along two "axes." One of them, the axis of combination, works in sequence: how do we put these words together, move from one point to the next? This is a matter of sequence and it takes place in time. We can call this, modifying Jakobson's terms, the *syntagmatic* axis, which is laid out horizontally.[26] The other axis, the metaphoric axis, vertically intercepts the syntagmatic axis, and it works off substitution: at this point what other word(s) might we select instead of the one that is in place? among all the possible words that could here satisfy the 'grammar' of the sequence, which do we choose? This axis, the paradigmatic axis, is essentially lyric, Jakobson assures us, since it is on this axis that the metaphoric substitutions essential to the lyric take place.

But there's an interesting consequence of adopting this approach: emphasize the axis of metaphor or substitution, which is synchronic, and you begin to remove the poem from time or, more accurately, you are well on your way toward extracting it from our experience of it in time, and toward laying it out in a field. Metaphor as substitution then. A replacing, re-/:placing. What we've been taught to prize, the metaphor in elegant cadences, metered perhaps, but even in free verse grammared & iambed & anapested. i am therefore i anapest.

So we run four, five centuries of metered verse & forget that the first English poetry was not stepped out in feet. We rhyme & metre all the better to remember you by. This, for centuries, in the absence of cheap books—ones we could keep & in which, not knowing a poem by heart, we could look it up. Even after, even after there are no mnemonic reasons for that prosody, we rhyme & metre. Partly for pleasure, partly from habit. A cast of mind. Conventions. We are still oral a long way into the time of written, then printed, texts. And we still think as if we were 'oral.' Still like to repeat ourselves. A lot. Read Walter Ong, he can tell you.[27]

Many years later rhyme & metre run out of steam. No longer fresh, or needed. Books do the remembering for us, no need for da-dum da-dum da-dee. Da-da then. Or versions, a-verse to the old. We string a new line, sub/verse/ ive lined up a new chorus of lyres. Barbara Herrnstein Smith taking, apparently, the most conservative use of free verse, but recognizing some principles:

> The distinction between metrical verse and free verse is a relative, not an absolute, one: it lies in the *range* of the formal features of language that are patterned in each, and in the *extent* to which the principles of formal generation in each are limited in variability. Free verse obviously cannot be "scanned" by the same methods we apply to metrical poetry, but that does not mean that no formal principles are operating in it. What it does mean is that traditional scansion, since it is concerned primarily with the distribution of relative stress-values, does not discriminate other linguistic features, such as pitch levels, the relative value of junctures, assonance, internal rhyme, and simple word-repetition, that are frequently more significant than stress in creating the formal structure and rhythmic effects of free verse.[28]

The principles change. And metaphor hangs on like quack grass. For a long time. In there freely substituting into a stable grammar, a nailed-down syntax, so you'd think the jig was up, the game was over, almost. Finally, a few guys start questioning metaphor, begin to think there might be something else. The Objectivists, leery of immanental thinking, start to swing/ onto syntagm. & all that jazz. string you along / a line. They try a new line.

Poets start losing interest in metaphor, start fooling around/ with the line. They begin to look to the syntagm as a basis for their writing and the action moves onto a new axis, they have new axes to grind. Into new combinations & permutations, underminings of syntax, instabilities that jar us loose. They redefine units, ask new strategies of us. Way those words start carryin on & carryin over & carryin you off/away like that all at the same time somethin doin with all them other ones like that is what i call wild man once they got a taste of it they are swappin right & left till you don't know your top from your bottom. And it's a whole new ball game. You know how it was—the glamour of those metaphors, those mincing and galloping stars. The big metaphor, the well-turned cadence—the power boys, the heavy hitters. For a long time they had things/ their own way, they were on   a firm footing. Sluggers.

But now the new guys. a new line—quick of foot. the stutter step, stop. stealing bases (we've quickquick stolen the entire bases on them, out from under) quick around the paths. quick-quick catchthemnapping. Stutter starts, big leads, bloopers (over their heads) the crossing over/ of feet. stops. start reading/ the pitcher. getting the jump. George would like this. this is for George. george be nimble george dont put   yr spikes on an iambic foot. hit & run. go with the make a break for it pitch quick. of wit. of tongue the line leads on, breaks down, stumbles rounding second just yr foot catches a second ties you up, tongue-tied. steals you blind. its quite a feat
        knowing just when to/

make your break
    get a step
        before
     go for broke
 they throw you
        quickquickgeorge you are
    short/ of breath
out
    they want to
      pick you
   off   the short
  stop catch you
way off base
     if you dont   way out of line
        recover
   in time
         you can always run
 on the bad pitcher/catcher you can
    ((do they have good arms(
   run them
       ragged
          second takes
    make them balk
      at yr clever foot
  work
 yor flailing a way
the way
      yr line drives

   them crazy   ) you caught
     the way it falls
       up/ in it
  never fails

    The syntagm is a line-up.

    You put yourself on the line.

    A crime: against poetry.

5.
reader as raider

Think of where this puts the reader. puts you off? Where it puts the poem. the poet. We set in motion a new series of relations. Realizations. When the new poem comes on line.

A radical de-centering. Away / a way from the poet as prophet. No more metaphor moses. We witness the migration of authority from author to reader. Unauthorized entries, entreaties. Oh where are you going said reader to writer, said reader to writing. No treaties—an agonistic relationship. Reader as hero, breaking & entering. The end to the poem as private property, of words in service to the previously known, the already named. But the writer admitting to work, a working with materials, to showing them at work. & yes, that too, showing off, of course. The flauntingly 'made' text admits to its status as text (it is not a book, embodiment of the 'real' world), does not lie in illusion, does not legitimize itself by something that precedes, determines, or overrides its making. Metaphor, we've noted, means to carry over or to carry across, and the image serves to bring forward something that is *there*. Either way—in metaphor or in image, *whatever* their differences—we are asked to observe in them a principle of conveyance. According to this very common poetics the poem would bring to us truths as they are located in 'life' or the 'world,' or truths and emotions as they are situated in the poet. The first argument is re-presentational (and Imagist), the second ex-pressive (and Romantic). Both serve what Derrida has diagnosed as a metaphysics of presence. They both suppose some ineffable or transcendental, certainly some prior, reality whose responsibility it is the poet's to recognize and to make public. We might come to recognize, however, that meaning is not simply represented or expressed in language, and that language actually *makes* meaning, provides an occasion for the reader to construct meaning.

The breakings—up/in—outrageously favour the reader as hero. They not only permit, they require the reader at the gaps.

In space. Gaping/groping. Unauthorized entry. We pry open the strong boxes. Across the reader's eye leapfrogs, the mind travels / travails—along these paths. Trails along in risk, adventure. Not knowing, ahead of time. in a head of time. Willing/ to make connections, get caught. We abandon the security of known procedures. Submit to uncertainty, a minimum of direction. Adjustments all over the place, at every turn

```
            the eye      the ear
      swung on the line      hung      acro
               (in suspension      in sus pense(ive
            batically      for a moment  G-less   & then
         we are carried
                                                          aahh
                           to extreme measures
            swung back      on the next
                  so thats it
      parabola
                  & on  on
                     to the next
```

A readjustment in our sense of what a poem is, of what reading is, then. Along those lines. Raymond Chapman tells us that in the past rhetoricians distinguished between two radicals. What they called tropes occurred in the paradigm as lexical deviations, and what they called schemes—shades of lineation—took place in the syntagm.[29] In much the same way, Roman Jakobson has said, in revision of his earlier definitions (mentioned above), "As a rule, in imageless poems it is the 'figure of grammar' which dominates and which supplants the tropes."[30] Jonathan Culler would concur:

> The typographical arrangement produces a different kind of attention and releases some of the potential [poetential] verbal energy. . . . We are dealing less with a property of language . . . than with a strategy of reading, whose major operations are applied to verbal objects set as poems even

when their metrical and phonetic patterns are not obvious.[31]

Particularly instructive are Jakobson's following comments:

> Notwithstanding some isolated exceptions such as Berry's recent reconnaissance [Francis Berry, *Poets' Grammar: Person, Time and Mood in Poetry* (London: Routledge and Kegan Paul, 1958)], the role performed by the "figure of grammar" in world poetry from antiquity up to the present time is still surprising for students of literature a whole century after it was first pointed out by Hopkins. The ancient and medieval theory of poetry had an inkling of poetic grammar and was prone to discriminate between lexical tropes and grammatical figures (*figurae verborum*), but these sound rudiments were later lost.[32]

Jakobson goes far enough to argue that "The essential literary-critical question of the individuality and comparative characteristics of poems, poets, and schools can and should be posed in the realm of grammar."[33]

Take almost any prose passage, even the most 'prosaic,' set it off in poetic lines as I have defined them & see if you don't, suddenly, find new potential in the words. Invited to read the words differently—as poetry—we do. We apply an appropriate type of attention. And we can do so simply because, contrary to common belief, there is no irreducibly 'poetic' language. The measure does not reside in any intrinsic quality of language (metaphor or image or rhythm), nor in the poet as origin or genius, but in the terms by which any text presents itself and the conditions, largely intertextual, we choose to apply.

If, as I have been arguing, that energy is released in much contemporary poetry along the syntagmatic axis, the implications are crucial. For one thing, our 'reading' then radically relocates itself in time. The act of reading has always taken place in time, I know. But for a good part of our century, we have been instructed to read along certain *lines, certain* lines, to talk about poems as if they could be totally available to us, interpretively,

in a given moment, as objects outside of time. As objects of interpretation whose primary interest is semantic and whose
'meaning' is virtually limited to semantics. Poem as noun. The
dominant aesthetic—hermeneutic—in effect spatialized literature and moved our discussions of it outside the actual experience of reading as the words come to us, one by one, one
after the other. This critical bias accounts for part of a decayed
interest in rhythm and sound, which must take place, can become known to us, only, radically, in time. in time they will become again available to us.

Re-focus the model and you value other things. Poem as verb,
as event. Match the aesthetics of line breaks with reader-based
criticism, which addresses what happens when we move
through a text, bit by bit, in some sequence, and interesting
things happen. Matters of consequence: following on or leading
to, hence laid out in sequence. Kinetic excitement, action at the
holes, the junctures—points of suspension, expectation. Syntax
becomes meaningful. We are asked to hear, really hear, right here
and *now*, what's happening. We must learn—I mean the verb to
carry moral weight—not to hasten irritably on, puritans of
paradigm, to 'important' (because traditional) matters, already
'knowing' what it is we are reading. If we can resist our training
and start to linger we may begin to appreciate other bases of
meaning. In the operations I am advocating the parts, put on an
equal footing, would be allowed value and dignity, given a fair
hearing. In a new democracy of grammar, insubordinate. We
might do some fancy stepping, not sure of where we stand. But
not helpless before the poem. No, and not outraged either. Willing to risk the 'trivial' and to hear the unelaborated, the minimal, the discursive, the cerebral—we can learn to read in a new
way. We no longer have to hold with Keats (mistaken even then)
"That if Poetry comes not as naturally as the Leaves to a tree it
had better not come at all."[34] It *never* has! And so we look for
other strategies. The recent developments in reader criticism
provide a way to understand the new poetry. More, they provide
a justification, authenticate it. They save it from the danger of

'significance' and high seriousness: of reducing poems to semantics, subject to a grammar so familiar it becomes almost invisible, and read as the timeless utterances of imperishable truths.

Question the privileging of metaphor, of semantic 'seriousness' or intellectual density, of familiar phrasing, 'high' allusion, poet as medium, of the spatialized text—and the conditions shift. Staggeringly. Into speech models, into unstable grammar, double talk, into surprise & betrayal, hesitation and awkwardness. Fully implicated, we get our lines crossed—crossing over, crossed up (would i cross u), in ravellings, unravellings. Broken DNA molecules, recombinant. the poem turning & turning under you / on you you on & in return it will turn you god knows i looked forward to this on second thot in hindsight shuttling backwards & forwards. for words. Reader/ riding on a roller-coaster poem.

The fear of

getting caught

out   at the end

of the line

find

no great   climax

Think of the lines scrolling up the computer screen. The bottom one pops up/ on you. upon you. It is not available/ to you, till presented. Try reading that way—the last line you are in as the last line, as the only line (for the moment). It will throw you for a loop. You'll be startled at the premature closures, the reopenings, the unexpected turns, double takes you'll go through. Beyond discomfort, to delight, if you give yourself a break. If you have reached the end of the line in confusion & delight finally for all the garden paths you're (mis)lead/read run down. It goes without saying, almost. You will be a mused. Along these lines. You can take it from me.

1. In an excellent book which I read some time after I had worked out this essay, and which therefore I include more marginally than it deserves, Charles O. Hartman, *Free Verse: An Essay on Prosody* (Princeton: Princeton University Press, 1980), pp. 72-4, shows that many readers and poets, especially early in the history of modernism, assumed that in free verse lines must coincide with phrases if poetry were to have any rhythmic or prosodic basis. Hartman invokes Sculley Bradley to explain that the belief was almost inevitable historically and that it had to occur before lineation, once important in metrical verse, could be reestablished on new principles.

2. I quote from John Hollander's witty *Rhyme's Reason: A Guide to English Verse* (New Haven: Yale, 1981), p. 15:

—Milton, in his blank verse, makes use of those:
His long, dependent clauses are enjambed.
A somewhat sharp effect, as well, is damned
Easy—when, reading on the reader learns
The maze of verse can have its sudden turns
And twists—but couplets take your hand, and then
Lead you back into end-stopped rhyme again.

Also see George Bowering's short piece honouring line breaks in Wordsworth and Yeats: "The End of the Line." *Open Letter*, fifth series, No. 3 (Summer 1982), 5-10. In *Seven Types of Ambiguity*, rev. ed. (New York: New Directions, 1947), pp. 49-57, William Empson gives examples of ambiguous line-endings from Shakespeare and Donne.

3. Excerpt from "What It Was—" in *20th-Century Poetry & Poetics*, 2nd ed., ed. Gary Geddes (Toronto: Oxford, 1973), p. 204.

4. Excerpt from *Leaves of Grass*, in *Complete Poetry and Selected Prose by Walt Whitman*, ed. James E. Miller, Jr. (Cambridge, Mass.: Riverside, 1959), p. 50.

5. Phyllis Webb, *Talking* (Montreal: Quadrant, 1982), p. 68.

6. "Language Made Fluid: The Grammetrics of George Oppen's Recent Poetry." *Contemporary Literature*, 25, No. 3 (Fall 1984), 313; my stress.

7. Excerpt from "Progressive insanities of a pioneer," in her *The Animals in That Country* (Toronto: Oxford, 1968), p. 38.

8. *Linguistic Criticism* (Oxford: Oxford University Press, 1986), p. 46.

9. The article, "Projective Verse," as confusing as it is celebrated, has appeared in many books, including Olson's own *Selected Writings*, ed. Robert Creeley (New York: New Directions, 1966), pp. 15-26. The piece originally appeared in 1950.

10. "A Critical Difference of View." *Stony Brook*, 3/4 (1969), 362. The piece (360-3) is a brilliant statement on the Williams-Pound tradition.

11. Webb, *Talking*, p. 69.

12. See Hartman's chapter "Free Verse and Prose," in his *Free Verse*, pp. 45-60, and his exemplary discussion in the next chapter where he shows how crucial to Auden's "Musee des Beaux Arts" is the lineation (pp. 75-80).

13. Paul Fussell in his *Poetic Meter & Poetic Form*, rev. ed. (New York: Random House, 1971), p. 81, has written to the point:

> if constant enjambement takes place—that is, if the sense and syntax
> of one line run on into the next so that a hearer would have trouble
> ascertaining the line breaks—we have a very different kind of free
> verse, a kind we can designate as meditative and ruminative or
> private. It is this kind of vigorously enjambed free verse which has
> become a common style in the last twenty years or so as a vehicle for
> themes that are sly or shy, or uncertain, or quietly ironic, or furtive.

As will be apparent from other essays in this collection, I don't use the terms "meditative" or "ruminative" quite as Fussell does.

14. From "Moonwalks" in *Draft: an anthology of prairie poetry*, ed. Dennis Cooley (Winnipeg: Turnstone and Toronto: ECW, 1981), pp. 29-30. Barbour has a beautiful set of moon poems that work off an adept line: *Songbook* (Vancouver: Talonbooks, 1973).

15. *Poetry as Discourse* (London: Methuen, 1983), p. 68.

16. *Poetry as Discourse*, p. 69.

17. *Poetry as Discourse*, p. 65.

18. Joseph Riddell, "Decentering the Image: The 'Project' of 'American' Poetics?" in *Textual Strategies: Perspectives in Post-Structuralist Criticism*, ed. Josue V. Harari (Ithaca, N.Y.: Cornell, 1979), p. 353. Gerald Bruns speaks astutely to the point: "It is in terms of the power of letters," Bruns writes (he is thinking most immediately of Mallarme) that " 'typography becomes a rite.' " Bruns argues that the rite of typography displays the world in the poem "not as a field of objects nor as a world of experience but as a totality of relations among a set of lexical structures." Bruns aptly quotes from Mallarme, then goes on to comment. First Mallarme:

> Everything will be hesitation, disposition of parts, their alterations
> and relationships—all contributing to the rhythmic totality, which
> will be the very silence of the poem, in its blank spaces, as that silence
> is translated by each structural element in its own way. . . .

Bruns:

> Not substance but form: not the imagining of a totality of objects but
> the unfolding, typographically, of a manifold of pure activities. . . .

"Silence" here is, in one sense, the silence that attends the written or printed word. . . . The spatial field across which the poet casts his words (or, rather, across which the words arrange themselves) is gratuitous in traditional verse, but here it must be understood to be an integral part of the poem itself, in the same way that silence forms an essential part of any musical composition.

Gerald L. Bruns, *Modern Poetry and the Idea of Language: A Critical and Historical Study* (New Haven, Conn.: Yale, 1974), pp. 112-3.

19. Umberto Eco, *The Role of the Reader: Explorations in the Semiotics of Texts* (Bloomington: Indiana University Press, 1984), p. 53. The quotation comes from a useful article called "The Poetics of the Open Work," which is well worth reading in its entirety (pp. 47-66).

20. *Of Grammatology*, trans. Gayatri Chakravorty Spivak (Baltimore: Johns Hopkins, 1974), p. 18. Derrida insists in this book that writing is based on spacing.

21. In W.W.E. Ross, *Experiment 1923-29: Poems by W.W.E. Ross* (Toronto: Contact, [1974]), p. 17. Ross is my nomination for the most underrated poet in the history of Canadian poetry. Interesting that date of publication, 30 years after the poems were written.

22. *Of Grammatology*, pp. 17-8. In the same book Derrida writes "writing, the letter, the sensible inscription, has always been considered by Western tradition as the body and matter external to the spirit, to breath, to speech." Writing is in that view an "artificial exteriority: a 'clothing'," a fall from the good word (p. 35). It is "an imperfect tool and a dangerous, almost maleficent, technique." It represents, to speech, a "contamination which has not ceased to menace, even to corrupt that system . . . as a series of accidents affecting the language and befalling it *from without.*" In Plato's world it is "the intrusion of an artful technique, a forced entry . . . : eruption of the *outside* within the *inside*, breaching into the interiority of the soul" (p. 34). I quote at some length to tease out connections between Derrida's designation of a position hostile to or at least suspicious of writing, and my own earlier characterization of those who would dismiss or denigrate the use of lines as a system of notation.

I am also aware that if I were to accept Derrida's argument wholly, which I don't, my celebration of speech models would be put in doubt.

23. *Figures of Literary Discourse*, trans. Alan Sheridan (New York: Columbia, 1982), p. 113.

24. Here, oddly, is Margaret Atwood's cryptic contribution: "As for the academic community, that segment of it that concerns itself with Canadian writing, it's heavily into metonymy and synecdoche, but they don't have a lot to do with what writing is about, unless you stop at the craft

and don't bother at all with the vocation or the art." "An End to Audience?" in her *Second Words: Selected Critical Prose* (Toronto: Anansi, 1982), p. 356. Since the piece conceives of the writer as witness and testifier, the strange opposition of art and craft may make more sense than is at first apparent.

25. "Closing Statement: Linguistics and Poetics" in *Style in Language*, ed. Thomas A. Seboek (Cambridge, Mass.: M.I.T., 1960), pp. 350-77. For an extended summary and application of Jakobson's terms see David Lodge, *The Modes of Modern Writing: Metaphor, Metonyms, and the Typology of Modern Literature* (London: Edward Arnold, 1977). It would be misleading, however, not to note that Jakobson is aware of grammar as an aesthetic principle, a claim for which we will soon see evidence.

26. Jakobson uses the term "metonymic" for the horizontal axis, but I am substituting, as do others, "syntagmatic" on the grounds that Jakobson's term is imprecise. One of those who makes the adjustment is Frederic Jameson, *The Prison-House of Language: A Critical Account of Structuralism and Russian Formalism* (Princeton: Princeton University Press, 1972), p. 37, p. 122. Jameson also challenges "the common-sense view of the work of art as mimesis (i.e. possessing content) and as source or purveyor of emotion" (p. 83). The preference for "emotion" in poetry can only lead to an insistence upon lexical operations—a being content with 'content'—and almost always to a suspicion of and even dismissal of other operations.

27. See, for example, his excellent book, *Orality and Literacy: The Technologizing of the Word* (London: Methuen, 1982).

28. Barbara Herrnstein Smith, *Poetic Closure: A Study of How Poems End* (Chicago: University of Chicago, 1968), p. 87.

29. Raymond Chapman, *Linguistics and Literature: An Introduction to Literary Stylistics* (London: Edward Arnold, 1973), p. 75.

30. Roman Jakobson, *Verbal Art, Verbal Sign, Verbal Time*, eds. Krystyna Pomorska and Stephen Rudy (Minneapolis: University of Minnesota, 1985), p. 43.

31. Jonathan Culler, *Structuralist Poetics: Structuralism, Linguistics, and the Study of Literature* (Ithaca, N.Y.: Cornell, 1975), p. 163.

32. Jakobson, *Verbal Art*, pp. 41-2.

33. Jakobson, *Verbal Art*, p. 51.

34. John Keats, *Selected Poetry and Letters*, ed. with an "Introduction" by Richard Harter Fogle (New York: Holt, Rinehart and Winston, 1951), p. 310. It is clear that Keats' comments come in historical reaction to the neo-classicals and to their insistence upon a long rhetorical tradition which, especially in Swift's celebrated version, opposed the admired bee (learned and respectful) to the loathesome spider (stupid and vulgar). Keats' comment about organic poetry, expressive to the core, comes in a letter dated Feb. 27,

1818. Only a few days earlier, on February 19 to be exact, he wrote John Hamilton Reynolds, cleverly rereading the two symbols:

> It has been an old comparison for our urging on—the Beehive; however, it seems to me that we should rather be the flower than the Bee . . . . Now . . . let us not therefore go hurrying about and collecting honey, bee-like buzzing here and there impatiently from a knowledge of what is to be aimed at; but let us open our leaves like a flower and be passive and receptive—budding patiently under the eye of Apollo and taking hints from every noble insect that favours us with a visit. (p. 309)

I quote Keats at some length to show that not even his claim comes as eternal verity but in part as necessary quarrel with literary ancestors.

THE EYE
IN SINCLAIR ROSS'S
SHORT STORIES

Consider secrets. Or discoveries. How central they are to the realist narrative, above all to the realist narrative of epiphany. And how hermeneutic such texts are, those that slide around some armature of illumination, how they ask us to enter into interpreting a narrative whose occlusion it is our part as readers to remove or over whose erasure we are to bear witness. Consider too that realism in its most conscious and often in its least self-aware formations, in many nineteenth-century and early twentieth-century novels, sought the removal of illusions which stood in the way of the social good. Author as moral hero, bearing witness: *this* is what I see. Testifying that we might see. The indignant eye. The narrative of personal revelation takes a quite different though, I hasten to say, no better form. Both structures aim at eliminating error in forms of the hidden or the neglected. Realist fiction, whether psychological or sociological, commonly observes as its ethos the stripping away of illusions that perpetuate stupidity and injustice.[1] Such narratives, especially when they are psychological, also suppose a stable essential self (as we saw in *The Stone Angel*) and further suppose that personal or collective change is both possible and desirable. It will not be my purpose to explore those points here. All realism, however, pretends there is a denotational object or field that precedes the connotational system and that governs it. This convention will enter into what I have to say.

A secret. What can be seen but what at least to one character is not apparent. What can be available to the eye, measured by the eye. We have a trunkful of words that say as much: looks bad, I'm in the dark, a little light went on, it's not at all clear, show me, let's see, evidently, a real eye-opener, mere obfuscation, obscure points, Columbus (or some other worthy) discovered America, let's clear away all this bafflegab. And so on. We could expand this list to the hundreds. The fact that we whisper, too, in keeping or passing secrets, in keeping them from big ears, or big mouths, does not discount the point. Overwhelmingly our vocabulary of knowing, or not knowing, endows the eye with those powers. Its pre-eminence has figured throughout this book and it has been my major project, against that weight, to speak for the ear in other essays. Here I want to consider the eye in what I take to be the finest of Sinclair Ross's fiction, and among the very best in a long line of prairie realist fiction which continues to this day in writers such as Guy Vanderhaeghe and Sandra Birdsell, Ross's short stories collected in *"The Lamp at Noon" and Other Stories.*[2]

My methods here will stray from most Ross criticism, which stresses character and setting and which concentrates on that complex and enigmatic novel *As for Me and My House.*[3] And as has been my practice, I will proceed not by survey but by dwelling on a few selections. I will also exclude for convenience' sake most of the superb stories of growing up—"The Outlaw," "Coronet at Night," "Circus in Town," and "The Runaway." It would be a mistake, however, to suppose the eye figures only in those stories I concentrate on. As it would be misleading to suppose that Ross's focus on the eye takes the form merely of occasional reference to narratives of disillusionment. The book is full of eyes and seeing. Silent. How silent they are: the texts with their moral reticences, their ellipses, oral occlusions, the laconic speeches (especially of the male characters), the reduction of speech,[4] often by the preferring of narrated and inner speech to directly reported speech.[5] That preference enables the narrator to preside more firmly over the discourse, simply because the mode of narrating is what Gerard Genette would call more diegetic than mimetic; in other words it narrates more than enacts scenes.[6] Lacking confidence in speech (perhaps more in speech as a resource than in their own abilities to use it), the characters who inhabit these stories speak with their eyes and judge with their eyes: "Glances were exchanged again" (48), "You could see in his glance" (88), "My father glanced at her sidewise without answering, and I saw the reproach in his eyes" (89), " 'Prettiest horses a man ever set eyes on' " (98), "They looked at each other for a few seconds, then she dropped her head weakly against his greasy smock. . . . 'Straighten up, quick before they see you!' " (80), "There are eyes here, critical, that pierce with a single glance the little bubble of his self-importance" (40). It would be easy and perhaps wearisome to compound these examples, for the stories constantly establish eyes as indices of knowing and desire.

Two of the earliest short stories in the book, ones which I mention only briefly, lay out the characteristic dissatisfaction of young farming couples ravaged by drought and cheated lives. "The Lamp at Noon" and "Not by Rain Alone" both establish their anguish and the distance it has put between them not by dialogue but by describing their eyes. "Not by Rain Alone," which Ross has constructed out of what earlier were two separate stories, tells of the young farmer whose "eyes were quick with a kind of anger and resentment" (52), whose "eyes screwed up against the blast of sun" (54), who "kept his eyes down doggedly" (55), but whose eyes when he contemplates some eyelash of joy in his marriage "strained suddenly with eagerness again" (57). The string of references knot suddenly when the farmer, appropriately named "Will," arranges to meet up with his future wife. When they get together we meet a density of references: "She glanced . . . then looked," "He turned quickly a moment to meet her eyes, then sat silent, staring. . . . He kept his eyes narrowed . . . not daring to look at her again" (59). The second part of the narrative, after a gap of some months, shows the now married and struggling couple staring blankly, averting their eyes from one another, glancing and looking down, reading eyes, looking out into the night and snow. The story ends when Will, returned through the threshold of the open kitchen door, finds the house full of snow and his wife in the midst of childbirth that kills her and that brings him to "a twinge of recognition" (67).

"The Lamp at Noon," the first story in the collection, signals in its very title how crucial a visual economy will be to itself and to the book of which it is a part. Its opening paragraphs delimit a terrible disparity between the lighting of the lamp and its occasion: "A little before noon she lit the lamp," the story opens, and proceeds within the next few sentences to describe or to imply acts of seeing. The figure stands at a window, the dust an impenetrable fog, and the paragraphs fasten onto a vocabulary of the eye—dim, visible, obscuring, seem as if, watched, dim and yellow, her eyes fixed and wide, the eyes strained apart and rigid. Wide eyes and closed eyes, all that watching, that tissue of opacity (13). All that seeing and not seeing—prolepse to a quilt of illusion and revelation. The plot is slow to devolve and minimal in its action, for these are characters as nouns[7] to which are attached more adjectives than verbs, more attributes than events; characters ensnared in a grammar of stasis.

Such as it is, the plot moves us into familiar Ross terrain—the desperate wife wanting some glamour in her life, the bewildered husband dogged in his loyalty. What's interesting about the twist "The Lamp at Noon" takes is the narrator's decision to draw out secondary meanings in the lexicon of vision. "Look at the sky—what's happening. Are you blind?"[8] Ellen berates her husband. As indeed he is. "Look at it—look at it, you fool. Desert—the lamp lit at noon—" (16). The narrative deftly invites us to draw into complicity these details and to contemplate Paul's inability to see, to consider the darkness that obscures their most intimate and deepest selves. The lamp, metonymy of duststorms, becomes transformed in a characteristic operation of Ross's fiction into a symbol of secondary meanings, here of human blindness. "Will you never see?" Ellen pleads at her most wheedling (17). Can we doubt that Paul will, we who have read Ross stories, who have read dozens of such stories, we who refuse to the story the very transparency by which it would move us and by which, despite our knowing, it does move us, profoundly?

The story continues to consolidate the general pattern and to strengthen the specific equivalence between human understanding and the lamp, mentioning for instance that Paul's "eyes fixed on the yellow lamp flame," that Ellen, "seeming to know how her words had hurt him," immediately tries to comfort him (17), and that Paul continues "staring at the lamp" (18). The narrative of Paul's disillusionment begins when, "without meeting her eyes," he enters the barn with its "cavern-like obscurity, into vaults and recesses" where he starts "losing" his anger "in the cover of darkness" (19). The caves of vision, the underworld of revelation. The darkness where light is found. From which they emerge, in wisdom. For almost at once Paul thinks he *has* been blind and when (this in his mind's eye) he sees Ellen's staring face (succinct joining that—his eyes, her eyes, his eyes that see her eyes in a double sighting) "He understood suddenly" (20). As in a terrible sense he does see, sees prophetically as if with an inner light, the spectre of a woman with mad eyes appealling to him. One check on Ellen finds her safe and he returns to his barn to reflect on their life together.

When at last the wind dies and he walks out into his fields after a significant "three days of blight and havoc like a scourge," the "naked" spectacle "struck his eyes to comprehension" (21). The barren landscape corresponds to his own nakedness, stripped of illusion. Now "Everything that had sheathed him a little from the realities of existence . . . [was] stripped away," and at that very moment Paul, answerable to Ross's narrative of pain and revelation, recalls his wife's remonstrances about the lamp she has lit at noon, as if looking for something, something with which she could penetrate the cowl of dust, drop some light onto their smudged dreams. But there is yet to come a third and more shocking recognition. He has understood and he has comprehended something about their marriage. Now, steeling himself against that awareness, against the truth of Ellen's resentment and the power of her case, he returns to the house, resolved to stick it out. Two hours later he finds Ellen, in grotesque fulfillment of his earlier vision, whose awareness he had pressed to the edges, their child dead ("The child was quite cold" we read in a devastating meiosis Ross so brilliantly uses) and she with her eyes "still wide in an immobile stare," an expression that takes us back, framed, to the beginning of the story, now closed in our recursive reading, where Ellen's eyes "were fixed and wide with a curious immobility" (13), as if in parody of an overwhelming vision whose experience ironically now is Paul's. Ellen, who time and again has scolded Paul to 'see,' falls into a madness that makes her oblivious to the simplest fact of her child's death. In the end it is a disturbing vision that carries Paul, "his eyes *before* him" (my emphasis), and Ellen's words— "You were right, Paul"—ringing in his head (23).

I have tried to show that the two stories, "Not by Rain Alone" and "The Lamp at Noon," elaborate a narrative of personal illumination achieved only after a series of illusions and partial or false discoveries. It is a common narrative in realist fiction and one that Ross respects in this series of related stories. One of the best, "A Field of Wheat," brings its principals, another farm family, through much the same brutalizing experiences, culminating in the wipe-out of the most promising field of wheat they have had in years. When, benumbed, the husband and wife walk out into their fields, "The sun came out, sharp and brilliant on the drifts of hail" (79). Martha, the farm wife, spares herself the pain of her children's presence by telling them " 'There's nothing anyway to see.' " And so she and John stumble through the ice and slime, stricken to a silence that neither of them wants or can break, for "the words they could find were too small for the sparkling serenity of wasted field" (80). A murmur in the heart of things, the story shivers. A silence that elbows into all these figures, as perhaps the whole colossal wreckage of the Dirty Thirties, in realist cause, stupefies all characters in these stories. More silence, more eyes in "A Field of Wheat"—glimpsing, hiding, hiding from, drying. And then the revelation, one that comes on Martha so suddenly, so shatteringly, she almost loses hold. John in the barn, John the strong one, who has never betrayed a weakness, never let himself be seen, vulnerable to the eye. John, against his horse, stricken. Ellen, seeking merely a "glimpse" of John, seeing more, staring, incredulously (81). "It would be unbearable to watch his humiliation if he looked up and saw her. . . . [S]he fled past him, head down, stricken with guilty shame as if it were she who had been caught broken and afraid."

And then after even this, this terrible knowing, comes another, a final revelation. The young daughter, Annabelle, emblem of her mother's dreams of something more civil and more beautiful in their lives, points excitedly to the sky, oblivious to what has happened: "Look at the sky! . . . look how it's opened like a fan!" (82). Is the sight she points to ironic, iconic of a cosmos that flaunts its beauty, its false covenant, in the face of human misery and misfortune? Perhaps. But it coincides, modestly (and Ross is almost always poignant in his modesty, his quiet understatement), with Martha's determination to carry on, all the same. She starts the fire again, lights the parlour lamp, slips a quaver of light into their lives, enters the future with her eyes wide open. She has seen the light.

* * *

I want to move now to two stories that complicate the narrative of disclosure. It's in no way surprising that one of them is told in the first person, retrospectively, and that both of them offer us a situation that is at once reassuring and unsettling, for we have in one instance ("The Painted Door") a narrative told by a duplicitous narrator and in the other ("One's a Heifer") an evasive narrative told ostensibly, years later, by its protagonist. I say ostensibly because in no narrative, and certainly not in any of these Ross narratives, can the protagonist and the narrator perfectly coincide. We perhaps can be fooled when we are immersed in the story, naively consuming it, into believing that the "I" who speaks is the "I" who acts. But clearly this is not the case and cannot be the case. The "I" who tells necessarily must follow on the "I" who acts in the story, for even the 'same' "I" cannot tell his story until after it has happened, until, in other words, the protagonist has been altered by the perspective he has gained and has arranged that experience to suit his present purposes. Another way of saying this would be to distinguish between the "I" of story and the "I" of discourse. The story "I" would be immersed in the events, which in the moment of telling them, have already passed. The moment of telling, the discourse, occurs in a present whose "I" then has been altered by those past events, and who therefore, being different, cannot be confused with his previous self about which he speaks.

The point may seem unnecessary or cumbrous. It's not. Knowing there is this gap we can watch for it, we can also be taken in by it and recover only later from our deception. No matter, we have in the two Ross stories narrators who choose strategically to hide their knowledge and to cultivate the gap, in other words to create illusions and to fool their auditors. Gerard Genette in his brilliant book, *Narrative Discourse*, explains why they would do so: "the narrator, in order to limit himself to the information held by the hero at the moment of the action, has to suppress all the information he acquired later, information which very often is vital."[9] As a result such discourse wobbles between devices (the narrator's intervention in the present) that put off revelation, primarily by hiding its imminence, and forces (the protagonist's experiences in the past) that would reveal the hidden essence, the already known but obscured truth.

These enigmas work, by the way, both for the protagonists and for the readers in the two stories I have in mind.

In a real sense we could think of "One's a Heifer" as a detective story enrolled with a vengeance in Roland Barthes' hermeneutic code, "by which an enigma can be distinguished, formulated, held in suspense, and finally disclosed."[10] It certainly dresses itself in mystery, and teases us with the possibilities of what we don't know. Is Vickers, the lonely old man who puts up the young protagonist for a night, mad? Or as we say, just queer? Is he hiding something significant in his barn? The body of his murdered common-law wife? How much does he know, in those crazed and knowing eyes? We traipse through the story, intrigued to be on the verge of uncovering some bizarre secret, the secret forever eluding us, a string twitching before a cat, in the unnerving actions of Vickers and the strange furnishings of his shack—a vaguely menacing grindstone, and the guns and traps on the wall. But a detective story all the same: "in every detective novel there is deception, for the best hiding place for hermeneutic secrets is the sequence that appears formal and inert."[11] We sift the clues, shifting before us, pick them up and study them. But what are the clues? Is this man merely mad, crazed by his extreme isolation? Or is he cunning, behind that demented face a treacherous and calculating keeper of dangerous secrets? Above all, what is in the locked stall, perfect symbol of what is hidden away and kept from the young protagonist, out of sight, and (to the degree we enter the discourse) to the increasingly intrigued reader? What's *in* there? And the narrative jackknifes into what Barthes calls a proaretic code,[12] a trajectory of action and suspense. No longer a question of curiosity, now a matter of growing urgency. Not just: what *is*? but: what *will happen*? Suspense. But what are the clues?

There are the familiar references to eyes, only more of them, a *lot* more. Apt sign for the protagonist's initiation when his naiveté collapses in disillusionment.[13] At the risk of losing your patience, I offer a fair though by no means exhaustive list of references to seeing, chosen only from early in the text:

it's not a tentative mistake he makes, he identifies the cattle "for sure," with absolute confidence.

Then that gap, where discourse speeds past story. There have been a series of mistakes—the protagonist's mistakes—and now this hiatus, as though the narrator has paused to take a breath, to let things settle, sort out the truth. It's as if the narrator has swallowed all the false leads—there will be no more of them— in silent summary, simply by setting them aside and holding them in removal. The ellipsis, as Genette demonstrates in his superb discussion of narrative speed,[14] serves to eliminate story altogether and to push to the margins of discourse a stretch it chooses not to regard, for the moment at least. This breach in story, with the visible absence it contains, would seem to assure us of the narrator's discretion, to guarantee that his sobriety, recovered in that shift, will put us back on track.

And then across the hole, immediately, that simple statement, so disarming in its simplicity: "And then at last I really saw them" (121). The pensiveness evidently gained across the juncture permits us gently to inflect the adverb, as if in apology and self-correction—"I *really* saw them." The narrator slides by us the consequence of the claim by phrasing it so quietly—a necklace of monosyllables, a little pulse of relief, a rising as the sentence ends to imply the boy's new lease, like the first perk of coffee. Then there's the innocence of the coordinate construction, initiated by that tricky "And," guaranteed to bring us the unvarnished truth. The same goes for the shortness of the sentence, its normative syntax, and its refusal of subordination or any qualification other than the treacherous "really." Who could doubt the artlessness of the speaker, he who practises such plain speaking? I can't answer for other readers but I can confess that I was taken in when I first read the story, fascinated by the trickle of false leads. What is especially treacherous is the narrator's masking of the double "I," for the narrating "I" knows full well what the protagonist "I" does not. Yet for his own purposes the narrator chooses to obscure this distinction, to speak of both figures as the same "I," and to bear false testimony. "The narrative voice [in several Ross stories] takes on a retrospective quality," Robert D. Chambers writes, "a distancing which makes us forget for a moment that we are listening to a youth."[15] The narrator tricks us by keeping back certain information and setting aside for the moment certain signs of sophistication (even as he teases us with hints whose function as prolepses only later becomes apparent). For, as Gerard Genette reminds us, "The narrator almost always 'knows' more than the hero, even if he himself is the hero,"[16] and "all forms of prolepsis . . . always exceed a hero's capacities for knowledge."[17] It is at just such a suppression, at the first crucial joint, that we either subscribe to the duplicitous narrative, complicit in our own deception (the narrator only masks his deception as ambiguity), or that we put ourselves on guard against what road the narrator would put us on. Tremors in the narrative, lines where the guileless reader slips, supposing the plates will fit without fault. It's a matter of surrendering to what contemporary criticism calls "story" or consciously holding oneself within "discourse" and the knowledge that what we read is not a presentation nor quite even a representation of life, but a making of it, a making that in turn invites us to share its shadings and shapings.

From here on the clues pile up, however obscured they may be within the illicit system. We might think of the hermeneutic code in "One's a Heifer" masked or nearly noised out by other hints or flickers. Together this interference establishes or allows us to establish a structure of meaning within which the details become known and subject to our interpretive readings. As we well know, whatever symbolic meanings we ferret out tend to fade when we roller-coaster on the "story" and allow ourselves to read as if these things really happened, as though we were gazing directly on life unhampered by an intervening intelligence.

The boy and his deranged host, Vickers, size each other up, if the disingenuous narrator can be believed, by looking, and often by looking into the other's eyes. As we have seen, this disposition can be found generally in Ross's stories. Here it becomes obsessive. The coding serves to intensify the very mystery whose duration it is the narrator's wish to sustain. Here is a quick sample of what happens between the two characters as they eye up their situation: "He peered," "I watched," "strange wavering look in his eyes," "I'll show you," "I glanced at the doorway," "Come on, then, and look around," or more fully: "It was plain enough: he was hiding the calves before letting me inside to look around. . . . I had time to reflect . . . that it might be prudent just to keep my eyes open"; or: "he tried to make me believe [these] were the ones I had seen, but, positive I hadn't been mistaken, I . . . glanced at the doorway" (these from p. 122). As the narrator leans on Vickers, he brings the references to eyes more and more into play. For Vickers, in this story that refracts around light, has odd eyes. He gives the boy the evil eye. In the kid's words, "there was something about them wavering and uneasy" (121), a notion he likes so much he returns to it on several occasions. He sees in Vickers "deep uneasy eyes" (124) and notices that "the wavering, uneasy look was still in his eyes. A guilty look, I told myself" (125). There's more to this than meets the eye. Still later he sees a "glassy, cold look" (128) and "a sharp, metallic glitter" (129) in Vickers' eyes, and decides after a harrowing night with the old man that "it seemed his eyes were shiftier than before" (131).[18]

The narrative conspires to elaborate the furtiveness that sticks like some residue of guilt to the odd-ball host. It thickens that sense by aligning the old man with his lantern and his pet owl. First the lantern. Weary with his vigil, the boy loses focus on Vickers and looks at "the lantern like a hard hypnotic eye." Moments later, when Vickers checks on his young guest, the narrator reports "He held the lantern to see me better . . . in such a long, intent scrutiny" (123). At the moment the two objects of light and vision come into correspondence, the old man takes on attributes of the uncanny. Later we learn that the boy studies the restless owl (traditional symbol of wisdom), waking in the corner far from the lamp, where—wonderful trope—"its eyes go on and off like yellow bulbs." And we uncover another association, verbally induced, when the boy, having decided "there was a sharp, metallic glitter" in Vickers' eyes, goes on to say "His eyes as I watched seemed to dilate, to brighten, to harden, like a bird's" (129). In the boy's fevered fantasies Vickers becomes a walking eye, his hallucinatory powers of surveillance extended as if in overflow into the objects he brushes.[19]

Even in the midst of our confusions, even in our participations in the kid's delusions, we do read evidence to the contrary in passages that may become evident only in later readings. "I fancied I could still see the wavering expression in them [Vickers' eyes], and decided it was what you called a dirty look" (124), he confesses, hop-scotching from fancy to decision with unseemly ease. If the slipperiness at first eludes us, it may be in part because the narrator distracts us with rhetorical tricks, flashes whatever will allow us to divert our willing eye, our desire to be taken in by a narrative of secrecy, when he appeals to our common judgment and to our commonplaces—to "what you called a dirty look"—when we have said nothing of the sort; the assessment is entirely his own. More refractive than reflective, our eyes take us in. It becomes apparent, too, in subsequent and more 'knowing' readings that though Vickers may well be some bug-eyed nut, he at times is lucid and on at least two occasions he reads the boy's thoughts.[20]

We cooperate in our own blindness only too eagerly because, knowing this to be a detective story whose dissolution we want to put off, we turn a blind eye to the secrets we realize are buried in the sequence which is the story line. In any case, the disclosure must be put off so the narrative can go on. We must be taken in, be willing to be taken in, for the sake of the story. An end to enigma would mean an end to action, and hence an end to the story, since the action lasts only so long as the occlusion holds. In Barthes' terms we would say that the proairetic code will collapse with the hermeneutic code.[21] At the same time, for all our savvy, we want to know—I want to know: are the calves in that stall that Vickers has boarded off? We want to pry open the door, peer into the box of secrets, know what is kept from our eyes.

But we don't want to know too quickly or too easily. That is the narrative contract into which we enter: only too conscious that the loss of a secret will collapse the narrative, mangle the suspension in which we swing, we choose to go with the sequence which will suppress the secret—an answer that is perpetually deferred. And so we tilt between desire and fulfillment.[22] The crafty narrator, more shifty than Vickers, happy to play on our desires, delays the end to prolong the suspense, puts off hermeneutic answers to keep alive the proairetic axis: what will happen next? He impedes revelations that would satisfy the completion of one system simply so that, by floating that incompletion, we might retain interest in the other. We want that thrill. Disclosure soon enough will end narrative, we realize, and gratefully we offer up our credulity to the narrator's strategems. Fool me, we in part say. And in large part he does.[23]

He fools through a series of expressions, inadvertently tucked into the account. Describing the protagonist's manoeuvres to outflank Vickers and to discover what he thinks will be his calves behind the closed door of the barn, the narrator, playing the role of the boy he once was, lets out some telling comments whose meanings undermine his own confident claims to discernment and veracity. Duplicitous or ironic, the words mount up. Determined "to keep my eyes open" (122), the boy decides "Vickers had queer eyes" (125), supposes at one point that Vickers had "just been seeing things" (130), idly tells Vickers "My aunt . . . says her eyes aren't good" (126), and in his panic to get into the stall before Vickers returns says he "worked blindly" (132). When his series of suppositions and misreadings together with his struggle with Vickers come to an end, he, about to peer into the stall, looks up to see Vickers watching him, and culminates the whole sequence with his last claim of assuredness: "I knew now for sure that Vickers was crazy" (133). Sure, just as he had been when first he got to Vickers' ramshackle farm. So sure of himself, he turns out to be the biggest dupe of all. He errs arguably because he has committed himself too fully to his own narrative—to *find* something in an act of initiation—and to the role he fancies in that narrative. As a result, he sets aside all impediments to his finding *something*. It may be he so sets the act ahead of all evidence, so succumbs to the proairetic, that he loses sight of the hermeneutic. However much he has kept his eyes open, he has been unable to see the truth. A truth more modestly available to his aunt Ellen who, when he returns home, opens his eyes to the truth (the calves have come home) and, as the narrative resolves, stands "looking at the stew" (134).

So, remembering that our own moment of recognition, managed by a less-than-innocent narrator, may well coincide dramatically with the protagonist's, we can say: of course, I should have known better. Or: who would have thought? It's impressive how Ross brings us suddenly (if we weren't immune to his narrator's machinations) to the re-cognition. When the boy arrives home to find his calves already returned, we, released in a climax where proairetic code and hermeneutic code click into joint, hit a sudden twist in the recognition: " 'But . . . if it wasn't the calves in there—' " (134). Catherine Belsey has written succinctly on this structure:

> Classic realism is characterized by *illusionism*, narrative which leads to *closure*. . . . [It] turns on the creation of enigma. . . . But the story moves inevitably towards *closure* which is also disclosure, the dissolution of enigma through the re-establishment of order, recognizable as a reinstatement or a development of the order which is understood to have preceded the events of the story itself.[24]

Yet, as at the intersection the recognition scene clears up part of the search (for the calves), it throws the rest of the narrative (Vickers' guardedness) into greater mystery. One mystery shuts only to leave us with the opening of another, resists the closure Belsey points us to.

* * *

Even in short stories which do not so obviously migrate around secrets, Ross opts for narrators whose business it is to repress the truth (specifically, information they already have when they begin their discourse) and therefore to betray us into the complicity of our own delusion. The strategy is hardly peculiar to Ross, for it functions in many 'well-made' stories whose purpose it is to build toward some climax or some moment of epiphany or both. By bringing the two trajectories—the protagonist's illumination, the readers' realization—into perfect and very late correspondence, Ross achieves special power. In "The Painted Door" the force of the disclosure in some ways is all the greater because we don't even know until the very end we are in suspense and because that awareness comes, shockingly, only in the very last word.

Arguably the best in a set of astonishing stories, "The Painted Door"[25] elaborates a favourite Ross theme—the triad of the frustrated wife, the dogged husband, and a dangerous but trusted third man. Here the drama circulates around Ann. Entrapped and cheated in her life, Ann develops some interest in a handsome young neighbour and, despite her appreciation for her husband, John, compares her husband unfavourably with his unknown rival. The narrative spins around an intricate series of wheels and wheelings, all of them serving to squeeze a fatedness into a narrative which lays claim to the characters. What perhaps typifies Ann's weariness, and her wariness, more than anything is her watchfulness at the window, icon of her contained life and repressed desires. The two themes—her fate, her vision—blend at times, as in the description of Ann after she has waited for hours for John to return across the wasted miles of a prairie blizzard: "Then she wheeled to the window, and with quick short breaths thawed the frost to see again" (105). Within her farm house the tick of the clock and the click of the fire mark off with sharp force her loneliness and her emotional simmering. But we note the window, and the wheels, above all the double wheel about the moon the previous night, a sign which finds its equivalence in the ovals Ann blows into the frost on the window.

There she nudges the small space she would open as if parenthetically, in silence, for herself and through which she would peer as if looking for something, something larger or more gratifying. Small openings into which she burrows in her rhythms of reticence and desire. The dashes that splatter the pages, that quiver and gasp through the narrative—they punctuate Ann's lapses (others' lapses, too, in other stories). Her ellipses tremble with conditionals, all the unutterable "if's" of their lives, all the hesitations into which she trails. Fallen silent. Spasms that define her divisions and mark off her measures, her language lurching as if she were a car driven with one foot on the brake and the other on the gas pedal.

An old story, yes, and the staple of these powerful Ross stories wound on the grimness of lost lives. A narrative which Ross shapes into a startling line of delusion and understanding. The complications set in when Ann lets Steven in out of the storm (*her* storm) and lights the lamp, one of the first and most telling indices of the pattern of seeing and not seeing which will figure prominently in the next long section of the short story. Shaken, she gathers herself "round a sudden little core of blind excitement" (110). Wanting badly for the moment to happen, for some gust of joy to enter her, Ann struggles for breath within the cramped existence that has hold of her. In enunciating that effort Ross decides, as so often he does, to use free indirect discourse. The strategy enables his narrator to display an intimate awareness of the protagonist and to edge around a mind that would otherwise be less accessible to the reader. Changing her dress (and we need not quibble over that as a sign of transition, and presentation), Ann fights to build a narrative that would permit her escape for the moment from her Puritan inscriptions according to which she is to play a character of unremitting denial. The terms of Ann's new construction are critical to our purposes: "There was something strange, almost frightening, about this Steven . . . but strangest of all was the familiarity: the Steven she had never seen or encountered, and yet had always known, always expected, always waited for" (111). That "always"—so emphatically repeated—isn't this her insistence, her anguishing out, as if by will, some form of conviction or self-justification?

Attached as it is to "known," the word takes on greater urgency and meaning in this narrative of seeing. We find from this point in the narrative, Ann's persistent return to the refrain. From now on she talks herself into another narrative, one that would endorse her actions even as it requires her self-deception: "because deep within herself she had known even then. The same knowledge" (112). She brings herself to the height of delusion in a passage with phrasings so stilted and abstractions so jaw-breaking they read like a parody of sociologese. It would be too easy, and I think mistaken, in a work so exquisitely written, to assign the clumsiness to Ross. The rhetoric alerts us to the strain and the falseness of her thoughts:

> She who in the long, wind-creaked silence, had emerged from the increment of codes and loyalties to her real, unfettered self. She who now felt his air of appraisal as nothing more than an understanding of the unfulfilled woman that until this moment had lain within her brooding and unadmitted, reproved out of consciousness by the insistence of an outgrown, routine fidelity. (114)

We recognize that in its infelicities, not least of which is the jostle of adjectives that bunch up (fans at the wicket) in explanation—these are the grievances, here are my points, let me list them—this is not Ann's register and that, essayistic, it belongs to someone else. She appropriates an alien discourse, latches onto it with a desire we can appreciate. And catapults herself now wholeheartedly into the fantasy: "For there had always been Steven. She understood now. . . . Her eyes were fanatic, believing desperately, fixed upon him as if to exclude all else, as if to find justification" (114). As in "One's a Heifer," the protagonist commits herself, certain in the accuracy of her perceptions, to a major mistake, to a profound but a perhaps necessary not seeing at the very moment when her rhetoric would suggest that she is most fully in possession of insight, that she is most fully 'herself.'

The text lapses into a discreet reticence at this point, elides the story of her affair with Steven, wakens only later when Ann herself, shaken out of sleep, shaken in her sleep it seems, 'sees' her husband as "one great shadow that struggled towards her threateningly" (114) in the dark. The uncertainty of Ann's vision—the narrator teases us with the thought this is a dream, begotten out of her stricken conscience—reinforces the story's rotation around sight. Remorseful, she once more steps into an orbit of 'insight,' now directed toward John: "She knew now . . . the face that was really John" (115), and then, a few minutes later, deep into her remorse, "she knew now—John was the man. . . . Looking down at [Steven] . . . she understood that thus he was revealed in his entirety" (117). The lexicon of certainty—"It was hard now to understand how she could have so deceived herself" (117)—so repeats its earlier appearance, the distressed repetitions of solidity within which Ann has encompassed Steven, that readers might now entertain some doubt about the veracity or at least the adequacy, the stability, of her new sureness about John. We might, too, having seen Ross elsewhere at work, suppose that in his love of prolepses and narratives of coercion, the narrator will not yet have closed and that, whatever certitude the protagonist may possess, we ought not to be so confident.

Any suspicions are soon confirmed when, across another lacuna in the text—this an eloquent silence that elides the narrative to bring dramatically into focus the next highlight—we read about the discovery of John's body frozen against a fence. The narrator then rapidly closes the discourse, one which we do well to remember has lingered and prolonged itself by stretching the narrative of Ann's temptation and by insinuating a tingle of suspense: will she, or won't she? In the end the plot carousels back on its beginnings, closes the hermeneutic circle, the cycle of secrets and revelations. It reminds us that there was a double wheel about the moon, and brings us deftly to the last act, Ann alone with the body of her dead husband:

> It was later, when they had left her a while to be alone with him, that she knelt and touched his hand. Her eyes dimmed, it was still such a strong and patient hand; then, transfixed, they suddenly grew wide and clear. On the palm, white even against its frozen whiteness, was a little smear of paint. (118)

What an astonishing ending! The narrator, who all along has secreted this last bit of information, now, at the climax, in the very last word, finally lets it out. By bringing the two trajectories—the protagonist's illumination, the reader's realization—into perfect and final correlation, Ross achieves an amazing power. Ann, she who as the discourse begins is trying to thaw (warmth connotes fulfillment throughout the text) "a clear place in the frost" (99), a pool of knowing, goes through a rapid narrative of seeing: her eyes dim, transfix, then go wide and clear. The dream frighteningly real, the illusion solidly true. Her eyes have been opened and in that last overwhelming moment she truly *does* see—the shattering realization, the dead certainty, that John *was* there at the door, that he crossed that threshold, entered into a room of knowledge so devastating that he wandered dazedly? deliberately? into his death.[26] Prepared though we may be for some disappointment to the characters, we too are stricken. Surprised. The last word, another word of seeing, crunches home with the force of a punch in the chest, or a breaking bone, when at one and the same—the very last—moment, the meaning which has snaked dubiously through a series of false recognitions consolidates and gathers strength from three different sets of conventions as they now nakedly emerge and merge—climax, epiphany, closure. Their convergence, their final swerve to completion after so long a delay, comes with enormous weight. Our reading of the 'story,' steaming forward with all the muscle of a train, derails in the end. The insertion disrupts the sequence, its explosion coming as an incursion into the syntagm, and we lose our footing. A vertical surprise that sends tremors through the representational line, throws us off track just when we are settling into the reassuring rhythm of denouement. Wham! and we are suddenly upset. It is a stunning performance. And the secrets end. In a way. If you see what I mean.

---

1. Here, for instance, is what George Levine has to say about realism:

> Realism ... can ... be defined as a self-conscious effort, usually in the name of some moral enterprise of truth telling and extending the limits of human sympathy, to make literature appear to be describing directly not some other language but reality itself (whatever that may be taken to be).

The Realistic Imagination: English Fiction from Frankenstein to Lady Chatterly (Chicago: University of Chicago, 1981), p. 8.

2. *"The Lamp at Noon" and Other Stories* (Toronto: McClelland and Stewart, 1968), "Introduction" by Margaret Laurence. Later references to this collection will appear within the essay.

3. The only single essay on the collection remains Keath Fraser, "Futility at the Pump: The Short Stories of Sinclair Ross," *Queen's Quarterly*, 77, No. 1 (Spring 1970), 72-80. Other essays include sections on the short stories: Gail Bowen, "The Fiction of Sinclair Ross," *Canadian Literature*, No. 80 (Spring 1979), 37-48; Paul Comeau, "Sinclair Ross's Pioneer Fiction," *Canadian Literature*, No. 103 (Winter 1984), 174-84; and Frank Davey's excellent "Sexual Imagery in Sinclair Ross" in his *Surviving the Paraphrase: Eleven Essays on Canadian Literature* (Winnipeg: Turnstone, 1983), pp. 167-181. Lorraine McMullen also devotes one chapter to Ross's short fiction, "Short Stories" in her *Sinclair Ross* (Boston: Twayne, 1979), pp. 23-55. Ken Mitchell includes a chapter on the stories in the only other book solely on Ross: Ken Mitchell, *Sinclair Ross: A Reader's Guide* (Moose Jaw, Sask.: Coteau, 1981), pp. 3-26. Robert D. Chambers includes an eloquent chapter, "The Lamp at Noon and Other Stories," in his *Sinclair Ross & Ernest Buckler* (Toronto: Copp Clark and Montreal: McGill-Queen's, 1975), pp. 9-24. All in all there's not much sustained criticism of the stories upon whose virtues critics seem largely agreed.

4. In Diana Brydon's words, "Ross's fiction is unusually concerned with absences, with what is left unsaid and with what cannot be said, and

with the non-verbal arts, painting and music." "Sinclair Ross" in Jeffrey M. Heath, ed., *Profiles in Canadian Literature*, Vol. 3 (Toronto and Charlottetown: Dundurn, 1982), p. 97.

5. Gerard Genette, *Narrative Discourse: An Essay in Method* (Ithaca, N.Y.: Cornell, 1980), translated by Jane E. Lewin, "Foreword" by Jonathan Culler, pp. 171-3, usefully distinguishes among "three states of characters' speech (uttered or 'inner')": 1. narrated speech, 2. speech transposed in indirect style, and 3. reported speech. The latter, reported speech, is what we ordinarily call dialogue and is what has formed the basis in a long preference for 'showing' or 'mimesis' in literature:

> Aristotle lost no time upholding, with the authority and success we know of, the superiority of the purely mimetic. We should not fail to appreciate the influence that this prerogative, massively granted to dramatic style, exerted for centuries on the evolution of narrative genres. It is expressed not only by the canonization of tragedy . . . but also . . . in that sort of tutelage exercised over narrative by the dramatic model, expressed so well by the use of the word "scene" to designate the basic form of novelistic narration. (p. 173)

6. In *Narrative Discourse*, pp. 166-7, Genette lays out the distinctions beautifully. I quote him at some length because the passage can be applied here and elsewhere:

> The strictly textual mimetic factors . . . come down to those two data . . . : the quantity of narrative information (a more developed or more *detailed* narrative) and the absence (or minimal presence) of the informer—in other words, of the narrator. "Showing" [mimesis] can be only a *way of telling*, and this way consists of both *saying about it* as much as one can, and *saying this* "much" as little as possible . . .—in other words, making one forget that it is the narrator telling. Whence these two cardinal precepts of *showing*: the . . . dominance of *scene* (detailed narrative) and the . . . transparency of the narrator. . . . Cardinal precepts and, above all, *interrelated* precepts: pretending to show is pretending to be silent. Finally, therefore, we will have to mark the contrast between mimetic and diegetic by a formula such as: *information + informer = C*, which implies that the quantity of information and the presence of the informer are in inverse ratio, mimesis being defined by a maximum of information and a minimum of the informer, diegesis by the opposite relationship.
>
> As we see immediately, this definition, on the one hand, sends us back to a temporal determination—narrative speed—since it goes without saying that the quantity of information is solidly in inverse ratio to the speed of the narrative; and on the other hand it sends us to a datum of voice—the degree to which the narrating instance is

present. . . . The narrator is present as source, guarantor, and organizer of the narrative, as analyst and commentator, as stylist . . . and particularly—as we well know—as producer of "metaphors."

7. Ken Mitchell has pointed out that few characters in Ross's short stories are given surnames: *Sinclair Ross*, p. 5. It's worth adding that many characters are named only in the most inconspicuous ways—by late naming or infrequent (to the point of single) naming. When we remember that Mrs. Bentley presides over her own narrative in *As for Me and My House* without ever gaining a personal name, and that Chris Rowe in *The Well* uses an alias that obscures his identity, we begin to project significance onto the absences. Does the lack of name reinforce the typicality—that is, the anonymity— of these figures? Does it imply lives so stunted and selves so denied that the characters stumble through precarious identities, that they largely remain undeveloped or unacknowledged?

8. McMullen has noted this pattern: *Sinclair Ross*, p. 32. She goes on to add that at the text's end "In an ironic reversal, now Paul sees the real world, but Ellen, who viewed reality too clearly to be sustainable, has passed into an illusory world" (33).

9. Gerard Genette, *Narrative Discourse*, p. 199.

10. *S/Z*, trans. Richard Miller, "Preface" by Richard Howard (New York: Hill and Wang, 1974), p. 19. In this dazzling book Barthes explores the codes that crisscross Balzac's 'realist' story. The most startling perhaps, certainly the most provocative, of Barthes' codes is the referential. Far from giving us the 'real' world or describing what *actually* is there, in accordance with realist precept, referential codes oversee "in a collective and anonymous voice" (p. 18) the dispersal of all the clichés, all that is 'common knowledge,' all the entries in a dictionary of received ideas. These culturally based codes upon which Balzac builds amount to little more than

> an anthology of maxims and proverbs about life, death, suffering, love, women, ages of man, etc. Although entirely derived from books, these codes, by a swivel characteristic of bourgeois ideology, which turns culture into nature, appear to establish reality. "Life." "Life" . . . becomes a nauseating mixture of common opinions, a smothering layer of received ideas. (p. 206)

As Barthes writes elsewhere in *S/Z*,

> The utterances of the cultural code are implicit proverbs: they are written in that obligative mode by which the discourse states a general will, the law of a society, making the proposition concerned ineluctable or indelible. Further still: it is because an utterance can be transformed into a proverb, a maxim, a postulate, that the supporting

cultural code is discoverable: stylistic transformation "proves" the code, bares its structure, reveals its ideological perspective. (p.100)

11. Frank Kermode, *The Art of Telling: Essays on Fiction* (Cambridge, Mass.: Harvard, 1983), p. 105.

12. *S/Z*, p. 19.

13. The emphasis on the eye in a story of childhood initiation finds another powerful expression in Alice Munro's "Heirs of the Living Body" where a young Del Jordan, groping her way toward insight in a story clogged with references to eyes, fastens, fascinated, upon the eye of a dead cow. In a horrific scene she traces a stick around the eye. Munro develops that symbol richly in the story and in the cycle to which it belongs: *Lives of Girls and Women* (Scarborough, Ont.: Signet, 1974), p. 37. The book was first published in 1971.

14. In dealing with narrative speed, Genette further distinguishes (94) among four basic forms of narrative movement by comparing story time to narrative time: ellipsis, where narrative time is much shorter than story time (In 1914 he left and he returned four years later with a broken leg and heart); summary (this 'story' projected into several paragraphs, pages, or even chapters); scene (where story time = narrative time, as in scenic presentation using dialogue); pause (as in passages of description or commentary which stop the action).

15. *Sinclair Ross & Ernest Buckler* (Montreal: McGill-Queen's, Vancouver: Copp Clark, 1975), p. 11.

16. *Narrative Discourse*, p. 194.

17. *Narrative Discourse*, p. 205.

18. Anthony B. Dawson, in a fine article, "Coming of Age in Canada," *Mosaic*, 11, No. 3 (Spring 1978), 47-62, has written in a section on Ross, "It is curious that 'One's a Heifer' is the only story in *The Lamp at Noon* that feels more like a fantasy than a realistic story—though most of the others end in disaster, this is the only one that has the quality of nightmare, and the only one too that is inconclusive" (50).

19. Two short pieces pick up on the uncertainty that sticks to Vickers: F.H. Whitman, "The Case of Ross's Mysterious Barn," *Canadian Literature*, No. 94 (Autumn 1982), 168-9; and Marilyn Chapman, "Another Case of Ross's Mysterious Barn," *Canadian Literature*, No. 103 (Winter 1984), 84-6.

20. Oddly, Brydon takes the boy's estimate at face value and writes of this as a story of "madness and murder" (99). So, even more surprisingly, does McMullen. Though she writes at some length about duplicitous narrators, she claims that "the box-stall contains the body of Vickers' murdered housekeeper" (47) and that "the boy becomes privy to secret knowledge which even the adults of his world do not know" (48). The secret is so

intriguing it has generated still other guesses from readers whose confidence scarcely wavers. Mitchell concludes Vickers keeps a dead cow in the stall (20).

21. I quote at some length this remarkable statement from *S/Z*:

> Truth is brushed past, avoided, lost. This accident is a structural one. In fact, the hermeneutic code has a function . . . . [J]ust as rhyme (notably) structures the poem according to the expectation and desire for recurrence, so the hermeneutic terms structure the enigma according to the expectation and desire for its solution. [So] . . . the problem is to *maintain* the enigma . . . ; whereas the sentences quicken the story's "unfolding" and cannot help but move the story along, the hermeneutic code performs an opposite action: it must set up *delays* (obstacles, stoppages, deviations) in the flow of the discourse; its structure is essentially reactive, since it opposes the ineluctable advance of language with an organized set of stoppages: between question and answer there is a whole dilatory area whose emblem might be named "reticence," the rhetorical figure which interrupts the sentence, suspends it, turns it aside . . . . Whence . . . the abundance of dilatory morphemes: the *snare* (a kind of deliberate evasion of the truth), the *equivocation* (a mixture of truth and snare . . .), the *partial answer* (which only exacerbates the expectation of the truth), the *suspended answer* (an aphasic stoppage of the disclosure), and *jamming* (acknowledgment of insolubility). The variety of these terms . . . attests to the considerable labor the discourse must accomplish if it hopes to *arrest* the enigma, to keep it open. Expectation thus becomes the basic condition for truth: truth, these narratives tell us, is what is *at the end* of expectation. This design brings narrative . . . [across] a long path marked with pitfalls, obscurities, stops, [one which] suddenly comes out into the light . . . ; it implies a return to order, for expectation is a disorder; . . . order . . . completes, fills up, saturates, and dismisses everything that risks adding on: truth is what completes, what closes. (75-6)

Elsewhere in the book Barthes further lays out the connections between denouement and disclosure which operate in what he calls the "classic" text (p. 52, p. 172, p. 187).

22. As Wayne Tefs has pointed out to me, Freud would say that in these primal scene fantasies we want *not* to know as much as we want to know, since in one critical sense we already know what's there and this viewing will only confirm it. Undoubtedly at some profound level the claim will hold, even for this story, but in light of what various readers have believed to be behind that barn door we must refine it a bit when we apply it to Ross's story.

23. McMullen makes an important point when she reminds us that "the double focus [between past protagonist and present narrator] is not here [in "One's a Heifer"] so apparent" as in other Ross short stories (46).

24. Catherine Belsey, *Critical Practice* (London: Methuen, 1980), p. 70.

25. Edward McCourt calls "The Painted Door" "perhaps the best of his [Ross's] short stories—and certainly one of the best in Canadian literature" in his *The Canadian West in Fiction* (Toronto: Ryerson, 1970), revised edition, p. 103.

26. Diana Brydon, in an otherwise excellent piece, makes this startling observation about the characters and about the ending of "The Painted Door":

> Although Margaret Laurence argues in her introduction to these stories that "Ross never takes sides" . . . the struggle with dust and drought ennobles Paul, whereas it ages Ellen without maturing her. Similarly, despite the lack of explicit authorial comment, the reproaching smear of paint that provides the shock ending of "The Painted Door" condemns Ann for her weakness as surely as it indicates her husband John's strength. The implication is that the struggle with the land brings out the essential qualities of each sex: the petty, nagging materialistic dependencies in women, and the serious, silent, idealistic strengths in men. (99-100)

Needless to say, I disagree. The story seems far firmer in its sympathies to Ann, whatever her delusions, than Brydon would allow. By the same token, in my reading at least, the story portrays John, though gently, in something less than positive light.

THE VERNACULAR MUSE
IN PRAIRIE POETRY

*

The Roman Empire was coterminous with a diglossic
or bilingual world of cultural communication [in which
"the written language is thought of as the 'real' language,
and the vernaculars as illiterate corruptions"]. There was
no primarily linguistic cause for change. But, given a
growing military and political instability, this world could
be transformed by the social revolution of a Jewish sect
called Christianity, which eventually established a special
variety of Vulgar Latin to replace the Classical standard.
A lower-class secret society of biblical true believers
developed a new anti-aristocratic . . . mode of communal
life, with its own jargon, neologisms and semantic shifts.
Coming from the eastern Mediterranean, Christianity's
first language was a vulgar Greek vernacular, or koine . . .
for Roman Christians themselves were at first largely
Greek-speaking slaves and immigrants. [The resulting
language was] . . . invented to avoid established pagan
usage. The ecclesiastical and liturgical use of this Christian

dialect of Vulgar Latin gradually raised it from the gutter, giving it a special new dignity and sanctity, much to the disgust of Classical pagan aristocrats, who were being replaced by Christian bishops as the leaders of the new society.[1]

* *

Several years ago I edited a collection of essays on prairie poetry. Many of the statements in that book celebrated the finding of a prairie sense of place. Some of them spoke of that discovery as a matter of voicing, as I did in the introduction:

> Ultimately, that release derives from William Carlos Williams. An answer to pentametre and conceit in our bare hands, handling the telltale words. A local pride— poetry in the commonplace, the cows and cars and tall tales in this place. As we say them. As we have our say. . . . Listening and listing, inventing the inventory. Placing ourselves / our poems in this place. In our name. Remembering the names of our places, remembering our place. . . . "I remember" the names and voices, hear them now. Here now, try them, wondering. Ear-marked for the Prairies. As if for the first time, putting things in place.[2]

In a review of the book, one critic wrote

> Is this, then to be the epitome of prairie poetry: common, plain-spoken, a trifle colourless; the antithesis of anything Romantic?
> [R.E.] Rashley is, I agree, an examplary case. . . . He was exemplary in his ruthless work on himself and his style, his devotion to poetry, his integrity. Not for him the passing fads! Yet his way, the Via Colloquia, need not be everyone's; and anyway, Rashley would not have wanted followers. My need and my pleasure adhere to a different vision. His poetry is not aggressively regional; it is both true to his experience as a westerner and true to his experience of the English language, a language that cannot

be avoided or pummelled into submission. Its bones and
flesh are centuries old, its genius predates Cartier and
Henry Kelsey. Prairie poets are stuck with it; their art is
made of words, not worthy intentions.[3]

His remarks created a brief debate, including a strange
contribution from a fine poet:

> As for me, I would like to state that I am very much in
> agreement with Mark Abley. For me there is no such thing
> as "prairie poetry." There is the prairie, and there is the
> poetry being written by people living in the region. In-
> evitably the poetry is influenced by landscape, but I
> believe we must give up this silly notion that only one
> kind of poetry should be written in this place. The prairie
> is big, but poetry is bigger. There is room for all kinds of
> work here, even "poetry celebrating irony, paradox,
> ambiguity."
>
> For some of us the prairie is a chosen landscape, one
> we expect to spend the rest of our lives admiring. Whether
> we choose to be blunt and spare with our words or allusive
> and ambiguous, whether we write about the outer or the
> inner landscape, let's not debase our region by offering or
> accepting mediocre work with the excuse that it is "prairie
> literature."[4]

The observations are well taken, but they largely miss the point
I was trying to make. It's no accident, I submit, that both these
remarks—the original review, and the letter in support of that
review—came from people with traditional views of poetry. It's
especially revealing, too, that they came from a facsimile
Englishman and a transplanted Englishwoman, and that the
poet singled out for praise was himself of British origins.

A few months later, another reader entered the scene, this in
the form of a review on an anthology of new prairie poetry I had
edited as a companion to the volume of criticism.[5] The reviewer
once again trotted out complaints about a "flat" poetry and the
need (the terms were not so explicit as I have made them) for

'good' writing in metaphor and symbol and elegant cadence. This argument, too, came from certain assumptions—very standard and unacknowledged assumptions—about poetry, apparently still current in some circles. These notes help to explain a paragraph in a letter I wrote in response to the review. (The paragraph was removed when the magazine, *NeWest Review*, with which the poet I just quoted was closely associated, published the letter):

> This is a common and a continuing fight—to be able to use yr own voice in yr own world. To get out from under the smother of an official culture that is imported and 'high.' To be at home in the world. To name and proclaim an unwritten part of ourselves, spoken but never written because the writing available to us would not accommodate our worlds. Because that 'high' writing told us, as its adherents tell us now, and will continue to tell us, we must speak only in its voice. Well I'm fed up with being patronized by snooty English imports and snotty imitation English(wo)men who suppose the language and the literature has deteriorated from some Ur-state that it once enjoyed (in some versions, still enjoys) at Oxford. I'm pissed off that I should be told, in righteous terms, by people who know little about contemporary poetry [or poetics] and know even less about life in the prairies, that my voice and my realities are boring or irrelevant. I'm tired—we're all tired—with having to grin and justify ourselves to ill-informed arbiters who assume they are in charge, that their standards—their notions, however reactionary or intolerant, of what is true and what is good—must prevail. As they have always prevailed. I've had it with accusations of parochialism and ignorance from those who themselves don't know and don't care to know what's going on.[6]

I narrate this debate at some length to show that the view I will be taking here is by no means admired, much less accepted, in all literary camps, not even on the prairies where you might expect to get and normally do get a sympathetic hearing for it. I would imagine the reservations registered in these responses are even more common in regions or institutions whose practices are more purely based in English models. The suspicion will especially hold among critics whose aesthetic favours the elegant, the erudite, the allusive, the exotic—in short, 'high' culture.

It must be difficult, even for the curious, not to perceive vernacular poetry as a failure of imagination or intelligence. It hardly offers, it seems, the shock of metaphor or the challenge of interpretation many of us have come to expect in 'good' poetry. Apparently, vernacular just sits there blinking and naked as a newborn baby, and (some would have it) just as dumb. (The disapproving critic who appeared in an earlier quotation decided that "For Cooley, richness of language and idea is something as foreign as lobsters; a truly patriotic prairie poet will be proud to do without.")[7] It would be unusual for readers who look for a more traditional poetry to find anything, other than a certain verve, to recommend such work (although some are not prepared to find even that). I know that.[8]

But there are good reasons for such writing. I will be arguing that vernacular poetry presents a crucial shift in our sense of what poetry can be, and that this break extends away from 'high' art in all directions, to new definitions of the poem, yes, but also to redefinitions of—these really are the same thing—of what a poet is and what a reader is. I will argue, further, that the use of vernacular can be read instructively as a special instance of a larger strategy in contemporary art—the use of found material. (I am aware that, practically or biographically speaking, in the actual process of composition this category may not apply to vernacular poetry. But semiotically it does: we can assume the appropriation and transfer of a 'text,' whether or not it literally exists or has existed). And, finally, I will argue that an art of appropriation participates in the still larger category of postmodernism which profoundly alters the most basic beliefs and values that for centuries have informed the Western mind and therefore its art.

My statement is polemical. It observes a moment when many prairie poets—poets elsewhere, too, I expect—are fighting out from under their inscriptions. My remarks enter that struggle and are addressed in part to those who as critics or writers feel no need to question or to face questions about their own practices, since they bear all the aura, and with it all the power, that accrues to the received. Their authority would seem to elicit a special hearing and guarantee that *they* will ask the questions and make the judgments, simply because they bring with them the clout of the already known and widely admired. Those who hold such assumptions find it easy to believe their procedures will prevail and will lead, properly, to consensus and harmony, free from unpleasant noise in the system. As a result, their tone— I say nothing about the more ill-tempered—need not be combative, seems beyond advocacy. That's not surprising. We witness the civility of the privileged who have consolidated their gains and who risk almost nothing. It is easy to be genteel and reflective when you know your presuppositions will automatically be honoured and when you know you are empowered to silence others by disqualifying them from what Jean-Francois Lyotard calls "the language game":

> The stronger the "move," [he writes] the more likely it is to be denied the minimum consensus, precisely because it changes the rules of the game upon which consensus had been based. But when the institution of knowledge functions in this manner, it is acting like an ordinary power center whose behavior is governed by a principle of homeostasis.
>
> Such behavior is terrorist. . . . By terror I mean the efficiency gained by eliminating, or threatening to eliminate, a player from the language game one shares with him. He is silenced or consents, not because he has been refuted, but because his ability to participate has been threatened (there are many ways to prevent someone

from playing). The decision makers' arrogance, which in principle has no equivalent in the sciences, consists in the exercise of terror. It says: "Adapt your aspirations to our ends—or else."[9]

So, the gestures toward reasonableness are just that—gestures. I would take it as a tautology that, since in literary criticism we pursue our 'interests,' there can be no uninterested scholarship. Without 'interests' we would do nothing at all, as Terry Eagleton takes great relish in explaining. He wonderfully explodes claims of neutrality:

> All of our descriptive statements move within an often invisible network of value-categories, and indeed without such categories we would have nothing to say to each other at all. It is not just as though we have something called factual knowledge which may then be distorted by particular interests and judgements, although this is certainly possible; it is also that without particular interests we would have no knowledge at all, because we would not see the point of bothering to get to know anything. Interests are *constitutive* of our knowledge, not merely prejudices which imperil it.[10]

What I will be proposing here is quite in keeping with Eagleton: that all definitions and all estimations are conditional; that is, that there can be no intrinsic value to literature, only what people choose to think or say about a piece of writing (and whose basis then is *always* historical and contingent), and that new propositions necessarily will be transgressive, often aggressive. Literary value resides, he argues and I argue, not as is often supposed, independently and inside the poem, but in how we decide to read the poem, and our thinking will vary tremendously depending on a whole series of assumptions, strategies, and claims we bring, however unreflectingly, to bear. And these terms vary, as historically they have altered, simply because the terms of literature are functional, not ontological. Once we redefine the poem, or extend the range of its possible forms, we can recognize the force of other discourses.

Readers who know what struggle Americans had in getting American writing into their own universities will recognize a shocking parallel. American literature—and making this point always evokes gasps in audiences—didn't 'take' in American academies until amazingly late, until well into the twentieth century as a matter of fact. Rene Wellek's experience was typical: "I remember that when I first came to study English literature in the Princeton Graduate School in 1927 . . . no course in American literature . . . was offered."[11] The usual sneers and dismissals were there, and there is no need to rehearse them in this paper; you know them or can easily supply them for yourself. What is less known, and in its reporting the cause of even louder buzzes in public gatherings, is the late entry of British literature into British universities. For centuries literature meant 'serious' literature, 'bonafide' discipline, 'challenging' texts, the study of the 'classics' and philology—certainly nothing so frivolous or ephemeral as Chaucer or Shakespeare or the Brontes (how readily they fall onto the page for us, so fully given they are needful of no more than their surnames). Eagleton outlines how English literature as an academic subject entered English universities only well into the Victorian age and how it did not become respectable until the twentieth century. At that, it was apt for some time to be addressed condescendingly and easily set aside as weak material for the 'superficial' minds of women who weren't quite up to the rigours of legitimate literature, which meant work written in Greek or more commonly Latin. Eagleton shatters whatever delusions might remain in our assumed histories when he outlines the connections between British politics and the curriculum it brought into being. He proposes that the xenophobia turned against Germany in WW I meant that philology, which came from German example, lost its glamour, and the fervid nationalism of the day turned the English to their own accomplishments. We further learn that the rise of English literature elsewhere, in other countries, coincided with the consolidation of the British empire.[12] Whether anything like the same pattern has held for the fortunes of American culture I leave to others to decide.

* * *

Consider several definitions.

> vernacular [< L. *vernaculus,* belonging to homeborn slaves, indigenous < *verna,* a home-born slave] 1. using the native language of a country or place . . . 2. commonly spoken by the people of a particular country or place (a *vernacular,* as distinguished from the literary, dialect) . . . 5. 1. the native speech, language, or dialect of a country or place 2. the common, everyday language of ordinary people in a particular locality

> vulgar [ME. < L. *vulgaris* < *vulgus, volgus,* the common people < IE. base * *wel-,* to crowd, throng, whence Gr. *eilein,* to press, swarm] . . . 3. a) characterized by a lack of culture, refinement, taste, restraint, sensitivity, etc.; coarse; crude; boorish b) indecent or obscene[13]

Slave language as bad language, inferior and unworthy, as latent corruption in the master's house, to his Latin. Latin: important language, (to the slave) imported language. Imperial. We might remind ourselves also that in an etymology which extends through Latin back to Greek "idiom" is a cognate of "idict." "Idiom," we read, is the language peculiar to an individual, a group, a district or a class. An "idiot" is a peculiar or a private person, one who is of the self and of the self alone. The cultural loading for us has become massive, especially when we note that in general usage the category of "idiom" hardly holds for the language of, say, BBC announcers or Oxford dons. (To say that for linguists it does apply to such speakers is in no way to refute my claim, since the popular, and academic, practice is to ignore linguists as much as possible.) And the reason "idiom" doesn't pertain—the logic is, I think, inescapable—is because one particular idiom or a few idioms have been elevated and projected into something approaching 'universality.' We can see the consequences in how superior an 'educated' British seems, even to this day, to its practitioners and imitators in Canada. Irving Layton in "Anglo-Canadian" comically exposes that thinking:

ANGLO-CANADIAN

A native of Kingston, Ont.
—two grandparents Canadian
and still living

His complexion florid
as a maple leaf in late autumn,
for three years he attended
Oxford

Now his accent
makes even Englishmen
wince, and feel
unspeakably colonial.[14]

Establishing a fastidious upper-middle class British, or some replication of it, as the supreme measure of poetry has led to some nasty exclusions. Anthony Easthope speaks to the point when he identifies the hegemony of iambic pentameter in the English tradition. He argues it is historically constituted in the Renaissance at the expense of an earlier accentual tradition. By promoting syllables between accented syllables, and by spacing them out fairly evenly, iambic pentameter helped to entrench the " 'Received Pronunciation' of Standard [British] English (the bourgeois norm). It does so because it legislates for the number of syllables in the line and therefore cancels elision, making transition at word junctures difficult."[15] It eliminates from 'serious' literature, other than for comic purposes, the drastically elided and, in some of its variants, the emphatic voices of working people. Quickly elevated to ruling status, blank verse delivered a canon that asks for a clipped, precise and fastidious elocution. Such pronunciation—one thinks of Laurence Olivier—signals 'proper' speech; that is, a class dialect. Pentameter aims to preclude shouting and 'improper' excitement; it enhances the poise of a moderate yet uplifted tone of voice, an individual voice self-possessed, self-controlled, impersonally self-expressive.[16]

The argument is compelling. Once established, blank verse

becomes a sign which includes and excludes, sanctions and denigrates, for it discriminates the 'properly' poetic from the 'improperly' poetic, Poetry from verse. In an unbroken continuity from the Renaissance to 1900 and beyond, a poem within the metrical [I would add the metaphorical] tradition identifies itself (in Puttenham's words), with polish and reformed manners as against poetry in another metre which can be characterized as rude, homely, and in the modern sense, vulgar.[17]

We might think, then, of assumptions commonly at work: what is a poem? or more immediately, and more usually: what is a good poem? The limits arise for most of us, I think, out of a belief that a poet must 'control' 'his' material, that the material must be rendered in striking images and arresting metaphors, that the poem must be laden with elegant phrasings and high allusions, that the text must be susceptible to multiple readings (i.e. 'for all time'), that the poet must deal with 'serious' issues (life, death, nature, 'reality') in a 'significant' (sometimes a 'poignant') way. But 'he' must not speak in any manner that will admit to the historical moment or jeopardize the deepest ethical, political, or metaphysical beliefs, including the inherited discourse we have learned to perceive as poetry. Let me stress this point because I don't want to lose it or have it confused with quite another argument. Our definitions of literature have always been able to accommodate unorthodox ideas, in fact many of us hold such transactions in the highest esteem. In reply to this observation I cite at some length a brilliant essay, "Feminists and Postmodernism," by Craig Owens, who finds even in modernism, certainly in other shapes of authority, systems that observe some representations but prohibit and invalidate others.[18] Owens argues that even so radical a critic as Fredric Jameson, the Marxist structuralist, yearns for a narrative of mastery:

> It is one symptom of our postmodern condition, which is experienced everywhere today as a tremendous loss of mastery and thereby gives rise to therapeutic programs, *from both the Left and the Right*, for recuperating that loss. . . . For what if not the emergence of Third-World nations, the "revolt of nature" and the women's movement—that is, *the voices of the conquered*—has challenged the West's desire for ever-greater domination and control?[19]

The point here is not so trivial as it may seem. I am maintaining that readers of many political persuasions are agreed on the rightness of a particular discourse by which we constitute and measure our society: that discourse being largely referential and prizing unity, high seriousness, linearity, and closure. Jacques Derrida puts the counter case succinctly. The academy, which by and large has defined and valued our literature, has become a prisoner of its own discourse, assuming that its preferences and its procedures are somehow natural, neutral, or permanent:

> What this institution cannot bear [as Roland Barthes soon found out when it turned savagely on his early writings], is for anyone to tamper with . . . language. . . . It can bear more readily the most apparently revolutionary ideological sorts of "content," if only that content does not touch the borders of language . . . and of all the juridico-political contracts that it guarantees.[20]

If these are the terms that obtain—mastery, hierarchy, ingenuity, high-mindedness, systems of overriding belief or structure—we can at best be entertained by vernacular poetry, which will seem insignificant by such standards, immune to the exercise of a hermeneutics in which we have been so deeply inscribed and by which we have learned to value poetry.

Take the example of W.H. Auden. When he introduced his radical politics into British poetry, the literary establishment had no difficulty in recognizing and admiring him as a poet. That's not surprising: Auden's voicing, for all its audacity, presented no deep affront to accepted discourse. Learned, intelligent, controlled, it bore all the signs of the literary. It used symbols, drew on myths (especially of pastoralism and of the apocalypse), observed (however sinuously) conventional prosody, spoke of serious things, inverted syntax, built to climaxes, marshalled its own metaphors, thickened with intricate binaries of meaning, fairly hummed with literary allusions. Its ironies could easily be forgiven.

Supposing, though, we alter definitions of the poetic. Suppose the current terms are themselves put into doubt. Once we begin to lose faith in an aesthetic that recognizes, even celebrates, systems of ascribed superiority, we begin to remake our poetics. We may no longer esteem the poet as a master who imposes order or, god-like, manipulates language. We are not so readily convinced then that poetry must be written in a foreign idiom, as though it were written solely by and (often, it seems) for dead Englishmen. We no longer feel compelled to write or read 'universal' texts and 'eternal' truths. We no longer believe there are verities outside a place and moment of conception. Or reception. (Try *Hamlet* on Australian aborigines.)

Here's Daniel Buren on the "Function of the Museum":

> The work is always limited in time as well as in space. By forgetting (purposefully) these essential facts one can pretend that there exists an immortal art, an eternal work. . . . And one can see how this concept and the mechanisms used to produce it—among other things the function of the Museum as we have very rapidly examined it—place the work of art once and for all above all classes and ideologies. The same idealism also points to the eternal

and apolitical Man which the prevalent bourgeois ideology would like us to believe in and preserve.[21]

Much the same can be said for establishing and preserving the canon in literature, as Barbara Herrnstein Smith so tellingly writes:

> What is commonly referred to as "the test of time" . . . is not, as the figure implies, an impersonal and impartial mechanism; for the cultural institutions through which it operates (schools, libraries, theaters, museums, publishing and printing houses, editorial boards, prize-awarding commissions, state censors, etc.) are, of course, all managed by persons (who, by definition, are those with cultural power and commonly other forms of power as well), and, since the texts that are selected and preserved by "time" will always tend to be those which "fit" (and, indeed, have often been *designed* to fit) their characteristic needs, interests, resources, and purposes, that testing mechanism has its own built-in partialities accumulated in and thus *intensified* by time.[22]

Smith goes on to explain what in practice this situation means for selecting and protecting canon:

> For example, the characteristic resources of the culturally dominant members of a community include access to specific training and the opportunity and occasion to develop not only competence in a large number of cultural codes but also a large number of diverse (or "cosmopolitan") interests. The works that are differentially re-produced, therefore, will often be those that gratify the exercise of such competencies and engage interests of that kind: specifically, works that are structurally complex and, in the technical sense, information-rich—and which, by virtue of those very qualities, are especially amenable to multiple reconfiguration, more likely to enter into relation with the emergent interests of various subjects, and thus more readily adaptable to emergent conditions. Also,

as is often remarked, since those with cultural power tend to be members of socially, economically, and politically established classes (or to serve them and identify their own interests with theirs), the texts that survive will tend to be those that appear to reflect and reinforce establishment ideologies.[23]

Buren's art museum and Smith's canon, both subject to the special and variable interests that inform human history, are commonly offered to us as organizations whose categories are secure. But, as Smith and Buren propose, the very palpable and provisional standing of art gets transformed through such mechanisms to become massive and immutable, its moments turned into monuments. It is instructive to follow Smith as she outlines how, in defence of entrenched tastes, dominant or privileged groups in our culture proceed. In a vocabulary appropriate to our topic, we can say that basically they enforce, or try to enforce, stable definitions of: 1) poetry (insisting on intrinsic and therefore fixed qualities that delimit it); 2) institutions that can legitimately host and credit literary enterprise; and 3) competence that determines which readers are qualified to do the evaluating.[24]

These are deluded conceptions. Being contingent, writing can never be a masterpiece outside of history, or enter a permanent canon, since these terms are themselves located in ideology and reflect the preferences of those who at any given time constitute themselves, or are otherwise constituted, as authorities, and whose estimations can and do give way to their successors'. Such institutions have largely lifted texts out of their original situations and enlisted them in the fiction of a sacred, ineradicable, and therefore unquestionable standing. Literature, this notion would have us believe, is something that has happened in other times, in other places, in other words. But the canon, much less literature, is a variable, not a fixed category. Texts leave and enter it all the time, depending on how we choose to read them. But if a text, even one single text, is found to be no longer sacred—I say nothing about sanctified texts whose authors never supposed would service the entire species, for eternity—the whole apparatus falls into suspicion. How can 'universal' texts ever lose their universality, and if they can, what confidence can we have in any other of the approved texts? Logically a canon—at least one that endorses the verities and scrupulously keeps its membership list—would be restricted to addition and exempt from deletion. Nor should a canon require special justification: the importance of its constituents ought to be self-evident if its claims are not to slide into uncertainties and instabilities where 'competence' becomes a criterion for establishing them and where the texts can no longer be 'universal' because they are accessible only to certain 'qualified' readers.

So, for others, literature now becomes vigorously rooted—in *our* time and in *our* places, subject to *our* values, *our* sense of what is real. It also becomes, for many, vernacularly based in the 'low' and the local, speaking from or for minority groups who have become marginalized (women, the Third World, the poor, the 'uneducated,' natives, working people, ethnics, those in 'the hinterland,' in short—central to my argument—the disenfranchised). Once the exiled and the shut-out begin to define their own literature, they put the institutions into disrepute. They break the silence the establishment would fix with shame upon them. The powerless start to talk back and answer with the crackle of *their* language, often, I'm arguing, in a vernacular that subverts the 'high' soundings they have been told are the measure of true poetry.[25] And that vernacular asks some basic questions of official estimations: whose poetry? written for whom? by whom? in what words? for what purpose? to whose satisfaction or approval? with what consequences? what exclusions?

Hence the strategy of bringing the oral into the poem. It marks the seeking of a usable discourse in a colonized world. As Robert Kroetsch says, the buggers can't stop us from talking. The strategy here is not so much a finding of the right image, a more correct description, a more fitting version of the colonized world (though it may include that). It means refusing the presented terms or the given boundaries of poetry. Instead, we construct other routes, seek new discourses, which reconstitute the poem beyond any capacity to enforce consent. One major resistance comes through the defiant and joyous sounding of voices which in the past have been considered noisy or sub-literary. Now, celebrated in poetry, they become eminently sub-versive.

It is helpful to put the argument in the context of contemporary theory. Allon White outlines what happens when a powerful group puts its language into preferred standing. Such discourse, once "established as 'the' language of the speech community, unified, centralized, authoritative, always mythic," carries the full authority of hegemony.[26] The privileged or 'high' form "is constituted as unitary through the agencies of scholars, lexicographers, grammarians and literary critics, thus becoming a centripetal force of language in a political process of centralization and incorporation."[27] In short,

> Grammar, poetics and unitary language theory are modes whereby the prestige language simultaneously canonizes itself, regularizes and endorses its system and boundaries, makes itself teachable and assimilable in educational practice and above all 'naturalizes' itself over against all competing sociolects, dialects and registers.[28]

In counter to the prestige languages, whose juris-diction their speakers and writers tend to expand, the subordinated languages try to avoid or subvert that control when they "systematically invert, negate and relexicalize" the hindering language.[29] In contra-diction.

The argument startlingly parallels those we are now hearing from feminists. Any groups which are pushed into the margins, whether by gender or income or education or culture or race, find that those who maintain admired discourses will neither admit nor honour *their* disreputable language. The alternatives open to such minorities are limited: they can simply ignore the dominant discourses and get on with their own; they can try to enter and use those inherited discourses to their own ends; or they can try to extend or even displace them by inserting their own into the system. I am here arguing for the third position—that of redoing the discourse—as are numerous feminists. There are already dozens of excellent statements that would apply. I cite only one, very briefly, to make the point. In "The Silence is Broken" Josephine Donovan[30] claims that the rise of the novel created an opening which allowed women to enter 'literature,' which has been more and more narrowly defined in literary history,[31] for the first time in a serious way. That opportunity occurred, she argues, because the novel was a new form and therefore free from the constraints of a classical tradition to which only men enjoyed access, and immune to appropriations by male writers who, given their inscriptions, largely avoided the form as disreputable. In a peculiar way women's exclusion from classical education, including its emphasis on a highly 'rhetorical' mode of writing, meant women as cultural outsiders were in a good position to write novels "in a vernacular close to the style in which they spoke without fear of critical chastisement" or of educational conditions that could "force them to automatic literary exile."[32]

* * * *

Many prairie poets use (but do not necessarily confine themselves to) vernacular—Lorna Crozier, Ed Upward, Birk Sproxton, Gary Hyland, Kate Bitney, David Arnason, Glen Sorestad, Jon Whyte, Stephen Scriver, I myself. (There are others.) As part of that strategy they will often resort to narrative and in some cases anecdotal modes that violate the post-Romantic convention of a timeless present in the lyric. Like as not, in these kinds of pieces they may—but not necessarily will—put vigour before subtlety, prefer passion to ambiguity. But it would be a terrible mistake to assume these choices signify laziness or stupidity. Nothing could be further from the truth, for many of these writers work the mode for sophisticated and ideological reasons. You have only to hear from, say, Robert

Kroetsch or David Arnason, to recognize the formidable intellectual basis behind their work.

For my purposes I will concentrate on only three poets—Andy Suknaski, Dennis Gruending, and Robert Kroetsch—using short pieces from each of them. The most apparent and probably most typical use of such voicing occurs in Suknaski's work, where he will appropriate a single voice—the poet's Ukrainian mother, or an Indian fisherman, or a friend in a poolhall at Wood Mountain, or someone living in St. Boniface, or in his most ambitious versions, such as *Montage for an Interstellar Cry*, a whole series of street voices trickling through the pubs and stores and bus stops the poet inhabits, bringing those sounds, ringing, into our ears.

You will see immediately how the voicing in Suknaski abandons the reflexiveness favoured in several centuries of verse, certainly in most versions of high modernism and the criticism that grew up around it. In its expression of self and in its overt appeal to audience, the Suknaski poem does not pretend to be, nor can it be construed to be, a disembodied voice thinking out loud and outside its moment of enunciation. In the now-familiar terms that Roman Jakobson has presented to us,[33] we can recognize that the speaker commits himself less to reflexive or expressive language, than—what is pertinent to my argument—to a vocative or pragmatic mode (addressing an audience with the hope of somehow affecting it). And so we bump up against a greater immediacy than commonly we get in the accredited language of poetry with its mediation and distancing—an approved poetics that is upset, for example, by the language of exhortation. We get, too, the emphatic parallels of the 'oral' voicing that involve 'exact' repetition of words, 'double' subjects, remarkable duplications in grammatical structures, and in some versions heavy 'rhymes' of one sort or another.

Here is a brief example of a single appropriation in Suknaski:

Lawn Outside Norcanair in Buffalo Narrows

yad dhat misterr weight
dhat misterr weight
he dohn giv us nuttin   for dhat fish
he *so* cheap
5 1/2 cent sometime   7 1/2 cent foh pike
50 cent foh pickerel
how kin fulla live on dhat?
many fulla   dhey dohnt say nuttin
jus work like dohgz
dheir family stahrrve
dhy dohn say nuttin   to dhat misterr weight
well i see dhat misterr weight
udder day   an ah speak
MISTERR WEIGHT
YOU KNOH SIRR
YOU NOT GIVIN US   NUTTIN
BY TIME WE PAY FOH BOAT
BY TIME WE PAY FOH GAS
YOU DOHNT GIVE US   NUTTIN!
i say dhat to weight
i jus cant   keep quiet
wen sometin on my mind
wen sometin on you mind boy
you gotta speak
oh you *die*   boy![34]

The trick for Suknaski is not to be densely allusive in homage to
'high' and therefore recognized European culture, gesturing
toward the storehouse of accredited symbols, nor is it to be heroi-
cally inventive, as the poet in our post-Romantic time is still supposed to be. Suknaski's virtue here lies in being humbly
attentive, bringing unassuming voices into the poem, acknowledging their power, allowing them weight, their dignity and integrity, asking a careful hearing of us—the pacing leading our
way through the experience, bit by bit, set to a new music that
is neither evenly nor 'tastefully' measured.[35]

The writer in this model doesn't make great things out of nothing, he picks up interesting possibilities from the neglected or rejected events in life. With poets like Suknaski, 'apoetic' materials—words from other discourses, with their own conventions, quite unlike those traditionally held to be essential in poetry—enter the poem and ask of us a special reading. Ask to be read as poetry. They ask us not to take the words for granted, as unworthy references, not to receive them only as familiar windows on the world, or conveyors of large and ineradicable truths, or messages of deep import, not even as exercises in verbal ingenuity, but as words whose pace and force, and whose secondary meanings, now make them richer and more telling. To really listen. And to bring forward those voices once excluded from poetry, attending to the felt step of their measures.

In their search for a style adequate to their needs prairie poets have hit upon one which only recently has become available but which still is not widely accepted, as my opening narrative was meant to show. Certainly vernacular has been used elsewhere— in Carl Sandburg, Edgar Lee Masters, Robert Frost, most notably in William Carlos Williams with his *Spring and All* in 1922. (In case anyone mistakes what I am saying: I am certainly *not* thinking of writers like Rudyard Kipling, Robert Service, or even Robert Burns, all of whom practised within traditional prosody.) But even readers aware of those precedents might balk at some of the shapes it has now taken on. The precarious standing of vernacular becomes deeply apparent when in some texts we move to an almost demotic English, as in this baseball poem by Dennis Gruending, where the transposed language of sport breaks into chant and where the post-Romantic lyric gives way to the poem as drama:

> chucker chatter
>
>> hudda buddy
>> hudda buddy
>> now you gonowyou go
>> fireball fireball

righthaner
shoot to me buddy
shoot to me buddy buddy
fireball now fireball
righthander

ohhh
now you smoke
now you smoke buddy now you smoke buddy
buddy
now you hot
now you hot shot ohhh
now you hot
buddy buddy

c'mon babe c'mon babe
c'mon shooter
c'mon shooter buddy buddy
you 'n me honey
all they is
honey
all they is honey honey
buddy buddy
way to mix
way to mix now righthander
now you work
now you work buddy
now you hot buddy
now you hot buddy
you push to me buddy
push to me buddy
push ball
push ball
you 'n me honey
all they is honey honey
all they is honey
buddy buddy
buddy buddy[36]

This is, I think, an extraordinary poem, entering the body of literature in outrageous violation of its sanctities (though I suspect, and other readers may suspect, with a start, Gruending is writing with Leslie Fiedler in mind—his notion of male bonding).[37] In any case, the severely limited and specialized vocabulary and its suspect semantic standing (as 'non-sense' or at least willful extravagance, risking vacuity) stands out. "Chatter," we learn, is merely suggestive of language, and is imitative in derivation, perhaps serving here as a noisy marking of territory or as a locating device (taking soundings). So, too, the flagrant celebration of phonetics at the cost of syntax and semantics and the hovering on the verge of babble (what is that word "hudda" but pure sound, generated by the familiar "buddy" and attached to it—consolidating the experience and validating it in a cluster of phonemes?); the almost total erosion of punctuation (marks which are part of a *book* world); the collapse in 'grammar' and polite levels of usage; lapses in 'taste'; the unvarying and utterly undiscriminating coordinate construction—these signify the orality of the passage. Insubordinate, talk of equals. We find much the same effect in the dizzy elision of phonemes and the graphemic strain of simulating sounds ("c'mon," "righthaner," "'n," "ohhh"); in the giddy speed of fused words ("gonowyou"); the bold somatic weight of words in the mouth, the whole body; the joy in idiom; the display of verbal excess and exaggeration. We find an oral voicing too in the heavy, almost manic, observance of expressive and vocative modes so extreme the voicing can perhaps be best understood as phatic (Are you there? I am here. Are you here? I'm here.) The piles of appositives with which the speaker plies his listener; the obsessive assertion of the speaker's presence, responsive to the occasion, extending, approaching, compulsively addressing—these too push the Gruending piece far from a complex and studied 'literary' shape laden with tropes and intellectual difficulties (namely irony, ambiguity, 'high' allusion, and metaphor) and determined by the world of 'literate' private composition for the page. They shove it, finally, to the edge of tribal song.

As a matter of fact, the piece *is* a version of sacred song. Rhapsodic, it speaks, compulsively, profusely, not so much of what the world is but of what the world ought to be, if only language could align life to its expression. It eschews the personal, meditative voice which elsewhere, in approved verse, we seem not (as here) to be hearing so much as overhearing, and which itself seems to be asking nothing more than understanding of us. Furiously oral, Gruending's voice is freed from the compulsion to 'mean' in a weighty way, and clamours for response, would provoke effect, catch attention. Pleading, cajoling, rejoicing, trying to form a reality (the pitcher's supremacy, the catcher's capacity to evoke and fuse with it) by an audacious act of naming, a brazen rush of ejaculations and imperatives (though it speaks more out of wish than command), the voice calls upon public powers to serve the tribe. Invested in passion, the speaker aspires to magic—to bring about a state of affairs that he would locate according to his desires. Such a condition, once brought into being, would guarantee the speaker's identity with what he addresses. So he speaks in the rhythms of solidarity and affirmation: this is our world, our ritual, our shared life. This is what we say. It is pre-eminently immediate ("now," "now," "now" the voice insists, beats out its snare, speaks only in the simple present, never in a present progressive which would reduce its vertiginous plunge).

Inserted into a ritual circuit of language, it tilts far therefore from the fine distinctions, the felicitous phrasings, that obtain in 'literary' writing. That distance is enhanced by the push of low back vowels muscling their way, hypnagogically, through the poem. A mad phonetic enchaining, frantic tumble of sound, that is at once generative in its sources and constrained in its range. The relative shortage of front or high vowels, and of nasals, glides and even fricatives, means there is little trilling or hissing, only minimal buzzing and humming here. We catch, instead, a constant explosion of velar stops (smoke, c'mon, go, work), alveolar stops (hudda, shot, hot), and above all of bilabial stops (buddy, babe, push, ball). We hear the throaty rasp of glottals (hudda, hot, honey, righthander, ohhh). Mainly the voice pumps along on a torrent of explosive grunts that knock into those in their way, a column of dominoes falling. The mind that calls the vocal apparatus into play, and the mechanism which releases and shapes the air, give it sound, speak in stress, beseeching and shouting, again and again, urgently propelled in a language of the fullest participation. No time for the considered word, the inward measure. Sounds plunge through this world, beyond the impedence of detail, oblivious to nuance. The enunciation slides into a 'nonsense' category where it has no need for thought, no occasion to linger in unthreatened leisure. Hurried, harried, it cannot take time to attribute, to qualify, to invert syntax, insert parentheses, construct ambiguities. Pitched in a syntax of desire. A friend, Margaret Allen, said to me, remembering her childhood speech, her love of poetry: "I like the feel of the sounds of the words in my mouth." Utterly palpable, culpable. Mouthy.

In "chucker chatter" we are far, we see, from the fastidious enunciation or solemnity Easthope has described as accruing to 'serious' poetry. We may well hear the poem with some embarrassment. A public drama, in action and reaction, it is pure performance, ritual as a matter of fact. The voice is so forthright, so extreme in its intercessions, so unreflecting, so rude and redundant, so silly in its simple enthusiasms (if only we could preclude them), we find little room to be the readers we have been taught to be and want to be—moderate, thoughtful, judicious, prepared nicely to interpret intellectual complexities and perhaps find some display of understated emotion. But this toboggan of sound will not allow us the comforts of our training; it scandalizes with its refusal to be meaningful or judicious or well spoken. We trail—confused? offended?—into regions that are semantically inchoate, rhythmically emphatic, phonetically occluded, relentlessly and loudly vocative. 'Let's not get carried away.' What, finally, we find most objectionable, what beyond our offended sense of subtlety we find intolerable, is this poem's presumption that it will 'mean' nothing and yet that it will make things happen.

Still, we note the trope on fire and heat ("fireball," "now you smoke," "now you hot / now you hot shot"). We hear the strong parallelism in the title (the disyllabic words, both trochees, heavily alliterated and phonetically stopped at similar positions, comparable in duration, and exactly matched in their second syllables), and we gain some sense, take some satisfaction, from that. We hear, too, a personal anguish creep in, underlying the ceremonial language. It emerges most overtly in the eruption of the word "honey" (four times, uninterrupted) in the middle of the chant. A term of endearment? Or how about that "ohhh" that punctuates the pell-mell repetitions, the litany of desire? Purely expressive, is it not ecstatic, orgasmic? Is it not miscegenic, allied with the 'illiterate' black idiom we find in "all they is honey"? We can find such ways to confer significance on the poem. So we might construe the "you 'n me honey / all they is / honey" as a solicitous cry that emerges again and again and that culminates in an end we might read as plea or rhapsody. In any case, we see how secondary meanings can be released by easing a peculiar discourse into poetry.

Tribal though "chucker chatter" is, we see how 'personal' it is and how it bears many deictic features that establish situation, locate the speaker in it, and orient readers toward it. Those marks include the prominence of the adverb "now" (fourteen times); the pile of first and second person pronouns; and the load of nouns of address (buddy, righthan(d)er, hot shot, babe, shooter, honey) that nominate, would denominate this world and bring it, Adamically, into order. The "you" is always located in the nominative case, in a position of power; the speaker, supplicative, is always in a position of reception and vulnerability, named in every instance in the accusative case, never enjoying the confidence of agency or possession. The singular pronouns—"you," "me"—never give way, not once, to the plural "we" and the speaker is left arguably much as he began.

His purpose all along has been to provoke and prolong power, but he ends perhaps in a continued state of supplication, suspended in song, because unable to make the singular collective or the relationship reciprocal. (The total absence of proper nouns further reinforces our sense of this as a relatively anonymous because tribal discourse—locked into the unspecified status of pronomial reference.)

We could, however, argue that the Adamic impulse is paramount. In the barrage of names, the dance of nouns, the speaker seeks ordination. Inordinately. He would transfix the pour of experience in his litany, turn verb into noun in the hope of entering the moment into some stable set of objects. Though the catcher implores with emphatic verbals ("go," "fireball," "shoot," "make," "c'mon," "mix," "work," "push"), he soon migrates toward copula verbs: the "is" in variations of "all they is honey," and the elided "are" in variations on "now you [are] hot." He also declares, twice, a situation devoid of verbals: "you 'n me honey." As if to dam the current of verbs that would erode his condition and betray him into time, the catcher ends on a raft of nouns ("buddy buddy / buddy buddy"), visually aligned (protected?) in perfect symmetry and pulling his speech into a state beyond acting. We are left with "you 'n me" in copula, a final insistence that gathers strength from the two opening lines ("hudda buddy / hudda buddy") which complement the closing and help solidly to frame in the rest of the poem where it can be no longer imperilled by the surge of time.

We also discover, perhaps with surprise, that only one adverb, "now," and only one adjective, "hot," ("righthan(d)er" swallows its attribute in compounding, transposes adjective into noun) qualify the avalanche of nouns, sliders, and verbals. No wonder. There is no time for reflection, no chance for discrimination. Pitched in such vehemence there can be no provision for refinement or distribution—not in this voice, not on this occasion. Basic forces lurch through this world, beyond detailing, immune to distinction, known only in their fervent naming. The surge of nouns serves to call on the powers, to call them by name,

call them forth, into being: this is what they are called, this is
what they are. It is the catcher's vocation (his calling) to evoke
(to call into being, into action). Himself 'called' into office, he,
priestly, 'calls' others into participation, provokes, addresses
himself to them, would catch the pitch of their voices. Vocative.
Naming as sympathetic magic—evocation. In turn the welter of
verbals directs and channels those powers: this is what they do,
what I will them to do.

We see how susceptible to formal analysis such a poem can
be, perhaps understandably can be if Andrew Welsh is to be
believed. In *Roots of Lyric* he says of chant, "We seem to be in the
business of recovering abandoned theories of language for the
service of poetics." Chant, he argues, is "pragmatic" and seeks
"not vision but power"[38] because, unlike the poetry of
"phanopoeia," which is visually based, chant as a form of
"melopoeia" moves emphatically through time. It serves not to
imitate mental processes but to produce effects. It is functional,
not informational, and located always in a context of real utterance. It seeks participation, relies on magic, is communally
based, commonly speaks in strong patterns of repetition (including catalogues), assumes the reality and value of social power,[39]
and "overrides language [in its semantic dimensions] to the
point of producing a large proportion of 'meaningless' elements."[40] Chant survives in temple-chanting, church litanies,
even in "The game-songs of children and the songs and chants
of football games or protest marches . . .—trivial examples, it
may seem [Welsh cannot fully shake his inscriptions], when
compared to the Navaho and Australian chants, but nevertheless rediscoveries of an old and powerful root of poetry."[41]

Chant also survives, Welsh tells us, in some modern poems
written by people like Imamu Amiri Baraka:

> It is easy to pick out their poetic roots: they are public
> curses and prophecies and calls to action built on the
> melopoeia of a pulsing, rushing beat, repetition and
> catalogue, and, most importantly in this case, the

> *communal rhythms of a "street voice" that can bring his*
> *audiences to their feet in recognition and identity.*[42]

The impact of such voicing is profoundly registered in prairie poetry too for those who feel with a rush that they are hearing, as if for the first time, *their* voices, not the superior and exotic intonations in which they don't exist, don't even have a say or get a hearing.

Welsh is well aware of what is at stake and of how far we must shift to appreciate the aural:

> In modern poetry the communal rhythm has become
> even fainter, and modern poets tend toward a language
> that emphasizes other things: the Image rather than a
> rushing rhythm; the precision of careful thought rather
> than repetition, catalogue, or incantation; autonomy and
> impersonality rather than the *participation mystique* of the
> communal voice. The root is still present, however, and
> every now and then a modern poem will surprise us with
> a sudden emergence of that basic, communal voice.[43]

That's not surprising, since the whole project of which such texts are a part counters the elevated and involved phrasings of the obviously 'written' text with the lurch and jerk of 'oral' speech. The important distinctions between oral, chirographic, and print cultures are laid out in the work of Walter J. Ong. In an astonishing book, *Orality and Literacy*, he develops a whole series of oppositions between language as it exists in an oral world, and language as it occurs in a literate society. Orally based expression (to mention only several of Ong's insights) is: formulaic and mnemonic; embedded in the flow of time; public and shared; beset with distractions and interactions between speaker and audience; susceptible to multiple voicings (as in Menippea); additive rather than subordinate in its affixing; 'exaggerated' in using heavy or type characters, common or episodic plots, and simple conflicts between virtues and vices. It is also: redundant, copious or fulsome; combative and illocutionary (full of bragging, tongue-lashing, praising, appeasing, commanding, praying, exhorting, teasing, denouncing, threatening, wooing, confessing, cursing); situationally based (as in the use of riddles or appeals to audience); unwilling or unable to make sharp distinctions between speaker and hero, or speaker and audience; rapidly narrated with few details (discourse time being far shorter than story time); located in a present that constantly redefines its past by shaking off memories that are no longer useful (i.e. without our sense of 'history'). Such language events are not at all what ordinarily we find in written texts. Written texts are more spatial and located outside of time; abstract; analytical; private; novel; dense with meaning; visualist; 'economical' because informationally rather than persuasively directed; portable and less bound by occasion; nearly and at times virtually devoid of speaker and listener; distanced; closed and self-contained, sequential, linear, and climactic; fixed and singular in point of view.[44]

My rough summary cannot begin to do justice to Ong's superb and finely elaborated statement, but it does give some idea of the possibilities. With no great effort, we can make extensive and compelling connections between the oral culture Ong describes and certain features of contemporary prairie poetry. I think immediately of his observation that "Print culture gave birth to the romantic notions of 'originality' and 'creativity,' which set apart an individual work from other works even more."[45] And I think of how custodians of received culture find prairie vernacular, which is communally based, to have failed in not reaching for those very qualities valued by a print culture. It would be well worth our while to trace out the numerous applications that suggest themselves, but for my purposes here I will leave Ong's dazzling account much as it stands, packed with possibilities we can use for poetry based on speech models. (I would add, however, and hope that readers will not overlook this point: *Ong does not promote, nor do I promote, oral culture above print culture.* Ong pointedly says "Orality is not an ideal, and never was. To approach it positively is not to advocate it as a permanent state for any culture. Literacy opens possibilities to the word and to human existence [the writing of critical essays for one thing] unimaginable without writing."[46] The point is to reopen some space for orality in the face of a print culture which, allowing for Derrida's larger argument, has consolidated itself as *the* measure of literature, and which in its applications on the prairies works in damaging ways.)

One thing is certain: what is spoken, or putatively spoken, now works as citation, and the pre-eminence of source moves from the literary canon or sanctioned cultural phenomena (a Mozart sonata, a Picasso painting, a Proust novel, a Shakespearean play, a Frank Lloyd Wright building) to the unassuming sounds around us. In every discourse quotation bears authority, and we see poets such as Suknaski displacing the canonical voices with new citations. The overheard, the found, present a new authority—what we might call a vernacular muse. Already in place (as is a semiotician's 'story' that precedes a text), the cited is altered by extraction and transferral. Relocated in a poem, that is, in another discourse, it is reconstituted, and is subject to new readings. Jonathan Culler is brilliant on this point. Arguing that there is *no* essential poetic language, Culler proposes that poems are those texts we choose to read as poems, nothing more, and he offers exemplary instances of his claim by using two outrageously 'unpoetic' discourses, one from Gerard Genette and one he has himself found, which he then realigns as poetry and puts to a poetic reading. The definition of poetry, then, resides not in any of its customary features (image, metaphor, tone, timelessness, rhythm, whatever), it rises out of our decision to treat or to receive the words in a literary way. Poetry, once thought to be essentialist, proves in this argument to be functionalist and much more capable of accommodating a wide range of practices.

Certainly in reading we are helped by visual aids, which prompt us to adopt a certain 'poetic' reading. Culler:

> The typographical arrangement produces a different kind
> of attention and releases some of the potential verbal

energy of 'thing,' 'is,' and 'simplicity' [all words suspended by themselves and projected to the right of Culler's found and rearranged material]. We are dealing less with a property of language (intrinsic irony or paradox) than with a strategy of reading, whose major operations are applied to verbal objects set as poems even when their metrical and phonetic patterns are not obvious.

. . . The primacy of formal patterning enables poetry to assimilate the meanings which they have in other instances of discourse and subject them to new organization.[47]

Culler goes on to quote from Gerard Genette to the effect that

poetic language would seem to reveal its true 'structure,' which is not that of a particular *form* defined by its specific attributes but rather that of a *state*, a degree of presence and intensity to which, as it were, any sequence can be brought, if only there is created around it that *margin of silence* which isolates it in the middle of ordinary speech. . . .[48]

* * * * *

The appropriated text (and we recall that the category of appropriation includes oral 'texts') takes on especially rich and perhaps therefore less unnerving possibilities when, as in Williams' *Paterson*, it enters a larger text where it resonates with other passages, some of them perhaps even recognizably 'literary.' One of the best examples of such strategy in prairie poetry can be found in Robert Kroetsch's *Seed Catalogue*,[49] where in defiance of / defence against urbane writing he lays claim to a series of non-literary texts—rural Alberta vernacular, anecdotes, testimonials, contemporary idiom, tall tales, kids' songs, jokes, sections from art books, literary essays, inventories, inscriptions on gravestones, oral histories, and (most outrageously) extracts wrenched from actual McKenzie's Seed catalogues. Resounds with them. Tickling his ears / his fancy.

The extravagant superlatives he hauls in: what could be further from the modulations, the hushed expectancies, of 'serious' poetry? These insertions are comparable to Duchamp's infamous act of perching a urinal in an art show and bestowing upon it a provocative name, ostentatiously entering it into the old class of 'art' and exploding it. In both cases the material is ready at hand, already made, and eminently 'unworthy.' It would be going too far to suppose Kroetsch is scornful of either his immediate sources or the literary tradition—he's fond of both—and in this respect he differs from Duchamp. Kroetsch, it seems plain, is more than willing to play with the texts and himself to play the fool, to laugh in the face of what is sacred, but he doesn't go so far as Duchamp who apparently saw his own transgressions as derisive comments on the whole enterprise of visual art.[50] Anyway, Kroetsch certainly "lifts" his material. He elevates it, yes, promotes it to special standing in his poem, prompts our attention; but he steals it too—grabs what he likes and runs. So Kroetsch's appropriations both esteem and 'improve' his findings. His open confiscation evidently leaves their identity intact, and if it damages them it does so only by opening a field in which they can root and grow. The individual sections (numbered, lettered: declared not to be lyrical because 'calculated') Kroetsch incorporates as parts of an elliptical structure and forces us to find principles of equivalence and contrast among them, among the criss-crossing of myriad styles. He rejoices in the dance of expressions, the preposterous collisions. Beyond the disapproval of puritans, wanting 'significance' and fearing that somebody is fooling around, having fun. Whatever their fate, when these passages appear in *Seed Catalogue*, they retain the stain of their extraliterary existence and shrink the distance commonly put between art and life. *Seed Catalogue* breaches other literary etiquette when in its carnival of noise and its residual orality, in its apparent indifference to plagiarism, it erodes the sanctity of private enterprise. Violates both property and propriety, those linked terms of possession.

(Startling to find that the word "plagiarism" did not enter the language until after the Renaissance and has no etymology, at least no recorded history before that. A neologism—like "ecology" in the Romantic period—manufactured to fit a new sense of 'fact' and value, it has taken us for the last few centuries away from the sense of a shared language whose ingredients were openly available in a kind of verbal communism—yours for the taking, the talking, the giving (gifting), being gifted. Kroetsch assumes it is appropriate to appropriate, to expropriate what is after all a national treasure, a public resource. Kroetsch's 'improper' raids on 'copyright' nudge us once again toward that oral world of free exchange—in a commonwealth, a well being, a common tongue in which we communicate, no goods withheld for private sale. Before books, with their system of extraction and distribution as objects that contain property, we shared the wealth.)[51]

The found as gift then. We receive it—freely, treasuring it. We are happy to find out what it is because, until the moment of receiving, it was in a special sense unknown and unimportant to us, unworthy until recognized and offered, having taken on value by virtue of special attention. In its assigned significance, the found or the retrieved comes as bestowal, which we can appreciate only if, setting aside suspicion and disapproval, we receive the gift with the spirit in which it is offered.

Here's a typical piece that will give an idea of the mixed and outrageously 'sub-literary' voicing that results when Kroetsch starts stealing words and throwing them around like some kind of literary Robin Hood:

3.
No. 1248—**Hubbard Squash**: "As **mankind** seems to have a **particular fondness** for squash, **Nature** appears to have **especially** provided this **matchless** variety of **superlative flavor**."

> *Love is a leaping up*
> *and down.*

                              Love
                        is a beak in the warm flesh.

"As a cooker, it heads the list for warted squash. The
vines are of strong running growth; the fruits are large,
olive shaped, of a deep rich green color, the rind is
smooth . . ."

But how do you grow a lover?

This is the God's own truth:
playing dirty is a mortal sin
the priest told us, you'll go to hell
and burn forever (with illustrations)—

it was our second day of catechism
—Germaine and I went home that
afternoon   if it's that bad, we
said to each other   we realized
we better quit   we realized

let's do it just one last time
and quit.

This is the God's own truth:
catechism, they called it,
the boys had to sit in the pews
on the right, the girls on the left.
Souls were like underwear that you
wore inside. If the boys and girls sat
together—

Adam and Eve got caught
playing dirty.[52]

We're looking here at something close to a documentary
muse. The sections taken over (translated) from seed catalogues,
where they were offered as commercial come-ons, become in
this new configuration wonderfully sensuous, downright sensual. Consider that second description of the squash again. It is
"warted," "the fruits are large," we read of a "deep rich green

color," learn "the rind is smooth." How tactile the passage is now, what heft the bare words take on—kinaesthetic to the hand's caress, tangible to the eye's love. The unblemished feel of skin, the fullness of fruits, the brush of ribs and nubs and contusions—the gourds become the eroticized body of desire, a winter promise that will come alive ("how do you grow a lover?"), "strong" and "running" in spring. The play of light ("green") taking on texture ("deep rich") and contour ("olive shaped"), the eye, lingering, gains a feel for things. The wonderful bulge and slide of them there in our hands, their largeness, largesse. The palpable joy we take in them, the rub—vegetables swelling and protruding all over the place. Prodigious. Where naming takes place. A garden of earthly delights (where are the tastes? the smells?) to replace the old garden, loaded with European myths (though Kroetsch cleverly manages to use 'high' European texts), oppressive, and needing to be bombed as later in the poem it is, the ancestral home bombed by a Kroetsch, and lost anyway, even to Europeans, because (the poem tells us) "*Adam and Eve got drowned.*" (That K. won't hold his tongue, know his place.) This rambunctious prairie garden / poem, blooms with bare bums and idioms, surges with hyperbole, hops with speech—the longing tenderness, the ecstatic vulgarity of these words, remotivated now as a love song to plants—a vernacular garden rife with eros. Adamantly. Sounds good. He cultivates that, K. does—a song of sensual delight, a vegetable love, that grows, in affront to (in front of) the high-minded that would stop this "playing dirty," this playing around. Imprudent, impudent, Kroetsch gourds up his loins. In body language, infatuated with time. Bawdy. He speaks of country matters, madam. What matters. Maters. (One person on hearing this passage described it to me as "our" form of pornography: the McKenzie's Seed catalogue, with its language of richness and plenitude, its excited, almost orgasmic, anticipations of fondling and celebrating, keeps us warm, expectant, in winter.)

Oral—of the mouth, what emits, comes out. Come on Kroetsch, admit it. Speaking. What you put in the mouth, no not the foot—eating, sucking, loving. What the mouth meets, greets, where it meets. Mouthy. Talking, always talking, taking in, giving out. In rapture, loving the words, the loving words. An overflowing, excess. The comic vision, cosmic in what it will admit, emit. Copious. A cornucopia. Cornu-copia—the horn of plenty. K. horny when his vegetable love does grow, sung, Orphically, into existence, K. orgasmic in his utterance, his outering. Making love, slippery. The spermatic word.

As we see, the catalogue passage, newly located, shakes off its original context, moves from a document of persuasion to a poem of celebration. The words lose their original power to inform (or misinform) and acquire marvellous secondary qualities (the text seems more spare than it is because it refuses to 'tag' its multiple meanings or to announce its antecedents). We read them differently now, as if for the first time, not taking them for granted as pointers that connect to some external world in which we buy seeds and grow vegetables, in which the original words urge us to buy and plant. Instead, we bring them into accord with other words in this madly elliptical and permissive text, words that speak of seeds (Germaine; the Germans, later; of what is germane to the text, Adam and Eve playing dirty; even of the germs the poet / gardener puts in the ground / on the page, spills on the ground, singing his masturbatory song and lamenting he has no one to receive his seeds / words, to carry them away pregnant with thought). We also note how the found words intersect with words that speak of growth (here the lover's, phallically, the beloved's, physically; but playing *within* the book, in a *literary* action—the town's growth, the poet's growth, ultimately the poem's growth too). How do you grow . . . a prairie town? a garden? a gardener? a poet? the poem keeps asking in lines that serve as refrain. In other words : to read them/ as *other* words. Or how about that corny puffery in the catalogue's hype: "As mankind seems to have a particular fondness for squash . . ."? Seems innocent enough, no more than an endearing reach for a large statement, a harmless, even admirable, hungering for the grand gesture. At first. But then we run across that crazy kids' song ("*Adam and Eve got caught / playing dirty*"), and we realize both quotations match the narrative line, each comes from a garden story, and informs Kroetsch's own ambitious, suddenly ambiguous, garden poem, as we put it into play with other and more rarefied garden poems. His poem enters into correspondence, slips into the intertext of all those other garden poems buried inside it or beneath it. Once we get on to these proportions, we rethink the apparent casualness of the profanity, twice-repeated: "This is the God's own truth." And we begin to marvel at what might be done in vernacular montage. In bare-knuckle vernacular.

* * * * * *

The shift I have been speaking of here represents a fundamental de-centering. The official language, the sanctioned texts, the recognized procedures begin to collapse when we hear voices from the margins. The voices have always been there, whispering and jostling on the side-lines. No one was listening. Ears tu(r)ned to another music could at best hear noise, ephemera, something haltingly inarticulate. But by speaking in the mother tongue, those who have been excluded can call into being an other, another world. In their dream of cultural autonomy, the depreciated language they speak enables them to resist the impositions of a father tongue, which is the respected and learned way of writing, duly installed in academies of one kind or another. The measure of speech, then, sub-versively conceived, resides with you, rises out of what you know most immediately, an intimate sense of your place and your people—the words you feel most at home with. That means, culturally speaking, you can celebrate the unbecoming voices of farmers or bingo players. You begin to make noises. To speak freely. You let go a veritable babble of voices (we remember "chucker chatter," "Lawnchair," *Seed Catalogue*) which, as George Steiner so approvingly says, we have "shouted or whispered to each other

across the bewildering freedom of the rubble at Babel."[53] Not
clumsy but new, strange to the ear, hard (for the time being) on
the tongue, to those hard of here-ing. In it Steiner locates creative
disorders:

> The teeming plurality of languages enacts the fundamen-
> tally creative, 'counter-factual' genius and psychic func-
> tions of language itself. It embodies a move away from
> unison and acceptance . . . to the polyphonic, ultimately
> divergent fascination of manifold specificity. Each dif-
> ferent tongue offers its own denial of determinism. 'The
> world,' it says, 'can be other.' Ambiguity, polysemy,
> opaqueness, the violation of grammatical and logical se-
> quences, reciprocal incomprehensions, the capacity to
> lie—these are not pathologies of language but the roots of
> its genius.[54]

With no trouble at all we can apply Steiner's argument to a single
'natural' language and to admired modes in its literature. As
Allon Whyte summarizes Mikhail Bahktin, such voices play

> against the tragic pathos and high seriousness of the
> dominant artistic, moral and political discourses of the
> period. In this view the 'earthy' folk word—scatalogical,
> irreverent, humorous and contradictory—becomes both a
> critique of, and corrective to, the lie of pathos. The lofty
> word of authority is 'brought down a peg or two.'[55]

And how comical they are, these vernacular pieces. Not
Suknaski's, true, not the particular one I have chosen, though
his, too, often are. And how right that they should be, for
humour provides a way of fighting back. By speaking out of turn
it sets the admired discourse on its heels, puts it itself into disrepute. In parody and mockery, in jokes and riddles, vernacular
can shift authority and rewrite the grammar of poetry. Having
nothing to lose, 'common' people and those who rejoice in their
discourse might well locate themselves not in elegy but bur-
lesque. For, as White tells us, we find "In polyglossia [such as

Kroetsch's] . . . the conflicts engendered when the dominant, centralizing and unifying language of a hegemonic group is contested by the 'low' language of subordinated classes."[56]

The discourse I am arguing for certainly is profane if not taboo in some quarters. It violates 'good taste' and niceties of expression. So Kroetsch can rejoice in "Effing the Ineffable."[57] Vernacular as graffiti. Talking dirty, playing dirty. With its inescapable reminders of sex and excrement, the most basic workings of the body, graffiti enters the sacred texts, shocking their (or rather, their readers') preference for the elevated and the transcendent. The writing is on the wall (toilet). Vernacular, in saying the unsayable, in speaking improperly, figures as Dirty Words, a trope of vulgarity. Bad mouthing. Profane, it transgresses the preferred texts and their attendant voices—priestly, learned, vigilant of apocryphal texts. (The irony of poets, radical or even vulgar in their own times, turned by critics into high-minded ministers of the status quo, authoritarian, speaking 'properly,' and berating the upstarts, cannot escape us.) Sacred texts, written by 'men' of 'genius,' cannot be challenged. They certainly cannot be altered or displaced, they *can* be admired and emulated. (The fact that the canon *is* subject to periodic readjustments seems not for many of its defenders to cause the major embarrassment it ought to.)

One might object, however, that George Crabbe or William Wordsworth, among others (Donne, say, or Browning) unquestionably had speech models in mind, and that early modernism was full of the very desecrations I list here. Certainly my examples owe their origins in some ways to Wordsworth, the first poet by the way to set up shop outside London and as a result to strengthen his radical decentering of poetry. Yet neither Crabbe nor Wordsworth, certainly not Wordsworth (shocking though his diction and syntax were, and in his time they *were* shocking), could be accused of succumbing to the vertigininous depths of the vernacular. Not even Donne or Browning, far more vocative and gristly than Wordsworth, entertained street language so fully as the authors I have mentioned. I would also point out that though Eliot, say, did have a fine ear for idiom and used it prominently, such voices were never the measure of his verse. Rather they stood in contrast, in very inferior contrast, to a high-minded voice ripe with allusion and grandiloquence. Joseph Riddell in "Decentering the Image" has diagnosed Eliot's nostalgia for a concealed source or a lost centre located in a commanding myth. As

> appropriated or fabricated system [it] would serve as an a priori source of images, a privileged point of reference. The timeless [and "totalizing"] fiction . . . not only lends authority to the signs or images appropriated from it, but signifies the general form of mastery or totalization . . . [which will] enact the gathering or regathering of the many into the One. . . . The "mythical method," and its primary strategies—reference, citation, allusion, and quotation—confirm art as "timeless" repetition of the Same, repetition as incorporation [into the "ideal order" of "existing monuments"].[58]

Like most of his contemporaries—Lawrence, Yeats, Frost, Graves, Pound (Joyce was an exception: being Irish, having a feel for the marginal and the colonial?)—Eliot believed in and sought some overriding structures of belief, often located in an approved past. In their passion for 'universals,' they became complicit in various versions of class rule or national expansion, for adherence to 'high' language is always imperialist. We might even speculate on their preference for official high-toned voices and periodic, subordinate structures, with their circular and closed systems of thought. It is tempting to see these features as signs of their hierarchic values.

What, after all, is this perpetual cry for 'universals' and 'standards'? Is it not a call, however unwitting, for *one* definition, *one* way of appreciating? Deviancy or unorthodoxy—in our terms: other discourses, noise—can be read only as 'merely local' and lacking in standards. I am arguing, on the contrary, that upholding standards in any unshakeable way willy-nilly serves imperialist visions of the world. It is authoritarian. And so we get not universality but hegemony.[59] We should not fail to appreciate that humanists (and some structuralists), who in our century have stood by literature as an antidote to the larger and largely objectionable culture, have in their respect for such 'universality' inadvertently served a corporate dream that would obliterate indigenous culture the world over. The consequences would be amusing if they were not so disastrous.

How revealing that the word "standard" derives from the banner or standard used to mark a rallying point in battle—it being neither benign nor universal, but a sign of power aggressively pursued and inevitably imposed. (It surely must come as a shock, for those who believe otherwise, to discover that Charlemagne consolidated his kingdom by forcing at sword point all his subjects to practise the Gregorian chant.)[60] So, too, for those terms—provincial, regional, and so on—usually placed in slighting counter to the legitimacy of the universal or in some versions the 'international.' Sceptical of such activities, Michel Foucault leads those scholars who recently have come to think that the extension of various forms of cultural legitimacy is never neutral and certainly never free of ideology and the exercise of power. In fact, power (in the form of 'authority') always lies behind any cultural order. In an interview several geographers ask Foucault about his use of spatial metaphors and wonder why he thinks of them so often as historically rather than spatially defined. His response is telling:

> Well, let's take a look at these geographical metaphors. *Territory* is no doubt a geographical notion, but it's first of all a juridico-political one: the area controlled by a certain kind of power. *Field* is an economico-juridical notion. *Displacement*: what displaces itself is an army, a squadron, a population. *Domain* is a juridico-political notion. *Soil* is a historico-geological notion. *Region* is a fiscal, administrative, military notion. *Horizon* is a pictorial, but also a strategic notion.[61]

And Foucault goes on, in that same interview, to tease out the military bases of these terms:

> The point that needs to be emphasised here is that certain spatial metaphors are equally geographical and strategic, which is only natural *since geography grew up in the shadow of the military.* A circulation of notions can be observed between geographical and strategic discourses. The *region* of the geographers is the military region (from *regere*, to command), a *province* is a conquered territory (from *vincere*). *Field* evokes the battlefield. . . .[62]

Region, we find, is a cognate of regimen and regiment; and a province was not only a conquered territory, it was one controlled by imperial Rome. Thought of in this way, as signs of imperialism and militarism, the terms come to designate not inferiority but subjugation, not superiority but brutality. They expose *the* tradition as in one sense a disguised form of cultural bullying. For what are these regions and provinces but colonized places? What are these 'standards' of the good and the real but the assumptions that the conquerers bring with them? They are not 'universal' but observed, for the simple reason they are mandatory. The conquering, of course, need not be military. In fact, we see (in Layton's "Anglo-Canadian," for example) that forms of cultural invasion—more covert, less naked in their show of force—can be devastating in their capacity to authenticate and dismiss.

Yet the "local," freed from its demeaning epithet, turns out to be not so bad. Like its startling (because virtually unrecognizable) kin—"stalk," "stall," and "still"—it refers to a rooted existence, one that stands in contrast to the deracinated perspective of centralists or 'cosmopolitans.' Now that the subscriptions have run out the locals are acting up, finding and rudely raising their voices. Jacques Attali has proposed a "profound identity between noises and differences, between silence and anonymity." A "space full of life," he explains, is charged with "natural noises, noises of work and play, music, laughs, complaints, murmurs" (he is speaking most immediately of Breughel's *Carnival's Quarrel with Lust*), but these sounds are silenced by "the Norm," "Austerity," a "herald of regiments."[63] Or again: "the institutionalization of the silence of others as-sure[s] the durability of power."[64] That has always been a strug-gle for Canadian poets—breaking the silence—particularly those of a nationalist or a left-wing bent. I'm thinking, for in-stance, of F.R. Scott in poems like "Old Song" and "Laurentian Shield" or Dorothy Livesay in her courageous poem, "Day and Night," a text I deal with elsewhere in this book. Both poets speak of smothered or undeveloped voices on the verge of an eloquence culturally denied them. The taboo against saying what you are.

Once those voices release, they turn the reader into a more active collaborator and out of a role as sedentary contemplator. 'Impure' and 'subliterary,' speech proves to be anti-authoritarian. The new voices reside in a mobile authority lo-cated, not inwardly as in the lyric, but outwardly in the pop and snap of public speech. Vernacular redefines and redistributes power. It goes in fear of universals or eternals because it observes only the most provisional authority.

The impact of public funding policies, of new de-centering technology, including (now) laser printing and personal com-puters, and the creation of new publishing ventures on the prairies—Thistledown, Coteau, Longspoon, Turnstone, *NeWest*, *Dandelion*, *Prairie Fire*, *Grain*—have enabled such writers to find outlets. And their voices. All manner of unmannerly voices.[65] They cannot wait on the rest of the world to seek or welcome their work, and so they have shaken off the terrible lie that ob-tains in English departments and many of their graduates, them-selves imperious, impervious, in controlling literary accreditation, once and for all: if a work is 'good' it will be received elsewhere, the measure always located 'elsewhere,' anywhere but here; *there* is 'universal' (telling cognates: univer-sity and universal) and significant, *here* by definition is 'provincial' and inconsequential. But as I have tried to argue, these presuppositions are not harmless, the actions not innocent. There is a massive delusion in such professions, as if cultural transactions were durable because arbitrated only in a disembodied and timeless way and were not attached to instruments of publicity, promotion, distribution, accreditation, or attribution. And as if those mechanisms were not themselves subject to the pressures of the marketplace or to the interests of those who control or would control them. At every turn, behind the sacerdotal zeal, other considerations enter: special aims, personal desires, class inscriptions, historical accident or incident (an aging professoriate for example), vested privilege, political passion, definitions of gender, ideological struggles, concentrations of population, ownership of media. We are invited to believe by those who subscribe to the literary system and by those who are beneficiaries of it that 'extraliterary' conditions have no bearing, at least no crucial bearing, on what gets honoured. We are told that nothing but aesthetic criteria enter into the decisions, not even when the conditions include a pervasiveness of certain national cultures in the popular media and even our universities. We are tacitly asked to overlook the realities of careerism and 'professionalism,' by which activity shifts subtly and sometimes not so subtly from some axis of enquiry to another axis of advancement where professors are taught to manoeuvre for rewards and influence through mystiques of expertise: what must I do to be promoted? celebrated? How few of them—this surely is shameful—think of themselves or speak of themselves as intellectuals instead of professionals.[66] And how many worry more about what 'sells' in accredited places than what in any ethical and intellectual sense matters?

Officially the system works openly and fairly, assures us we need not concern ourselves with the accents of confidence and authority ("my dear boy," "oh yes you are the local one"), the sniffs of derision, willful misrepresentation (Cooley has *no* ideas, Cooley *only* has ideas); as if we need not bother with dubious assumptions about what counts in the academy, or the near monopolies in many outlets and institutions, the limited access to organs of advertising and recognition (the CBC, the *Times Literary Supplement*, the literary conference and its attendant lobbies, professional organizations such as the MLA or ACUTE, librarians' journals, government and private funding agencies, university governance, prestigious American and British presses, *The New York Review of Books*, English Departments, newspapers). As if it makes no difference that colonized and colonizing academics in Canada—many of them from elsewhere, important places—show a bizarre reverence for 'international' publications (almost always, by definition, located elsewhere—overwhelmingly the U.S.—and an expression of somebody else's estimations) and 'reputable' journals (by necessity old and familiar, with a track record one knows how to rate because it already is rated for one). And so on.[67] I used to believe this; or a fair bit of this. My point is *not* that the objects of their scrutiny are unworthy (though some of them may be), rather that what texts they endorse gain access to the system in ways that grant them a special hearing.

Given their inscriptions, their loyalties to "*The* Tradition" (not altogether a bad thing), it is not surprising a lot of English professors locate literature once upon a time, in faraway places, and tend to see *other* arguments as special pleading. Literature's over, finished, caput, and depends for its continued existence on us as custodians. The canon, the masterpiece, the monument, the genius or master, the museum, the academy—all these institutions, though their constituents might not admit or intend as much, in effect lift texts out of their original situations and inscribe them in a category of immutable art virtually immune to history and geography. Free, thank god, from sweaty contention. Above all that.

The writing I am discussing challenges the assumptions that inhabit us and that have come, in habit, to inhibit our thinking about literature. Vernacular offsets the demand for semantic weight and contemplative tone. In vernacular poetry the eye, centered in dense writing for the page, gives way to the ear, as I have tried to explain in other essays in this book. The spatialized text, profoundly specialized and hived off from its origins, is supplanted by the oral text that, no longer under such supervision, at every turn declares its location, its time, and jeopardizes the generic boundaries of poetry. Such texts, in their very roughness, their rude intrusions, suffusions of noise, lose 'perspective.' That means they are not detached and viewing at a distance, as if the world could be turned into objects and held in some gaze of power (abstracted). In sound we gain nearness. We feel the rasp and buzz of the vernacular, receive it almost tactilely with all its burrs and jags, its local grain resisting the abrasions of propriety, the silver polish other models would put upon it. Popular, populist.

Such writing is postmodern. It does not aspire to what is timeless or placeless. It seeks neither absolute authority nor fixed definition. It locates no special genius in the poet, no exquisite sensibility alone with its thoughts and generating subtle meaning for other fastidious souls alone, in leisure, with their refined minds. Postmodernism, at least in its vernacular forms, moves outward and upsets the comforts of the contemplative voice. It deeply suspects powers, especially inherited ones, and therefore does not presume to determine measures for others. Against a writing that in large part stations itself as high, there, then, and which is bolstered by the formidable power of shame, it disquietingly situates itself in the low, here, now. Outside the reach of institutional power to compel assent, to dictate language, it escapes an 'expertise' that would cow prairie poets and, by finding them 'unqualified,' banish them into silence. The voices that wheeze and clang through vernacular poetry like as not were once vehemently enrolled in the most 'non-literary' discourse—ferociously vocative, ejaculative, baldly informational, phatic, expressive (in Jakobson's, not Abrams', sense), flatly metalingual. Seldom 'formal' or 'literary.' Of the body, shamelessly. Festive with local knowledge. Loco. Leery of hierarchies and exclusions, the poem moves toward tolerance, inclusion, equalities. In good health, hale, on a sound footing. Decentered, it is permissive and dispersing. Eccentric, off-kilter, out of whack. It is liable to value the ready and the appropriated as much as the rare and the original.

To the belief that art has happened, and happened somewhere else, vernacular poetry replies in a very old and in a very contemporary poetics. And vernacular, like so much postmodern poetry, turns our interest from what Roman Jakobson calls the axis of selection or substitution to what he calls the axis of combination,[68] from the timelessness of metaphor and the synchrony of much contemporary theory, to the sequential experience of language in time, diachronically, as it is spoken and as it speaks from the history of a place. From semantics to syntax. It shows little interest in building to a climax, either, and will often (close your eyes) stop. With only the most modest closure.

---

1. Elias L. Rivers, "Prolegomena Grammatologica: Literature as the Disembodiment of Speech," in Paul Hernadi, ed., *What Is Literature?* (Bloomington, Ind.: Indiana, 1978), pp. 84-5.

2. "RePlacing," *RePlacing* (Toronto: ECW, 1980), p. 17. The book was issued simultaneously as a special "Prairie Poetry Issue" of a literary journal: *Essays on Canadian Writing*, Nos. 18/19 (Summer/Fall 1980).

3. Mark Abley, "Laying down the Law: Notes on the *Prairie Poetry* Issue of *Essays on Canadian Writing." Grain*, 8, No. 3 (November 1980), 53.

4. From an untitled letter by Anne Szumigalski, *Grain*, 9, No. 2 (May 1981), 56. The previous issue of *Grain* (9, No. 1) contained two other contributions to the debate: a facetious piece by David Arnason and a cryptic entry by Robert Kroetsch.

5. *Draft: an anthology of prairie poetry* (Toronto: ECW, Winnipeg: Turnstone, 1981).

6. The letter, dated January 3, 1983, appeared in a mangled and reduced form in *NeWest Review*, 8, No. 5 (February 1983), 2. The review to which it refers was written by Susan Gingell and appeared in the December, 1982, issue of *NeWest Review*.

7. Mark Abley, "Laying down the Law," 53.

8. T.D. MacLulich has written an illuminating article, "Colloquial Style and the Tory Mode," *Canadian Literature*, No. 89 (Summer 1981), 7-21,

on what he discerns as a wariness toward colloquial writing in the history of Canadian fiction. Until recently, he says, our novels have been written and in large part still are written by those, such as Hugh MacLennan and Robertson Davies, who prefer British to American models and who see the author as an educated gentleman whose duty it is to lead us to good taste and a hierarchy of ideas honouring the tradition. They, like Mark Abley, find vernacular writers and their apologists to be intellectually wanting and speak of them in tones of suspicion. Here is part of what MacLulich has to say:

> The colloquial style is a no-nonsense, pragmatic manner, tending towards informality and even chattiness. It is suited to convey transitory emotions, immediate physical sensations, and spontaneous thoughts. In contrast, the Tory mode is a vehicle for considered reflections. Its tone is formal, educated, and precise. It specializes in elaborated descriptions, rational synthesis, and qualified generalizations. The Tory mode does not capture the mind in motion, but presents the carefully arranged results of prolonged cogitation. (16-7)

No wonder some still resist vernacular *in poetry*.

9. *The Post-Modern Condition: A Report on Knowledge*, trans. Geoff Bennington and Brian Massumi, "Foreword" by Fredric Jameson (Minneapolis: University of Minnesota, 1984), pp. 63-4. See also page 46 of this book.

10. *Literary Theory: An Introduction* (Minneapolis: University of Minneapolis, 1983), p. 14. Eagleton's emphasis.

11. Rene Wellek, *American Criticism, 1900-1950*, Vol. 6 in *A History of Modern Criticism 1750-1950* (New Haven, Conn.: Yale, 1986), p. 146.

12. Eagleton develops the argument in chapter one, "The Rise of English," *Literary Theory*, pp. 17-53. Walter J. Ong, *Orality and Literacy: The Technologizing of the Word* (London: Methuen, 1982), p. 163, drawing on various authorities, makes much the same point. See also Raymond Williams, "Literature" in his *Marxism and Literature* (Oxford: Oxford University Press, 1977), pp. 45-54. Williams writes

> It is in no way surprising that the specialized concept of 'literature,' developed in precise forms of correspondence with a particular social class, a particular organization of learning, and the appropriate particular technology of print should now be so often invoked in retrospective, nostalgic, or reactionary moods as a form of opposition to what is correctly seen as a new phase of civilization. (p. 54)

13. All definitions and etymologies, sometimes abridged, in this paper come from *Webster's Ninth New Collegiate Dictionary* (Springfield, Mass.: Merriam-Webster, 1985).

14. The version I quote comes from F.R. Scott and A.J.M. Smith, eds., *The Blasted Pine: An Anthology of Satire, Invective and Disrespectful Verse Chiefly by Canadian Writers*, revised and enlarged ed. (Toronto: Macmillan, 1967), p. 75.

15. *Poetry as Discourse* (London: Methuen, 1983), p. 68.

16. *Poetry as Discourse*, p. 69.

17. *Poetry as Discourse*, p. 65.

18. *The Anti-Aesthetic: Essays on Postmodern Culture*, ed. Hal Foster (Port Townsend, Washington: Bay Press, 1983), p. 59.

19. *The Anti-Aesthetic*, pp. 66-7. My emphasis.

20. Jacques Derrida, "Living on: Borderlines," in *Deconstruction and Criticism* (New York: Seabury, 1979), pp. 94-5.

21. *Theories of Contemporary Art*, ed. Richard Hertz (Englewood Cliffs, N.J.: Prentice-Hall, 1985), p. 192.

22. "Contingencies of Value," *Canons*, ed. Robert von Hallberg (Chicago: University of Chicago, 1984), p. 33. Smith's emphasis.

23. *Canons*, pp. 33-4.

24. *Canons*, p. 22. In this same collection is a piece by Arnold Krupat, "Native American Literature and the Canon," pp. 309-35, that makes a case for considering native literature in terms that current systems of canonization do not recognize.

25. Two of the examples I later cite are identifiably male, I think. They are generally loud and rambunctious—one of them minimally in its register of a besieged culture, one very much so in its tapping of tall tales and pub talk, the third profusely so in its ceremonial song of solidarity. The world of high orality, as Ong reminds us, traditionally (but not now, not in an age of electronic amplification that shines into our homes intimate with tête-à-têtes) falls to male dominance for a number of reasons, one of them simple and physiological—the greater volume of sound males normally can muster in public assembly. See Ong's *Fighting for Life: Contest, Sexuality, and Consciousness* (Ithaca, N.Y.: Cornell, 1981), pp. 140-1. In *Orality and Literacy*, pp. 159-60, Ong argues that women writers have tended to be less oral or less oratorical than male authors and have "helped make the novel what it is: more like a [quiet] conversation than a platform performance."

26. Allon White, "Bakhtin, Sociolinguistics and Deconstruction," *The Theory of Reading*, ed. Frank Gloversmith (Sussex: Harvester, 1984), p. 136. White's emphasis.

27. *The Theory of Reading*, pp. 144-5.

28. *The Theory of Reading*, p. 143.

29. *The Theory of Reading*, p. 125. White adds a sobering note about conservative consequences that often extend from Deconstructionism:

> Without ever diminishing the Utopian ideals of play and pleasure which Deconstruction embodies, Bakhtin nevertheless shows up, through and through, the ludic narcissism at the heart of the Deconstructionist project. Even more, he reveals the naive complicity Deconstruction may have with social control and domination, and the consequent role that dialogic resistance must play to disrupt this. (p. 144)

In *Criticism and Social Change* (Chicago: University of Chicago, 1983), p. 51, Frank Lentricchia refines that argument by finding Paul de Man to be an essentialist thinker who is in search of transcendental warranties and whose practice willy-nilly "translates into that passive kind of conservatism called quietism; it thereby plays into the hands of established power. Deconstruction is conservatism by default. . . ."

30. *Women and Language in Literature and Society*, ed. Sally McConnell-Ginet, Ruth Borker, and Nelly Furman (New York: Praeger, 1980), pp. 205-18.

31. Raymond Williams, "Literature," in his *Keywords: A vocabulary of culture and society* (London: Fontana, 1976), pp. 183-8. The major shift moved the definition of literature from matters of general and polite learning to concentrations on 'imaginative' writing. It gained impetus with new notions of authorship as profession that began to develop in the late seventeenth century. Peter Stallybrass and Allon White have traced the emergence of the 're-spectable' author on into the eighteenth century in *The Politics and Poetics of Transgression* (Ithaca, N.Y.: Cornell, 1986), especially in chapter 2, "The Grotesque Body and the Smithfield Muse: Authorship in the Eighteenth Century," pp. 80-124, and in a shorter section, "Smithfield and Authorship: Ben Johnson," pp. 66-79.

32. Donovan, *Women and Language*, p. 212. *Orality and Literacy*, pp. 159-60, picks up a related argument. Ong also argues that the dominance of Latin, "completely controlled by writing," and totally in the hands of males, for centuries profoundly silenced "the swarming, oral vernaculars" which were mother-tongues, "thus reducing interference from the human lifeworld and making possible the exquisitely abstract world . . ." (pp. 112-5).

33. "Concluding Statement: Linguistics and Poetics," *Style in Language*, ed. Thomas A. Sebeok (Cambridge, Mass.: M.I.T., 1960), pp. 350-77.

34. *Draft*, pp. 148-9.

35. After publishing an earlier version of this essay in *Prairie Fire* I received a delightful letter from Aydon Charlton ("July 13/87") about his experience with "Lawn Outside Norcanair." He raised an issue that surprised me but that made me realize, all the more, how susceptible we are to dismissals of our 'improper' language:

> Because I am incapable of reading Suknaski's poem aloud without sounding like a cross between a Swede and Tennessee Williams, I tried to get an Indian to tape record the poem for me, and asked Bernie Selinger at S.I.F.C. [Saskatchewan Indian Federated College] to show the poem to some of his buddies. However, *none* of them would agree to read it onto tape; apparently, they felt it was "racist"! Although such responses seem to me to be based on elementary (mis)readings of the poem & failures to distinguish between the speaker and the poet, perhaps Bernie's Indian friends are onto something valid. I agree with you [that the poem attends on new voices] . . . [b]ut the Indians obviously feel slighted that their language is presented as non-standard dialect. . . . It may not be accidental that the best readings of the poem aloud in class are by the (white) students who are practised at telling Indian jokes in dialect. However, Suknaski's poem triumphs (for me) over such racist uses of the dialect when the native fisherman concludes: "wen sometin on you mind boy / you gotta speak / oh you *die*   boy!"

36. *Draft*, pp. 70-1.

37. Aydon Charlton, again, in the same letter (as above) writes about Fiedler and Gruending:

> I may have mentioned to you that I did have occasion to ask Dennis about his *intentions* in writing the poem. He told me that he wrote the poem at a workshop at Fort San after a ball game there that reminded him of the ball games of his youth in small town Saskatchewan. His initial "intention" was simply to evoke those games by capturing that aspect of the vernacular. However, he said that a few months *after* writing the poem, he was watching an NFL game and suddenly realized the Fiedlerian, homoerotic significance of the words & syntax of "chucker chatter."

38. *Roots of the Lyric: Primitive Poetry and Modern Poetics* (Princeton: Princeton University Press, 1978), p. 180.

39. These distinctions are laid out in the chapter called "Chant," *Roots of the Lyric*, pp. 162-89.

40. *Roots of the Lyric*, p. 164.

41. *Roots of the Lyric*, p. 175. Easthope, sympathetic to the very games and songs that embarrass Welsh, says "The ascendency of pentameter

relegates the older accentual metre to a subordinate or oppositional position in which it has remained ever since: the appropriate metre for nursery rhymes, the lore of schoolchildren, ballad, industrial folk song and even more recently, the football chant" (p. 65). As for children's games, Easthope finds that Freud's perception of them as childish simply indicates how much he shared high-minded notions of his day and how little that age (ours too) could appreciate the love of word play among say the Elizabethans (p. 34).

42. *Roots of the Lyric*, p. 188. My emphasis.

43. *Roots of the Lyric*, p. 187.

44. *Orality and Literacy*. The arguments are distributed throughout the book.

45. *Orality and Literacy*, p. 133. It will be evident how reserved Ong is about Jacques Derrida's assault on the spoken word. (See pp. 165-7, for example.) While accepting the value of Derrida's work, the basic validity of his argument, for that matter—"Derrida is of course quite correct in rejecting the persuasion that writing is no more than incidental to the spoken word" (77)—he finds Derrida's work crucially tied in its inception to the very typography and book culture that Ong believes to have come into eminence with the Romantics.

46. *Orality and Literacy*, p. 175.

47. *Structuralist Poetics: Structuralism, Linguistics, and the Study of Literature* (Ithaca, N.Y.: Cornell, 1975), pp. 163-4.

48. *Structuralist Poetics*, p. 164.

49. *Seed Catalogue* (Winnipeg: Turnstone, 1986), pp. 1-28.

50. Charles Tomkins, *The Bride and the Bachelors: Five Masters of the Avant Garde* (Hammondsworth, England: Penguin, 1976), p. 26. First published in 1965.

51. Ong says "Print created a new sense of the private ownership of words. . . . With writing, resentment at plagiarism begins to develop. . . . Typography had made the word into a commodity." *Orality and Literacy*, p. 131.

52. *Seed Catalogue*, pp. 8-9.

53. *After Babel: Aspects of Language and Translation* (Oxford: Oxford University Press, 1975), p. 235.

54. *After Babel*, pp. 234-5.

55. *The Theory of Reading*, pp. 131-2.

56. *The Theory of Reading*, p. 132.

57. "Effing the Ineffable," *Open Letter*, Fifth Series, No. 4 (Spring 1983), 23-4.

58. Joseph Riddell, "Decentering the Image: The 'Project' of 'American' Poetics?" in *Textual Strategies: Perspectives in Post-Structuralist*

Criticism, ed. with an "Introduction" by Josue V. Harari (Ithaca, N.Y.: Cornell, 1979), p. 346.

59. The term originates with Antonio Gramsci, locked in a Fascist prison in Spain. Raymond Williams gives a very readable note on the term in *Marxism and Literature*, pp. 108-14. Hegemony includes both deliberate and unconscious forms of value and control, and it is not at all limited to what most readily can be identified as overtly or professedly political. "It is a whole body of practices and expectations, over the whole of living: our senses and assignments of energy, our shaping perceptions of ourselves and our world" (p. 110).

60. Jacques Attali, *Noise: The Political Economy of Music*, trans. Brian Massumi, "Foreword" by Fredric Jameson, "Afterword" by Susan McClary (Minneapolis: University of Minnesota, 1985), p. 14. Originally published in French in 1977.

61. "Questions on Geography," *Power/Knowledge: Selected Interviews and Other Writings 1972-1977*, ed. Colin Gordon, trans. Colin Gordon, Leo Marshall, John Mepham, Kate Soper (New York: Pantheon, 1980), p. 68. The italics are in the Pantheon text.

62. *Power/Knowledge*, p. 69. Emphasis in the printed text except for the first, which is mine.

63. *Noise*, p. 22.

64. *Noise*, p. 8. Attali has written a fascinating claim about how 'noise' constantly subverts 'harmony' in the history of music. The case he makes suggests remarkable parallels to the kind I am pursuing here. He speaks, for example, of the power to silence others in the world of mass-produced recorded music as "preventing direct, localized, anecdotal . . . communication" and connects that silencing, "the elimination of noises" [my 'prairie vernacular'], to a denial of the body: systematically "silencing drives, deodorizing the body, emptying it of its needs, and reducing it to silence" (122). Shades of N.O. Brown. Even earlier, in music composed for the concert hall, and available only to a small, well-to-do audience, official music put aside "dissonances" (the expressions of the suffering and the exploited) by insisting on tonality and melody, a strategy which "amounts to an attempt to make people believe in a consensual representation of the world" (p. 46).

65. As "In the sixteenth century, printing allowed the vernacular [as opposed to Latin] languages to spread and be reborn, and with them came a reawakening of the territorial nationalities" as "a profound danger to the existing powers." *Noise*, p. 35.

66. Burton J. Bledstein in *The Culture of Professionalism: The Middle Class and the Development of Higher Education in America* (New York: Norton, 1976)

establishes the social and economic basis to the professions, including the professoriate. Although his documentation comes from American experience, we can, I think, with some caution transpose the basic argument to what has happened in a lesser way at Canadian universities. Here is part of what he says:

> Successful careers depended upon the continual application of . . . thoroughness to limited, specific tasks at specific stages in the course of an occupational lifetime. But these limited, specific tasks easily degenerated into repetitive professional exercises which primarily served to hurdle careers upward and to distract from the serious intellectual problems at hand. In the 1880s, for instance, the recently formed profession of economists by and large cringed at Richard T. Ely's advocacy of socialism [favoring strikes, assisting strikers, and teaching radical ideas]. To protect his own academic career and answer the charge of unprofessional conduct, Ely in the 1890s recanted his earlier views and became a squeamish academic careerist. No accusation more intimidated the youthful, bold professional than that of being unprofessionally enthusiastic [or, I would add, for our situation: of being 'merely local' or 'merely popular' with students]. . . .
>
> As Ely harshly learned, academic professionals spoke a different language from social reformers. The containment of ideas in the university placed them in a context where they could be managed in functional terms rather than radicalized in a socially demanding ideology. Universities determined the instrumental directions in which the majority of educated Americans in the twentieth century would turn their mental energies. (pp. 328-9)

Since English professors might find it easy to step over these observations, I would briefly addend more pointed remarks by Patrick Colm Hogan. Comparing the university to an American corporation, he speaks of the English professoriate, but especially of its junior faculty and graduate students, as susceptible to inordinate and increasing demands for productivity. Their precariousness as well as their ambitions mean that governing bodies in universities, where most literary adjudication is now done or endorsed, can more readily extract from them work that is useful for their survival or advancement within the system. The options, he says, are "whether one will write for salability, and thus make literary study a mere means [what I am calling professionalism or careerism], or one will write for truth (which I take to be an end in itself) [the intellectual], and risk swift, or slower, academic death." "The Political Economy of Criticism," in Gerald Graff and

✓ Reginald Gibbons, eds., *Criticism in the University* (Evanston, Ill.: Northwestern, 1985), p. 179.

67. One of the sad consequences of these prejudices is that the dullest article on Disraeli, a mediocre paper on a trivial Shakespeare topic, a talk on Spenser so bone-crushingly numb it would petrify blood, even patronizing dismissals of students' enthusiasms by those who have such impeccable standards they anaesthetize whole classes—any of these transactions, these testaments to The Tradition, if only they appear in approved sites, might be and too often are valued above other activities. Ranking literature with the avidity of a rabid skunk.

68. "Concluding Statement: Linguistics and Poetics," in Thomas A. Sebeok, ed. *Style in Language* (Cambridge, Mass.: M.I.T., 1960), p. 358.

DOROTHY LIVESAY'S
POLITICAL POETRY

But the real problem . . . is not how to get a sense of history.
. . . The real problem is how not to be overburdened by the
pressures of residual cultures and their traditions: how
not to be so positioned that our choices are always already
made for us. The real problem . . . [is] how to avoid being
professionally constituted a conservative.[1]

* * *

It is striking that although Dorothy Livesay has been long
esteemed as a major Canadian poet there is little serious criticism
on her work.[2] There is even less on her socialist poetry published
in the 1930s and 1940s. True, *Day and Night*, which contains much
of her political poetry, did receive the Governor General's medal
for 1944, W.E. Collin in *The White Savannahs* sympathetically emphasized her socialist verse,[3] and a number of essays in a recent
collection speak generally and approvingly about Livesay's
political work.[4] Yet very little has been said about these poems
as *poems*—at least not in a sustained and scholarly way.[5] That

silence, I would argue, rises not so much from fair assessment of the work, or some sobering second look that has found it unworthy of its first recognition. There seem to me two explanations for the situation: one having to do with Livesay's biography, the other with literary ideology.

Livesay's poems of the 1930s were inspired by her personal experience as a welfare worker, shaped by the radical politics she was at the time acquiring, then heightened by the formal lead she discovered in W.H. Auden and Stephen Spender.[6] When these poets, or at least their example, heaved into sight, Livesay watchers must have felt something odd had happened to her. Gone (actually only *almost* gone) were the signs of the early work—romantic lyrics based on themes of love and nature. Years later, with the reappearance in her work of a fairly tight imagistic writing, especially in the 1960s when Livesay went through another of the several resurgences that have characterized her literary life, it must have seemed at least to some she had returned to her earlier and true metier. Beverley Mitchell, for one, has made this argument. Although sympathetic to Livesay's larger aims in the Thirties, she regrets a loss of lyric in those poems:

> Miss Livesay uses a variety of technical forms in her poems of social protest and, from the point of view of technique, they are impressive. In my opinion, however, these are the least satisfying poems in the collection, for they lack the conviction of the more personal poetry. Perhaps Miss Livesay is naturally a "private" poet and therefore her "public" voice sounds contrived. . . . Whatever the reason, these are the only poems in the collection which appear "dated"—at times, they also appear ludicrous.[7]

Applying lyrical standards, Mitchell finds parts of the poems unconvincing (because 'insincere') and even bathetic. She argues "their emotional impact is dissipated and the poet's voice made impersonal. The reader has the impression that the poet is 'observer' rather than 'participant' in the events of the depression'."[8] Much of what has followed in Livesay's career would tend to confirm such a reading of her work—the socialist verse as some form of aberration in what is a body of metaphoric, romantic writing.

Livesay herself has had something to do with promoting this view. In interviews and in essays, in personal conversations and public talks, she often advocates what she takes to be the best and at times it seems the only legitimate form of writing: poetry that 'sings' or speaks 'magic.' The terms to which she is sometimes committed prefer one kind of poetry at the expense of others, including much of the work she herself once did as a socialist in the Thirties.

But the major obstacle to appreciating Livesay's radical poetry has been a definition of poetry that has prevailed in Canada for many years, and that still persists in some versions despite developments in poetry and criticism. For the most part the received terms serve Livesay's pre- and post-Thirties poetry. So if we want to see what is at stake in the socialist poems we can do so by placing them alongside the latest and especially the earliest poetry she wrote. To focus the exercise I will concentrate on two representative and, I think, strong poems. I will briefly summarize the qualities of an early poem, "Green Rain," then consider the shift in poetics that brought Livesay into "Day and Night." Approaching these poems as discourse will enable us to hold in reserve, at least for the moment, the terrible temptation of our prejudices (our pre-judgments) to decide too easily on what is 'good' poetry. It may be possible, given the provisions of contemporary criticism, and without simply falling back on political approval, to recuperate a mode that has not been amenable to common methods of reading. "Much of the interest of literary reading," writes R.A. York, and it will be my interest to argue here, "lies in the gap between real reader and implied reader, in the reader's learning to become—or in his refusing to become with any seriousness—the reader he is meant to be."[9] Not the reader I *am*, and not the reader I may *want* to be;

but the reader I *need* to be if I am going to appreciate the text I am reading.

Though "Green Rain" is well-known, and deservedly so, it would be useful to have it before us:

> I remember long veils of green rain
> Feathered like the shawl of my grandmother—
> Green from the half-green of the spring trees
> Waving in the valley.
>
> I remember the road
> Like the one which leads to my grandmother's house,
> A warm house, with green carpets,
> Geraniums, a trilling canary
> And shining horse-hair chairs;
> And the silence, full of the rain's falling
> Was like my grandmother's parlour
> Alive with herself and her voice, rising and falling—
> Rain and wind intermingled.
>
> I remember on that day
> I was thinking only of my love
> And of my love's house.
> But now I remember the day
> As I remember my grandmother.
> I remember the rain as the feathery fringe of her shawl.[10]

I count myself among the many admirers of "Green Rain," so what I say here is meant in no way to diminish its accomplishment. Nor is my purpose particularly to evaluate or to 'read' the poem (though I will do something of both). I want, rather, to describe its conventions and to locate it as a mode of writing, one that with the persistence of Romantic definitions of lyric continues to enjoy favour to the detriment of other kinds. The details of my description perhaps will surprise no one, though my general conclusions might.

We might first note the imagistic basis of the poem. The warm house, green carpets, the chairs, the rain itself—these we recognize as the heart of such poetry. It is substantive. Here we find beauty and implication in the poem's procedures. We happily take in the 'imaginative' tropes: the "veils of green rain," "Feathered like the shawl" (a double trope), perhaps, gently, the "waving" trees. The same goes for the symbols: the trilling canary (the bird / the poet / the inner self), the road, the warm house; and the recurrence of key words: "green," "I remember" (six times). We certainly notice the 'musical' phrasing typical to this and to later stages of Livesay's writing. And typical, too, of the lyric is its structure of language—sounds summon sounds, grammar conjures equivalents, metre induces its own extensions—so that all the parts are internally motivated and intimately related. The poem is ripe with rhymes, especially of an alliterative, assonantal, and consonantal sort, including Livesay's life-long love of CvC rhymes ("horse-hair chairs," "full of the rain's falling"). The density of nasal consonants— "n" and "m"—lend a sonorous quality, a solemnity that borders on the sublime. And though this poem, among Livesay's early pieces, is one of the most open rhythmically, it is far from irregular. For one thing, the line boundaries without exception correspond to syntactic boundaries, creating a sense of assured hovering in the poem. For another, the rhythms serve the expressive range of traditional prosody ("her voice, rising and falling") or approximate an even measure in the line ("But now I remember the day").

As a matter of fact, the last line—Livesay is fond of this—acts as an exquisite anapestic closure: "I remember the rain as the feathery fringe of her shawl." In that line, the most significant details, recapitulated and placed in a position of finality, bear extra weight. Thematically and structurally they consolidate the poem, stiffen it the way a slack muscle, suddenly engaged, brings the body to a sense of itself. The final line reinforces the frame when the opening and closing prove to correspond by reaching across the poem to one another. In a similar way, the rhythm of the last line, reinforced by alliteration (remember, rain, feathery fringe) in which three of the active syllables coincide with metrical stresses, declares in a regularity that departs from earlier lines, that previous variations and hence the poem itself have come to an end. It brings us, if only mildly, to a halt and marks the poem off as self-sufficient. Such a long gentle line—almost breathless—in its elongation of the base line ("I remember") whose culmination it is, alerts us to formal closure. Since it in effect swallows all those earlier lines, it all the more firms up the end of the poem.[11]

The frequency of unvoiced consonants further heightens the sense of serenity, as do the references, limited as they are to domestic or nearly domestic details. We are struck by the unharried, unhurried voice, by a world delicately, securely alive. The quietness of the poem finds its source in nostalgia and the now/then organization it shares with many such Romantic poems. "I remember," the speaker says—six times, three times in the last stanza, and once, punctually—invokingly? prayerfully?—at the beginning of each stanza, where the words act as anaphora to anchor the poem rhetorically and to trigger more material, to amplify the poem paratactically, with little regard to cause or sequence. *These* reiterations cannot be simple indicatives or mere demonstrations for, once said, in an informational economy the clause has made its point. Any recurrence would in that circuit have to be redundant. If the words are to be functional, therefore, we have to place them in some other network. The most likely would seem to be expressive: they sing of desire as much as confidence—that this *will* be, that the speaker will call some thing or some condition into being, out of caves in her mind, into her presence. The reprise is a sign that she is on to something, assuring herself that what she petitions and re- petitions is at hand, subject to the talismans she dangles before her.

We know that in Greek mythology Mnemosyne was the mother of the Muses. We also know, in these Derridean days, how such narratives privilege the prior, the 'original,' the already known. Livesay's poem looks to the past, puts some distance between the occasion of its speaking and its source. The text dwells on recovery operations, animates its moment by what it can salvage from the past, affirms personal continuity between what the poet is and what in her own source of herself she has been. No harm in that, it's perfectly common in writing of this sort, perfectly Wordsworthian.

Grammatically, "Green Rain" is in its main thrust indicative. That mood is common to the lyric, perhaps so critically related that it amounts to a generic marker, for it supposes poems provide definitions. The lyric—this is especially true of the imagist poem—seeks to define by de-scribing and therefore presumes that its subject can more or less be made known on a secure (which is not to say, on an easy) basis. As we shall see, the indicative mood, with its presumptions of neutrality and of speaking naked truth, a few years later gives way in Livesay's development to political poems built, necessarily, on a different rhetoric.

But let me posit a point we are perhaps less inclined to observe in reading "Green Rain." Consider the speaker. What is the occasion of her address? What marks the situation of her speaking? The actual details she observes or, more correctly, remembers, yes—but what audience does she *address*? I think the answer is none, overtly that is. Certainly, as in all poems, there is an implied reader here, the one who will one day come along, unknown and unknowable to the poet, to read the poem, much as we are doing. But I am thinking of somebody more locally: there is *no* figure to whom the speaker immediately appeals. We have, rather, a voice that pretty much talks to itself (here, at the window, removed in space as she is in time from the subject she describes)—a voice, in short, we have come often to expect in the post-Romantic lyric, a bird singing to itself, perhaps to be overheard. This voice never seeks explicitly to engage anyone. There are no "you's" in the poem, only the language of first and third person—again a language of some distance from any listeners.[12] That's pretty much what we'd expect in an "expressive" work, one that ex-presses or presses outward what resides within, and which observes the trope of Livesay's first book:

> Remember; it's *Green Pitcher*, the jug. "In a pitcher I have
> my songs in store; / when I uncalk [sic] it, out they pour."
> . . . That was how I felt, it was there locked up inside me
> and all one had to do was pull the cork and the poems
> would come.[13]

Naturally.

There are further signs of Livesay's detachment from any identifiable place which is right at hand and out of which she might speak in the moment of language. Iconic, "Green Rain" concentrates on images, especially visual ones, which work in an evidentiary way by pretending to point to the larger world without themselves in any way occluding or deflecting it. As a result they mask the work words do by seeming to line them up with their referents. But the poem is even more iconic in its focus on the observing "I," who spatializes experience and therefore turns it into a visual terrain known to the eye as organ, but also to the mind's eye. The speaker here reflects, she does not especially respond to or provoke any body or any thing in her immediate environment. In fact, she is without any discernible situation *as she speaks*. She talks out of the present moment, that we know, that much is clear, but there is not one single sign of where *she* is located. That's not surprising, either, because it is quite in keeping with the traditions of which the poem is a part. Poems of reverie can and often do locate themselves, and many of Livesay's own poems name their situation, but "Green Rain" is slightly more invested in a post-Wordsworthian moment that would seek spots of time induced out of emotion recalled in tranquillity. All details in the poem derive from a past—lost, disappeared, attenuated—as the speaker brings it into the present, makes it present. In that unchanging moment she sites herself, centering it. The recollecting, assessing "I" serves as the measure of all things—the past entering to enhance lyrical intensity, not to enlarge or alter wisdom in any public way, and certainly not to impel the speaker or anyone else into action. She is almost immobile, is moved only by the observations and the associations she is able to summon for personal appreciation.

Here we prize the poignancy of the speaker's presence, defer to the author who by virtue of her sensibility vindicates experience. Accustomed to the conventions at work—the speaker uttering / outering her most inward and intimate thoughts—we readily draw the correspondence between inner and outer that they institute. We may align the Livesay poem with what M.H. Abrams has called "the greater Romantic lyric." In the place of an amplified voice, verbal sententiae, and allegory, it offers

> the possibilities in the quite ordinary circumstances of a private person in a specific time and place whose meditation, credibly stimulated by the setting, is grounded in his particular character, follows the various and seemingly random flow of the living consciousness, and is conducted in the intimate yet adaptive voice of the interior monologue . . . [and that] unites the possibilities of both colloquialism and elevation.[14]

In many of its manifestations, including "Green Rain," this outer world confines itself to external 'nature.' The major siting abides in the stance of Livesay's speaker, and locates the self not in the public realm, nor in the urgency of action, but in the slowness of meditation, in the slide toward illumination, pulling out the images tenderly, one by one, secured by the absence of the second person, and heightened by the pleasant distance of the past. The inner and outer are brought into a congruence most obviously realized in the light which suffuses the room and which at the same time emblemizes a personal light—eye, memory, and illumination brought into one in the meditative mode.[15] In turn the natural world is so at one with itself that the rain is green: it takes on properties of other phenomena, here the colour of the trees and grass.

At the height of recollection, and quite in keeping with the lyric mode, the speaker dips into identification with her subject. When speaking of the originary moment, she opens and closes in past tense. But at the instant of fullest recovery, for one brief instant, she slips into present tense—"Like the one which leads to my grandmother's house"—goes back into the remembered, and brings it precarious, precious as breath, into her time. Much the same holds for the deictics in "Green Rain." I'm thinking especially of the articles and demonstrative pronouns. In working toward illumination, and in coming out of it, the speaker announces some distance between herself and the objects of her contemplation in her choice of "the" and "that"—"the shawl," "the spring trees," "that day," "the day." But in the middle stanza, the locus of vision, where she most intently commemorates presence, she delimits her discovery with indefinite articles—"A warm house," "a trilling canary"—and accordingly grants us the magic of immediacy and intimacy which, the rhetoric would have us believe, as in a sense we do believe, she briefly lights. In the primary operation of the poem, the cozy interior (hers, the house's, the poem's) rings with reassurance. Dream pod, seed chamber, it centres her meditation and begets it. The source guarantees her dream of totality.

So the speaker brings into being a world whose terms are comforting, whose gifts are reassuring as we leave the poem renewed in our sense of personal fineness. This poetic world presents itself as intact, nearly, and as autonomous in its emphatic 'literariness,' its firm closure, its expressive mode, its safe subject—exquisite soul is reconciled with love and nature, solitary genius brings us to resolution. The experience is harmonious, so freed from 'noise' it is nearly silent.

It is a poem whose major predicates and therefore whose actions, all mental, reside in the resurrection of a serene past. It's surely telling that (if we except gerunds and participles) there are only two predicates in the entire poem. (I've already mentioned the six appearances of "I remember"; the only other predicate occurs in "I was thinking.") Neither of them designates single or completed action. There's not much action at all, certainly not when the text speaks of mental processes or conditions.[16] There is not much change, either, in such verbs of duration or of incompleted action, which by virtue of their tense inaugurate on-going states or actions.[17] In tense, as in mood, the insistent predicate—"I remember"—stations the poet in confidence. The indicative mood, as we've noted, more or less projects the utterance as simple statement of fact. As is typical in such lyrics, the indicative crowds out the subjunctive and shoves it into some category of taboo where speculation, dissatisfaction, and desire are regulated. The simple present, too (as opposed to the present progressive), implicates the speaker in revealing action: this is what I do, what is characteristic of me, I *remember*, that much endures. In its semantics of grammar, the poem uses the simple present in its refrain, a tense that carries with it hints of habitual and hence defining actions. The tense conveys (though it does not insist upon) a peculiar sort of meaning: I remember, that is what I am, I do it all the time. The structure is known to us in the speech of kids who, we assume, are empowered to discern the essence of a subject in its predicate: cows moo, pigs grunt, critics presume. I remember. The predicates in such constructions establish characteristic and therefore defining acts.

The introspective world that the verbs constitute find their coordinates in other parts of the discourse. For one thing the poem trusts in reference. Out of its fidelity to a world meaningful on its own and needing only to be recognized by attentive people, the poem nominates the originary moment in a levy of nouns and in the bevy of adjectives attendant upon them. States and attributions. Amplifications. The effect of this load of 'things' is to lay out a stasis almost immune to change or movement.[18] We encounter a flurry of qualifiers largely given to the eye ("long veils," "green rain," "green carpets," "shining" "carpets"), but to the other senses too: the ear ("trilling canary," the sound of the rain falling, the wind blowing it) but also—and this surely contributes to a sense of intensity and intimacy, to authenticity too—touch ("feathery fringe," "warm house," "horse-hair chairs") and kinaesthesia ("her voice, rising and falling"). But essentially silent. The bird's song, the swish of the rain—these gain force by virtue of the acute silence in which they bob; as I become aware, writing this alone at night in Dorothy Livesay's old cottage, of the wind and one hundred feet away the lake I could not hear under the sounds of day.

In its brevity (which implies there is no need to justify the discourse), but above all in its care for intense emotion—here of a somewhat wistful sort—the poem speaks in measures of 'sincerity.' Such poems pretend that the enunciating "I" (the one who speaks) is identical with the enunciated "I" (the one who is spoken about). We are invited to perceive that the poet who wrote the poem and the persona who speaks the poem are one and the same, that the poet herself speaks directly, or almost directly, to us and in her own voice. The poem includes other signs of the 'authentic.' Its normative syntax, its subdued diction, and (compared to metrical verse) its slightly irregular rhythm would seem to indicate as much, since these traits commonly denote for us, so habituated to them have we become, unmediated experience.

But we are even more susceptible, with our residual Romantic notions, to crediting as 'genuine' first person and present tense. We are so familiar with "I am" as a mark of sincerity—this is really happening, right here and now, before my very eyes—have become so accustomed to its usage as signifying what is 'natural,' as opposed to what is 'mannered' in avant-garde poems, that we have come in our duller days to accept the most outrageous artifice as evidence of immediate event. We find it convenient then to ignore the impossibility of a poem's moment ever coinciding exactly with its subject's moment. The gap between these events holds even for the most radical postmodern pieces (though the point does not discredit postmodern suspicions of premeditation). There has to be *at the very least* a hair's breadth between the coming of a word into consciousness and the emergence of that word, physically, upon the page, or phonetically in speech. For the word cannot come into existence (I say nothing of revision or generic determination) in the poem until it has found its articulation, however recently, in the poet's mind. If we can discern a lag even here, in the most processural writing, how much more will the delay obtain for other poetry, such as Livesay's?

And in Livesay we do find a gap between the "I" who speaks in present tense and the "I" who exists in past tense. That wedge of time, common to the Romantic and post-Romantic lyric, destabilizes claims to 'sincerity.' It admits a discrepancy because the speaker possesses understanding that the past 'self' could not have had, and we are forced to acknowledge that the experience is mediated in a very profound way—that it is not, that it can never be, simple direct expression. Yet if we are not mindful, we are only too prepared, under the weight of convention, given our habits of reading, to receive such lyrics as naked cries from the heart, and hence as utterly natural. "Green Rain," solidly in a familiar tradition, gives us every chance to believe in its speaker, even to identify with her, when she says "I remember," again and again.

The poem itself is so accomplished and the speaker is so certain that as a matter of course we will share her perspective, we feel confident in the end that whatever bumps we hit in flight we will touch down safely. Reassured by her endorsement, her affirmation and well-being in the world, by her belief that her intimacy will exonerate her, we can readily accept the premises. The mode has been so firmly established in our minds, that only with some effort can we recognize it observes one among many options. We find it hard to remember that its conventions, far from being 'natural' or superior, are merely different and peculiar to its own operations.

Although my tone might suggest otherwise, my point is not to disparage this poem, or its conventions. Rather, it is to make its conventions known, to save us from the invisibility of our easiest assumptions. I am proposing that the definitions most of us have at hand will likely lead to a sympathetic and ultimately a favourable reading of "Green Rain." But it's just those conventions—as I've outlined them—that get in the way of reading Livesay's radical poetry of the 1930s.

* * *

About Livesay's intention in that new work as it erupted and her sense of a new direction there can be no doubt. Ensnailed like a foetus in the earlier poems, she later is chanelled through doors and windows into a birth of a new keeping.[19] In the social poems she becomes ensnarled in history and answerable for it. We have her telling statement, years later, about that shift and of her feelings, at once exhilarating and painful, as, having only a few years earlier moved away from lyrical poetry, she then swerved off orthodox Marxist discourse:

> All these three social work years I had abandoned writing any poetry which was personal. But in . . . trips to Greenwich bookshops I delved about—perhaps seeking some relief from the orthodox Marxian literature I had been consuming for so long—*Masses*, *The Daily Worker*, and countless pamphlets and political tracts along with some heavier economics and Engels, Lenin and Stalin. What was my astonishment and unbelief to find some slim volumes of English poetry—revolutionary poetry but full of lyricism and personal passion! C. Day Lewis first, then Spender, then Auden and MacNeice. There was nothing like it in America or Canada, but it was a movement that followed exactly where I had left off with my Paris thesis—it threw Eliot aside and proclaimed a brave new world. I think I must have wept over this discovery, but there was no one of my friends and comrades who would have taken any interest in it. All I could do was write a poem myself, celebrating the new horizon.[20]

There is nothing like a crisis in belief to bring a poet to the realization that the word and the world do *not* coincide, that the world we seem to inhabit is misnamed and that we cannot take the pure lyric (or, more accurately: the signifying system we know as lyric) for granted. The lyric cannot *by itself* stand as adequate measure for anyone who finds that inner desire and outer conditions fall far apart. The lyric cannot work when a state, and a poetics, jeopardizes the humanity of its citizens. Once that gap opens, it becomes difficult to invest energies exclusively or even mainly in freeing an experience of poignant significance from the page. Livesay's political conversion can be seen then as a crisis in language and literature as much as a crisis in social formation. Once she doubts the alignment of signifier and signified she loses faith in singular coherence and in a rhetoric of description (which assumes the word will stand, and should stand, for the world). She finds the Romantic lyric wanting for her social purposes since it implies an acceptance of 'what is,' and since in bodying forth experience it would have us believe that truth precedes writing and is therefore nearly ineradicable or resistant to change. So the political poetry which Livesay in the Thirties starts to write supposes that, on the contrary, truth follows on writing, and is made by it. Radically disjunctive, it is pre-scribed, comes into being, 'as it was written,' the signifier preceding the signified in reversal of imagist example. In this new model, consistent with the bent of contemporary linguistics, the world is not received, it is produced, in discourse. That means authority begins to drift away from the poet toward the signifying system, though Livesay has never been so prepared as are some contemporary poets to take that course very far.

What's at stake here is something more, actually something other, than old left complaints about 'bourgeois self-indulgence.' How puritanical, how fatuous, they sound. For surely the meditative lyric is nothing we would want to forgo or, I would argue, nothing we have to forgo, despite powerful attacks on it and its humanist vision. Livesay has on occasion put the shift sociologically as a matter of access to an expanded or new audience. I'd prefer to put the argument differently: we need better or at least richer reading strategies, ones that would allow us to appreciate a whole range of poetic possibilities, including lyrical and polemical writing, and preferring none in any final or exclusive way. In "Day and Night," unfortunately much too long to reproduce here, that would mean granting Livesay her new rhetoric. And it is a new rhetoric, much more innovative than Jonathan C. Pierce would allow when he says

"The public poem, far from being fundamentally different to Livesay, is the extension of private concern to a larger sphere of thought, feeling, and action."[21] Wanting now to engage and direct, she moves her attention from the sender to the receiver, as these concepts are outlined in Roman Jakobson's communications model.[22] As a result the verbal text serves not to reveal the interior of a speaker, to show us how she is feeling; it counteracts that aesthetic, contracts to act upon listeners, and takes on all the rhetorical signatures of that arrangement. Whereas once, in the lyric, language was expressive and descriptive, it starts to become pragmatic and prescriptive. It migrates from the reminiscent to the programmatic. Where once, in its relationship with audience, it was indicative (in presumptions of defining, of putting into place definitely, definitively), the rhetoric turns interrogative and imperative (instigating, challenging). At the same time, the verbs (toward the end of "Day and Night") become subjunctive and conditional, pointing forcefully to what might be and what in Livesay's Utopian vision *will* be.

It's interesting, by the way, that in Livesay's own words, the most immediate release for her was formal. *Poetry* set her free. It's not as if there were no other radicals to inspire her, there were for awhile no radical *poets* to help her write and no models from which to work. In *The Documentaries* Livesay wrote: "This discovery [of models] moved me deeply. I could share it with no one, but from that moment on there was planted within me the desire to write poetry once more—this new sort of poetry."[23] We find, then, a situation which we might crudely think of as 'translation': a political experience, already articulated in certain kinds of discourse (in letters, essays, orations, charts, debates, scholarly papers, resolutions, journalism, conversation) in search of a poetics that would be consonant with that vision. It is important to think of giving voice to the new stage as translation so we can avoid supposing intelligible experience precedes language and exists in some state before it is made legible.

In any case, the result of Livesay's search for a poetry that would answer to her political passion has never in public ways been accorded much credit, not at least since its initial recognition. The silence perhaps has come not so much for reasons of overt political dismay—though that would have something to do with it, critics in Canada being less radical than is commonly supposed among Chambers of Commerce and editorial writers for monopoly newspapers. It's my contention that the neglect *is* ideologically based, but that it has acted and continues to act in a hidden way, on the basis of assumptions that are more or less taken for granted. What is at issue here is not so much whatever ideologies each of us as readers may consciously profess, but what unacknowledged ideology is at work in our criticism.

In a feisty speech Margaret Atwood has argued that in Canada we prefer to think of artists as tortured neurotics and to value art as harmless diversion: "We are not good at analyzing it in terms of . . . politics, and by and large we do not do so." According to Atwood "our critics sneer somewhat at anything they consider 'heavy social commentary' or—a worse word—'message.' Stylistic heavy guns are dandy, as long as they aren't pointed anywhere in particular. We like the human condition as long as it is seen as personal and individual."[24] It's fine if unique, unlike any other, and hence not social or—what would make us blush—political.

The American poet, Denise Levertov, who in many ways resembles Livesay, wisely writes in "On the Edge of Darkness: What is Political Poetry?":

> whereas critics and the public are not dismayed when autobiography, psychological explorations, or at the other extreme, trivia, appear in lyric semblance, yet the political is often looked at askance and subjected to a more stringent examination.[25]

She goes on to say

> we have come to identify the short poem with the lyric *even when it lacks lyricism*, and consequently, often fail to

recognize the lyric *spirit* if it appears in company with the didactic. Thus a totally unlyrical poem passes muster, even though it is flat and banal, merely because it is short and deals with a noncontroversial personal experience; whereas the passionate partisanship of a political poem may block the reader from responding to its sensuous and emotive power simply because expectation does not link these elements with political convictions.[26]

In "Green Rain," we remember, the speaker meditates, in her 'own' slightly elevated voice, on personal emotions, gently, without seeing audience or seeking audience; speaks briefly in mediating rhythms and rhymes, choosing her words for their euphony and their phonetic continuity, dwelling on the romantic themes of love, nature, and absence. The poem offers 'beauty' and serenity, and locates those virtues in a past she calls into her presence. In all these ways, which align the outside with the speaker's sensibility, the poem promotes inwardness, doubly so in its description of the hushed intimate interior of the house. We are able to recognize and to appreciate such writing since it is in keeping with definitions of the poem that have obtained for much of this century—the sensitive romantic lyric, here in one of its most common modes, the brief melody in a contained object of contemplation.

In *Recodings*, a superb book on art and ideology, Hal Foster addresses himself to "The Expressive Fallacy." In that essay he describes the assumptions at work in poems like "Green Rain":

> expressionism denies its own status as a language—a denial that is necessary given its claim to immediacy and stress on the self as originary. For with a denial of its rhetorical nature goes a denial of the mediations that threaten the primacy of individual expression (e.g., class, language), mediations which are usually dismissed as mere conventions, as cultural not natural. Such a "transcendent attack on culture," Adorno wrote, "regularly speaks the language of false escape, that of 'nature boy.' " And so with expressionism: it speaks a

language, but a language so obvious we may forget its conventionality and must inquire again how it encodes the natural and simulates the immediate.[27]

Yet this notion of self-expression, which governs the common idea of modern art in general, derives, as Paul de Man noted, "from a binary polarity of classical banality in the history of metaphysics: the opposition of subject to object based on the spatial model of an 'inside' to an 'outside' world"—with the inside privileged as prior.[28]

What Foster then has to say about those presuppositions bears even more on what I have been arguing:

Contrary to expressionist belief, the unconscious is not at our transparent disposal; indeed, on the Lacanian reading not only is the unconscious structured as a language, it is also the discourse of the other. . . . [F]or even as expressionism insists on the primary, originary, interior self, it reveals that this self is never anterior to its traces, its gestures, its "body." Whether unconscious drives or social signs, these mediated expressions "precede" the artist: they speak him rather more than he expresses them. . . .

The expressionist monologue, then, is a form of address, one that suppresses its rhetorical nature, it is true, but a form, a formula nonetheless. And to deconstruct expressionism is to show precisely how it is constructed rhetorically—that *the expressionist self and sign belong to a preexistent image-repertoire.* . . .

The expressionist quest for immediacy is taken up in the belief that there exists *a content beyond convention, a reality beyond representation.* Because this quest is spiritual not social, it tends to project metaphysical oppositions (rather than articulate political positions); it tends, that is, to stay within the antagonistic realm of the Imaginary.[29]

"Green Rain," in fact, ideologically fit what shortly after its first publication in 1936—coincidental, ironically, with the composition of "Day and Night"[30]—was becoming in Canada, though to a lesser degree than in the United States, the Cold War orthodoxies of New Criticism. The formalist bias of New Criticism led to an insistence that literature by definition was, or by virtue of aesthetic value ought to be, self-contained and therefore beyond politics somehow. To take one example, a recent student of Auden shows how Cleanth Brooks, in projecting Eliot's conservative program, once set up "a buried 'contrast' between ideology and lyric form, and a buried judgment that the two are incompatible."[31] In some versions of the argument literature was to be 'pure,' which meant uncompromised by life or 'rhetoric' that would seek to make things happen (as if any poems could be free of 'rhetoric').[32] Writing that actually sought to effect change was inferior if not illegitimate: it was 'propaganda,' invested in a history whose contamination it was the business of canon-makers to resist. Invidious though these notions are, they, or ones much like them, still work their way through criticism. Some readers (this is less true of those working on Canadian literature or in contemporary literature than of other critics in Canada) like to think they are immune to 'politics' and engaged in some 'high' pursuits in an 'eternal' realm of 'universal' art, toward which all literature is struggling and in which it could be accorded fitting status. Once inside such a realm, literature should not and can not be tied to a world of political contention. These suppositions, which would ordain the personal lyric and endow it with special standing, have got to be reassuring to those whose interests lie in preventing change. How pleasing for them to hear Keats, in reaction to neoclassicism, in commitment to the page, say dismissively, categorically, "We hate poetry that has a palpable design on us."[33] Frank Lentricchia lays out the unwitting complicity of such thinking in its support of the status quo, when we act

> as if "the intellectual" really represented an autonomous class, crystallized and separated out from socioeconomic matrices. To ask the question of the intellectual in that way [supposing the intellectual *is* separate from social interest

and class] is already to accept what [Antonio] Gramsci called the "traditional intellectual" on his own terms; it is to accept uncritically his idealistic vocation as a student of ideas and a keeper of culture. . . . The question will have to be rooted in what [Michel] Foucault calls the "specific intellectual," working from a particular social and historical experience, within a specific place in the institutional network: the question must be so framed even though the intellectual (the academic intellectual in particular) will tend to regard himself as a cosmopolitan, universal figure, dispassionately attached *as intellectual* to the society in which he lives, speaking for the ages, and . . . [tending] to think that when he serves culture he stands outside power.[34]

I am reminded of Yeats' silly apothegm: "We make out of the quarrel with others, rhetoric, but of the quarrel with ourselves, poetry."[35] Fine if you live in eternity. Lentricchia again:

Almost always overtly opposed to the historical and the rhetorical (and therefore to the political), the idea of the literary as the uncontingent, the universal, a kind of mimesis that is always pretty much above it all, has dominated, and continues to dominate, the history of criticism.[36]

It does so because traditional humanism pretends to separate culture and power and covers up the political work of all texts, including—perhaps above all—the politics of "the great books."

One action profoundly reveals the ideology of that practice—denigrating the rhetorical and elevating the 'imaginative'—and that is the defining of literature in narrower and narrower terms until, other than in the most indirect ways, it does not concern itself with such lowly matters as public life. Raymond Williams has written revealingly on the history of the term "literature." He notes that in the Middle Ages it meant simply texts one might write or read, by virtue of one's capacity to read and write, and that into the eighteenth century it referred to 'polite' or 'humane' learning. By the twentieth century the term had taken on rather rarified limits with

> first, a shift from 'learning' to 'taste' or 'sensibility' as a
> criterion defining literary quality; second, an increasing
> specialization of literature to 'creative' or 'imaginative'
> works; third, a development of the concept of 'tradition'
> within national terms. . . .[37]

Williams comments toward the end of his statement on the ideological implications of presenting literature so narrowly:

> It is in no way surprising that the specialized concept of
> 'literature,' developed in precise forms of correspondence
> with a particular social class, a particular organization of
> learning, and the appropriate particular technology of
> print, should now be so often invoked in retrospective,
> nostalgic, or reactionary moods, as a form of opposition
> to what is correctly seen as a new phase of civilization.[38]

Although not all the details of Williams' argument apply well to Canadian experience, the terms we too have been led to observe would ensure that literature, thus excavated from history, inadvertently reinforces the prevailing powers, hence covertly serves an ideological function even as its champions declare their distaste for it.

For it is in history, and only in history—never in eternity—that the possibility for change and change itself occurs. We can see how crucial it is that the lyrical "I" whose expression once usurped the whole of Livesay's poetry, and whose self-sufficiency would abrogate history, should give way to quite another and nearly invisible persona. Eternity—how convenient for the powerful and the privileged—cares little for the hot struggles of the anonymous (and therefore invisible) poor, they being ephemeral and of little consequence in the grand scheme of things. Why indeed should such people care how many slaves died in the building of the pyramids so long as the pyramids are there, things of beauty forever? Although Livesay never has been insensitive to human misery, in her early lyrics she supposes the author works, idealist begetter, beyond politics, outside the exigencies of life. But in "Day and Night," her self emptied out into the public arena, she locates people in time, obdurately insists on processes and struggles which envelop the individual and in whose circuits, responsive to the world and responsible for it, we are inscribed. The poem offers no comfort to those who don't want anything to happen and who would have to face what would happen if their verities came tumbling down. They would then have to contend with an unpleasant world of doubt and provision, subject always to redefinition, where neither poetry nor nature, much less human nature, can be for all time.

There is no conspiracy in their professions, no knowing collusion. In fact, most literary critics, especially those in Canadian literature, would almost certainly oppose the stupidities and inhumanities of our social order, would in many cases consider themselves progressive or left-wing. That's why doubt about Livesay's accomplishment cannot be assigned to conscious rejection of her politics. The resisting ideology does not assert itself, it nestles implicitly in the assumptions and procedures built into a formalist literary criticism that would foreclose on obviously political writing, obvious because radical (conservative rhetoric seldom being conspicuous because it is in place where it can be and usually is rendered invisible and therefore thought to be natural). That aesthetes, authors and readers alike, inadvertently reinforce conservativism means they are complicit in a system's coercions, never in direct or physical ways, certainly, but in line nevertheless with such power, however much it might personally appall them. The virtually unknowing reinforcement of orthodox wisdom resides in hegemony, which is

> fundamentally a process of education carried on through various institutions of civil society in order to make normative, inevitable, even "natural" the ruling ideas of

ruling interests. The hegemonic process is a way of gaining "free" assent, productivity, and cooperation within a ruling political structure without recourse to violence (the domination of bodies through the means of the military and the police). Hegemonic rule is therefore the mark of the stable, "mature" society whose ideological apparatus is so deeply set in place, so well buried, so unexamined a basis of our judgment and feeling that it is taken for truth with a capital letter.[39]

* * *

In poems such as "Day and Night" (*CP* 120-5), which I take to be representative of Livesay's socialist poems and one of the most daring among them, Livesay moves to challenge that hegemony. She does so by dramatically altering the discourse, by renouncing the private stable self and the mode that legitimized it. Willing to relinquish her accomplishments in the lyric, to jeopardize her standing as a poet, she sought to develop a style that would be adequate to her deepening sense of moral outrage. In her own words, she hoped to face life more fully and to make poetry more accessible to ordinary readers. That redefinition produced a drastic shift in her work, from interiors to exteriors. Livesay is reported in a 1936 newspaper as having claimed literature had become obscure and elitist, "miles away from the common man":

> But it was a mistake to think that all art must be propaganda. The artist was more or less bound to be more sensitive, to see farther ahead than the average man and to be a social realist. But there was no outstanding example in modern writing to show that Canada was reacting to these influences. . . . As a concrete example of the growth of many young writers along progressive ideas, Miss Livesay spoke of her own case. Mere poetic expression of a new world of nature no longer satisfied her, she said. Poetry would never be popular until it was close to

the people and for the most part Canadian poetry was sadly lacking in this quality. (*RHLH* 222-3)

(If the report is accurate in every respect, we elsewhere read in it, incongruously, of Shelley as a model. Shelley with his often dense and abstruse writing!)

Whether Livesay's political poems are any closer to, or any more accessible to, or more commonly read by, 'the common man' than are her earlier or later lyrics, is doubtful. Nevertheless, she did enlarge the discourse of poetry and insert voices which at the time were largely sub-literary or anti-literary. If "Green Rain" rolls on reverie, on various forms of inward power—lodged in a rhetorical repertoire that encodes 'authenticity'—"Day and Night" reaches outward (one of her fine poems out of the Thirties was called "The Outrider"), into a rude babble of public voices—jingling, exhorting, narrating, singing, instructing. Everywhere they proliferate and contend. The voices, because they are motivated by intention, perhaps offend those schooled in New Criticism. This is a noisy poem, far from the melodious phrasings of "Green Rain." In it we abandon monophony for polyphony, harmony gives way to clamour. "Green Rain" is eminently polite, decorous, poised, refined. "Day and Night" is vulgar, bad-mannered, transgressive—engaged in verbal struggle. In effect it reverses a long-standing trend in the history of English literature. Peter Stallybruss and Allon White have examined the origins of the author as spectator and of literature as high-minded activity in the Restoration. Dryden, among them, participated in "an overall strategy of expulsion which clears a space for polite, cosmopolitan discourse by constructing popular culture as the 'low-Other,' the dirty and crude outside to the emergent public sphere." In contrast to Shakespeare and others in the Renaissance, new authors wanted "to homogenize the audience by refining and domesticating its energy, sublimating its diverse physical pleasures into a purely contemplative force, replacing a dispersed, heterodox, noisy participation in the *event* of theatre by silent specular intensity."[40] Livesay steps in the other direction, from silent watching to noisy dispersal. The speaker in "Green Rain" takes her world for granted because she sees no need to alter its most basic structures. Hence the assurance and elegance of her voice, with its mellifluous inner music, seemingly self-induced and self-sufficient, its guarantee that the most basic suppositions will remain intact. Once she is unmoored, however, and is unanchored from single and visual knowing, the poet begins to take soundings and, largely effaced, to listen to the chug of voices around her.

There is one other crucial difference in the narrators of these two poems. In "Day and Night" the poet knows from the outset she is *not* in search of vision, though in the Romantic lyrics she would seem to be working toward it. The convention of epiphany in such poems teaches us to prefer a trajectory by which the speaker drifts toward some vaguely religious change or in which the speaker at least locates herself in need of illumination or enlarged vision. (How coy such poems are in pretending to an initial innocence they do not have: as if the speaker when she begins to speak were yet unenlightened). But in the pragmatics of her new work Livesay for the most part knows, and tacitly admits that she knows, *before* she writes how ethically—but not linguistically (the poem is not written until it is written)—she sees things, or wants to see things. And so its rhetorical thrust, its entire proceeding, takes a different direction. Fully aware of where *she* stands, she hopes to bring *others* into that standing, her under/ standing.

Now, with the crisis in Livesay's measure of things, melody begins to jangle and we are in a new world. Right at the outset, in the abrupt first line of "Day and Night," the poem signifies a new verbal order: "Dawn, red and angry, whistles loud and sends." The brief first eight-line section that opens the poem observes a basic iambic. As a matter of fact, the line unit is blank verse (the syllables count out perfectly), as befits a serious theme in metered verse. But the voice inside that line seizes up like an overheated bearing, refuses the ease of sustained metre. Look at

that first line again: *six* stresses, not five—with an opening spondee ("Dawn, red"), its double stress intensified by the heavy
silence that falls into the hole opened by the comma. There is the
slight shock of that opening stress ("Dawn"), an emphatic hit—
bam; then, the pause, its suspension, and the tiny expectation it
insinuates; and then—bam—another beat. BAM silence BAM.
In inception, in her first breath, this speaker, jerking, declares
tension, that she is *not* at ease, not at one with the world. The
pacing lurches, with the insertion of the comma, into the third
foot. These feet do not step lightly, in easeful dance or joyous
beat. Responsive to another music—"a humming, whirring
drum"—they falter and stumble. Though the iamb as a rule sees
each line to a uniform and perhaps comforting close, in the first
stanza every line but the seventh shows in its aberrations a telling duress. Line six slides in its middle foot into another iamb
broken in two over the silence of its comma ("its, ev"). With the
exception of line two, where the metrical disruption occurs in
the trochaic fourth foot, the lines open with resistance, insistence. Line four buckles with a shoulder-shrugging spondee in
the second foot ("must move"), and four others begin with
trochees: "Scream of," "Men in," "Move in" "Men do" (this last
foot we might scan differently). The very rhythms, then, prove
to be part of an emancipatory discourse and actively to promote
it.

Semantically we confirm this new music. We found in "Green
Rain" a trilling canary, now we read of "loud" "whistles," a
"scream" of steam, the hum and whirr of drums. And the green
world gives way to "red," the serene setting to an "angry" dawn
(the epithet "angry" startles in its inversion of our cultural
associations with dawn as moment of promise).

We find, too, a new domain of coercions and imperatives: life
must move, arms *command*, drums summon and enlist (mechani-
cally, militarily). In shrill violence the steam and whistle *stab* the
air. What is fluid is reduced to the static, what is multiple to the
single and the fixed: "Men in a stream" "Move into sockets." We
have not only the animal mechanized (as belts, sockets, bolts,

possibly drums); we have, perhaps even more chillingly, the inanimate animated: the angry dawn that whistles, the (mechanical?) arms that command, the factory whistle that screams. A horrific shift occurs as if a non-human world were taking on power by draining it from the human order. The implications of such an exchange in power—its basis and its consequence—the rest of the poem proceeds to explore.

We encounter, then, in this opening section, a drastically altered voice in Livesay's writing. It addresses not gratifying personal memories, but the madness of urban economic life. Livesay, escaped from her agoraphobia, steps out into the marketplace, the economy. In rhythms of strain she articulates the new imperatives of power, including procedures of surveillance ("searching the air"), in a world now infected with noise and brutality. Unreconciled, the poem declares itself not by contemplative intimacies nor by romantic metaphors, but by the intellectual bite of irony ("The fun begins"). By shifting from 'imaginative' to 'intellectual' tropes, the poem opens a gap between itself and a contrary discourse that would commemorate the personality of speaker. For in using verbal irony, the poet converts from one who in the lyric ostensibly speaks to herself. Now she becomes one who testifies to her understanding that these words—"Then the fun begins"—actively enroll someone else in the discourse. Livesay, in assuming or taking over a voice that we realize cannot literally and directly be hers, admits to the existence of audience, one that might have heard such expressions, may in fact have used them. In so doing, Livesay glances up from the page to look us in the eye, to say in effect, 'I speak merely as you might want me to speak, or as you have heard people speak. How do you like it now?' Verbal irony implicates the reader: 'you, thank god, would harbour no such thoughts,' says writer to reader; 'we're with you all the way,' says reader to writer.

The newly found discourse emphatically announces a new subject and a new treatment: a more discursive voice focused on the urban, populated, discomforting, and socio-economic realm.

These men indeed "do a dance" to the beat of a different drum, the shift caught in the title's pointed inversion of Cole Porter's romantic words "Night and Day." A "moving human belt" (the first qualifier, "moving," surely speaks of the men's lives physically *and* of the effects on them emotionally), these men enter a grotesque series of objects and powers that encircle and enslave them. They churn into belts and sockets, revolve in the machinery of drums. Even the sonic repetitions—"Scream after scream," "move . . . / . . . a moving," "a humming . . . drum," "belt" / "bolt"—reinforce the acute sense of closure and repetition. So do the parallel structures: red and angry, whistles / sends, must move / [must] command, humming / whirring. In either case, phonetic or grammatical, we find a formal enclosing and recurrence that enforces the semantic locking. Put into telling positions of equivalence, the words establish a motivated relationship, one that assigns to them a thematic continuity.

* * *

The first part of "Day and Night," though remarkably different from Livesay's earlier lyrics, presents no crisis in readership. The discourse, though 'unlyrical,' offers a prosody and density we can recognize and act upon. We are less sure of where we stand, or less able to appraise the poem along given lines, when we move into subsequent sections. The very principle of numbering sections announces a shift in discourse, a hitch in decorum: what feeling can there be in numbers? what sense of transparency? sincerity? spontaneity? honesty? The poignant lyric ordinarily would not abide such devolutions. Take the very next part of "Day and Night," six simple stanzas laid out in the most emphatic rhymes and rhythms. Doggerel, we might say:

> One step forward
> Two steps back
> Shove the lever,
> Push it back.

Their dance, presumably. "I insist," Livesay writes elsewhere, "that the nursery-rhyme and ballad pattern are essential elements in poetry, not to be ignored."[41] Yet, the stanzas flirt with banality as they thump and jiggle along. Embarrassingly, they offer little resistance to our 'understanding,' few metaphors that would jolt us to astonishment. (They do, however, send shock waves through readers who are unaccustomed to finding 'subliterary' lines in poetry and who, I suppose, would feel a terrible and sudden sense of violation in them.)

Then there is part 3 which, in contrast to the appositional style in "Green Rain," moves emphatically into successive time: "Day and night are rising and falling / Night and day shift gears and slip rattling / Down the runway." But this discourse soon departs from what looks to be an effaced and objective source, an invisible narrator, into a voice invested with judgment, one that speaks of what can "remember / The record of evil." And it then breaks into the collective pronoun "we": "We move." Once more, we might recall that among the deictics of "Green Rain," the pronouns figure exclusively in first and third person: it is "I" and "my" (the frequency of the possessive case underlying the speaker's personal claim to the world), and it is "her" and "herself." What's missing—"you"—betokens the introspection of this kind of poem, lifted out of a given situation or, more accurately, removed into a situation whose discourse can neither beget nor abide an interlocutor, since it presents itself as utterance without audience. The conventions of such poetry, as Walter Ong so ably has shown, derive from the power of the *written* text,[42] which by its very technology pries the speaker in a special sense free from the second-person of oral, situational speech. Oral speech locates itself radically *in* time and space— no transcendence here—declares its interest in reading and in shaping history. Hence the emergence in part 3 of what Roman Jakobson has identified as a "conative" voice, though we might more simply speak of it as "affective" or "pragmatic."[43] To be sure, all parts of "Day and Night" participate in the literary status of the poem, or at least in what Jakobson calls the "literary" functions. We nevertheless can fruitfully locate elsewhere in Jakobson's model this new speaking, knobbly with challenges and interrogations ("And where is the recompense, on what agenda / Will you set love down? Who knows of peace?"). As we already have noted, the reverie of "Green Rain" implies someone is talking to herself, as if in diary (though the listening "I" in diary itself represents a highly fictionalized "I"). In this later poem the speaker acknowledges audience, actually seeks it, hopes to provoke it. And so the speaker in part 3 moves into a more declamatory and exhortative style.

But I want to move on and to summarize briefly further shifts in voice that follow in the poem. We note, in part 4, more narrative, which is also 'oral' in its appeal to "we" and in its explanatory question, directed to some auditor, "We were like buddies, see?" The speech model soon surrenders pre-eminence to yet another discourse—the black spiritual:

> Lord, I'm burnin' in the fire
> Lord, I'm steppin' on the coals
> Lord, I'm blacker than my brother
> Blow your breath down here.

Part 5 of the poem as it appears, amended, in *Collected Poems* and in *Right Hand Left Hand*, returns to the discourse of part 1, then— in what reads as the most startling redirection in the poem— reverts to the rhetoric of Livesay's earlier mode in two stanzas about nature. The section closes on another simple song, though even this passage sways with imperatives and generalized language. The sixth and final division reinserts the romantic discourse. And then we come across the emphatic beat of song brimming with injunctions and the telling emergence of future tense.

The poem meshes through a chain of mixed voicings, which it links in radical discontinuity. Livesay, in search of a poetics that will be adequate to her new vision, abandons most of the conventions that served her so well in "Green Rain." There, as we saw, the speaker seeks authenticity or the aura of sincerity in a source of power, alone and in retrospect recovers personal experience, gains access through the resources of the past tense and monologic voice located in her as a separate and consolidated speaker. In "Night and Day" we find a new enunciation, one that is accorded present tense and, in the end, future tense, one that acts not to redeem the past but to proclaim the future. We move from the diegetic (and lyric) mode of "Green Rain" to the mimetic (and dramatic) mode of "Day and Night," where the narrator cannot readily be located. Surrendering belief in a simple organizing agent, Livesay disperses authority throughout the text and opens up new sites of knowledge and power, new forms of discourse to which readers must rapidly and radically adjust. So too for the supervising 'narrator.' Her voice must be susceptible to adjustments and readjustments that show she is addressing and above all reacting to an audience, in dialogue with them. Years later, in a paper called "Canadian poetry and the Spanish civil war," Livesay describes a Kenneth Leslie poem, "The Censored Editor" (inexplicably omitted from his collected poems),[44] as "a dramatic poem for voices. Interspersed between the long, supple lines [of speech] . . . the drama unfolds interspersed with short questioning songs" (*RHLH* 254). Livesay goes on in further explanation of Leslie's poem to note the "stark simplicity [of song] . . . interwoven with much more complicated rhymes and images" (*RHLH* 255). Much the same can be said of Livesay's own poem of the Thirties. It too demonstrates varied and flexible voicings, so the play of discourses creates a small drama. That possibility was brought vividly home to those who were fortunate enough at the 1983 University of Waterloo conference on Livesay to hear an enactment of one of her agit-prop plays from the period. The effect was startling: words that seemed to lie on the page in the full deadness of melodrama, sprung into our ears in rapid play of sounds and voices that made that performance electrifying.[45] The result was what is sometimes called choral.[46] In that mode no one voice and no one section is asked to stand on its own, as if it were self-contained. As parts of a long poem, they are permitted to interact and to take on colouring tonally, rhythmically, rhetorically. We are required to span the ellipses.

Livesay herself has written an influential essay, "The Documentary Poem: A Canadian Genre," which can be applied to her own "Day and Night." In it she argues that such poems represent "a conscious attempt to create a dialectic between the objective facts and the subjective feelings of the poet. The effect is often ironic. . . ."[47] She explains that

> the Canadian longer poem is not truly a narrative at all— and certainly not a historical epic. It is, rather, a *documentary* poem, based on topical data but held together by descriptive, lyrical, and didactic elements. Our narratives, in other words, are not told for the tale's sake or for the myth's sake; the story is a frame on which to hang a theme. Furthermore, our narratives are told not from the point of view of one protagonist, but rather to illustrate a precept.[48]

And again:

> Such poems record immediate or past history in terms of the human story, in a poetic language that is vigorous, direct, and rendered emotionally powerful by the intensity of its imagery. Thus we have built up a body of literature in a genre which is valid as lyrical expression but whose impact is topical-historical, theoretical and moral.[49]

These comments all apply to "Day and Night," as must be evident, and as should become increasingly so. What is notable, for my interests, is Livesay's further claim: "it could be proved that since the 1930s our narratives have followed the experimentations originally made by Grierson in film: they are documentaries to be heard aloud, often specifically for radio."[50]

Parts of "Day and Night," I have suggested, and most readers will find, are easily assimilable to conventions of reading that we can apply to Livesay's imagist poetry of the 1920s. Those expectations meet with impedence, however, in the songs and in the insistently pragmatic passages that form such a large part of the political work. The temptation for readers so informed must surely be to consign the songs largely to the category of doggerel and to perceive the exhortations as belonging to the domain of propaganda—well intentioned but hardly amenable to poetry, perhaps by their very terms confined to mediocrity. Those lines in section 5, where an anonymous worker prods and pressures—surely these are not 'high' poetry. Nor are they, in one sense, meant to be, unless we see them as expressive parts of a larger structure; or unless we recognize and receive them as communal song whose voice comes with the power of tribal chant, declaring purpose and solidarity, and exempt therefore from demands for lyrical subtlety. Alternatively, they may well participate in the long tradition of hymnody which cultivates religious fervour in 'plain' poetry, not unlike psalms in times of trouble.[51] We find corroboration of this possibility when we begin, as soon we will, to reflect on the religious terms of the poem.

Even as we do that we need to move from a "realm of natural, fixed, or eternalized meaning [with which 'great' 'literature' is so fraught and which enables it to sit elevated and shining above the sordid sweat of mere politics] to the human arena where meaning is made and unmade, enforced and subverted, assented to and resisted in collective acts of will, where nothing (or very little) is natural, fixed, and eternal."[52] Not even poetry. There being no timeless definitions that can fix poetry in evanescence, only the shifting terms of our making and appraising, the jags and spasms that mark its history, we cannot be held to any exact definitions of its nature or its value. That is why, to return to the start of this argument, we get in "Day and Night" a redefinition of the poem. It will not in our reading abide the better known and widely recognized terms that lie beneath "Green Rain." It refuses any pretense of the timeless or the apolitical, enters a world of struggle in full awareness of its own rhetoric.

Once mobilized, it is more interactive and public than the introspective lyric, set apart from life and never once addressing it with any thought of changing it.

* * *

So there's that critical point—the necessity to step out of our old shoes. Yet we need not leave all resources behind. Even as we learn to accommodate a very different voicing that makes no bones about its ideology, we can bring to the poem a desire for coherence, which includes the possibility of complex systems of equivalence and opposition. And while it is not my intention here to give an extended reading of the poem, it would round out the argument to sketch some principles of cohesion at work in "Day and Night." Despite its pragmatics, the poem certainly is rich in secondary meanings and rewardingly susceptible to reading it with such expectations in mind.

A major thematic centre resides in the marked references to arrested or twisted voices (evident throughout Livesay's poetry, as Peter Stevens has shown),[53] possibly including the screams and angry whistles in part 1. We find many subsequent mentions: "Your heart-beat pounds / Against your throat / The roaring voices / Drown your shout" (part 3); workers operate "without words" (part 4); admit to being "overalled [dressed in overalls, subjected to an overall power] and silent" (part 6). Those lost voices enter a larger category which we might call conscious speech and of which the workers' stolen history forms a part. So one worker says "We move through sleep's revolving memories," and it is only with colossal acts of courage or effort that they manage to record or "remember / The record of evil."

We have, as early as part 3, a call for other voices to speak in discordance and contra-diction. An anonymous speaker calls on "love" to "Set your voice resounding / Above the steel's whip crack." And in part 4 we hear in the blues spiritual the cry of workers, of suffering humanity, cast into a hell of the ungodly. "Oppositional criticism," Lentricchia writes in a passage which serves as fitting gloss on Livesay's radical poem, is

> always an active possibility within capitalist society
> because ruling ideas—situated as they are in a ruling class
> and distributed from that site through other sites in the
> society—are nonetheless not situated everywhere, not
> distributed from every social site. . . . Ruling culture does
> not define the whole of culture, though it tries to, and it is
> the task of the oppositional critic to re-read culture so as
> to amplify and strategically position the marginalized
> voices of the ruled, exploited, oppressed, and excluded.[54]

These countering voices take on special sanction as Livesay draws on the moral authority of prophesy. (In doing so she is careful to eschew certain religious notions, dear to some, that the poet must not point fingers and must not pass judgment. Unfortunately, when believers in collective sin insist that the poet, as fellow sinner, must not speak of 'them' and must not dissociate herself from others, they can easily end in enforcing reactionary politics.) Those consigned to the inferno of a modern industrial capitalism—Shadrach, Meshach, and Abednego—"burn in the furnace, whirling slow," in the unspoken completion of the Biblical story in Daniel, 3, biding their time, apparently, and awaiting deliverance. The reach of the Bible, felt in phrasing ("Use it not") and put to new but not altogether new purposes, emerges too in a neighbouring allusion to the Crucifixion: "they cut him down, who flowered at night / And raised me up, day hanging over night."

The opposing voices begin to carry the day when toward the end of part 5 a pressing, imploring figure insists that with a full reckoning (they will "Add up" "figures") he and his audience can make "The page grow crazy / Wheels go still, / Silence sprawling / On the till—." Just a few lines earlier, we learned, "There's a hush—" that momentarily halts the industrial din. Ordinarily that racket would have prevented men from speaking and calling their own world into existence—in dialogue, in song, in nomination, in attribution. The powerful exercise control not simply over the means of (physical) production, they also—and it is exhilarating to find this knowledge in the mid-

Thirties, when old-line Marxists enforced their own kinds of orthodoxies—decide upon what makes legitimate speech and enforce the linguistic codes. They try to silence those who cannot or will not observe a dominant discourse.

Presumably the comic resolution so endearing to someone like Livesay, who as she says "has not rejected the possibilities of a Utopian society,"[55] signals the end of the poem with the workers' sudden victory. It is entirely appropriate, in reference to cycles and turnings, that their revolution (we recall the word's root) consists of overcoming the wheel: "The wheel must limp / Till it hangs still." The machinery of power grinds to a *halt*, yes, but in completion of references to sound, it also falls *silent*, losing its capacity to shout commands and to obliterate other sounds, namely the workers' speech. Noise (meaningless sound, stupid sound, obstructing sound) gives way to creative language.

We may very well suppose we are reading a Manichaen struggle for this world. The story from Daniel reminds us of the godly Shadrach, Meshach, and Abednego, whose collective pain and longing we evidently hear in the worker's (workers'?) song. What better expression of solidarity than a black man's song, a cry of the abused and enslaved? Those lyrics tell us of burning and shrivelling, the reductive misery of workers in an industrial foundry that figures as modern hell. They also reveal a "smothered" humanity awaiting a breath, first God's, then, in telling sequence—supplanting the Lord's—the Boss's breath that might save them. Nebuchednezzar, we remember, serves the evil powers of this world. In the end, when the three true believers whom Nebuchednezzar casts into the furnace survive because they are sustained by belief, Nebuchednezzar realizes the errors of his ways and comes over to their side. The completion of the Biblical narrative may be implicit in Livesay's poem, with its emphatic and hopeful anticipation, typical of such poems, of a future that will bring "Day and Night" to a close.

Livesay strategically invokes the Bible on several occasions. She alludes to the Crucifixion, to the burial service, and she

speaks of "the knives against my back." One of the least obvious
references enters with the early description of voices stuck in
throats and then the worker's/workers' song of exhortation:

> We have ears
> Alert to seize
> A weakness
> In the foreman's ease
>
> We have eyes
> To look across
> The bosses' profit
> At our loss.

We must for a moment be startled when we put the following
words alongside Livesay's:

> 4 Their idols *are* silver and gold, the work of men's
> hands.
> 5 They have mouths, but they speak not: eyes have they,
> but they see not:
> 6 They have ears, but they hear not: noses have they,
> but they smell not:
> 7 They have hands, but they handle not: feet have they,
> but they walk not: neither speak they through their
> throat.
> 8 They that make them are like unto them; *so* is every
> one that trusteth in them. (Psalm 115, 4-8.)

The Psalm goes on to speak of divine protection and a bountiful
future.

Livesay carefully has drawn on the Bible to establish a
narrative by which her people are put into exile and subjected
to evil powers, but in which they also are promised a new land.
The title of the poem points to one set of binaries by which
Livesay constructs that theme. Day, for the time being, belongs
to the Bosses. Patriarchs. At the outset day ("dawn" actually)
shrilly summons the workers, later "Light rips into ribbons /
What we say," and one speaker calls on love to "Be with me in

the daylight / As in gloom." We note, in counter, that one black worker "flowered at night" in a world with "day hanging over night," and that the activist works "after evening." The workers go into corners of darkness because power in the contemporary order resides in the eye. Surveillance, as Michel Foucault has shown in *Discipline and Punish*,[56] enables institutions and their officers (the overseers) to compel assent. Under their aegis the eye subjects what it sees and turns it into object. In response, the powerless sustain themselves by secrets kept from the eye, whispered in the ear. We are into a period of temporary release from the foundry, obviously, when Livesay's workers can do something else, such as organize themselves. "Indeed," write Stallybrass and White, "a valuable way of thinking about ideology is to conceive of it as the way discursive traffic and exchange between different domains are structured and controlled."[57] We appreciate for the men in their site that this is a time of camouflage or secrecy when, beyond reach of the boss's gaze, the forbidden becomes marginally possible, when the tabooed can be spoken and take on power. In the ear. This is a time when the men can begin to find their voices, just barely, whispering their clandestine dreams. It is also a dark world and a fluid world. Secret, secreting. A matriarch. The men, as though finding solidarity in a shared cult, furtively reconstruct their lives in matrix of dream, in reverie, in song, chant. Knowing that, it may be satisfying to read their rallying song as chant. If so, we would view it not as failed lyric, and it would enter the poem on a different footing. Heavily oral, it would speak redundantly, pragmatically, mnemonic in its prosody. In the place of personal poignancy it would offer communal desire, not individual psychology but tribal ceremony, not contemplation but action. Above all, the voices would find themselves in some sort of dark underworld, the source of oracular or revolutionary powers in romantic mythology. In the domain of the political unconscious, repository of contradiction and dissatisfaction, rallying in the margins of legitimate discourse, these voices in agony (which is

in part 5 with special and absolving effect in a passage I earlier mentioned:

> Now I remember storm on a field
> The trees bow tense before the blow
> Even the jittering sparrows' talk
> Ripples into the still tree shield.
>
> We are in storm that has no cease
> No lull before, no after time
> When green with rain the grasses grow
> And air is sweet with fresh increase.

The discursive lurch[59] alerts us to the generic mix Livesay has so intelligently deployed in her search for structure. She has recently said that "Establishment criticism" has dealt with her lyrics and dismissed "the other side of my work," but that her aim has been "to merge the political and the lyrical,"[60] a practice that Paul Denham has confirmed.[61] She has produced a form which has not yet been widely recognized, much less in her own work. In "Day and Night," as in most of her Thirties poetry, we find at work a strategy that Herbert F. Tucker has identified as central to the Browning monologue, within which "the alien voices of history and of feeling come to constitute and direct one another."[62] It's precisely at what Tucker calls "a paratactic pocket, an insulated deviation from the syntax of narrative line" that the lyrical intervenes "through a recurrent and partial overruling" of the prevailing discourse. One of its effects in Browning, Tucker explains, is for the interpolation to align the poem it enters with other Browning lyrics and with other genres whose presence threatens to dissolve the text in question.[63] Following the structure of Tucker's analysis, we can read Livesay's lyrical interventions as intertextual glosses which bear the full but implicit weight of her pastoral poems.

True, this 'pastoral' world is beset by storm, and lexically we fall upon signs of struggle. So the trees "bow tense before the blow," the final noun registering the double sense of a wind's motion and its shock. We are struck too by the "jittering" of the sparrows and the "shield" that is a tree. We do not find total harmony, yet there is unison. The point gains on us when we locate the passage locally. "We are in storm," the speaker says, "that has no cease." The absence of green in the industrial and capitalist workplace heightens our sense of that world as demonically anti-pastoral. So do the references to pastoral growth and increase, which stand in stark contradiction to the many signs of diminished or sterile existence. Interesting, too, that the 'memory' piece which delivers the pastoral into the poem, moves by its second stanza into a mellifluous phrasing of almost perfect iambic tetrameter (only the first foot, "We are," is excepted), a common prosody in romantic song, especially in its foregrounded and therefore favoured passages, and countering the staccato rhythms of the workplace that fill the previous stanza.

Much as these passages revert to an earlier practice, they still depart from it. Particularly crucial is the stance of the "I" in the lyrical interpolations, perhaps inspired by Pablo Neruda or by Garcia Lorca, to whom in *Day and Night* (1944) Livesay dedicated "Lorca" (*CP* 125-7) as a symbol of lyrical poetry countering political and military brutality. Whereas in "Green Rain" the speaker sought a transcendent moment and identified with the object of her meditations, in "Day and Night" she abandons all quests for private fulfillment, even within the lyrical interpolations. At first glance we would seem in them to have the same old centering on the personal to the exclusion of all else: "I called," "I remember," and (in a later passage) "I commend." The text seems sufficiently studded with the first-person singular. But there's the collective "we" in "We are in storm," and in each of these passages the erosion of expressive practice. It's still there, but it begins to give way to the prophetic, most notably in the third verb "commend," with its reminders of public ritual. Even though the "I" is personal here, it presents itself as speaking not on its own behalf but for what David Lindley elsewhere has likened to "the 'I' of Watts or Wesley, for a collective awareness."[64] In the voice of testimony, for a larger self, on behalf of others' understanding.

Once the 'failure' of pastoral or at least its inaccessibility has been presented to us, we entertain it as an option that enjoys special status. We become all the more aware of the monstrosity which has supplanted it. The pastoral—as in other Livesay poems of the time, such as "Speak Through Me" (*CP* 106)—symbolizes what once was and what might again be. It functions as vestige and as symptom of preferred life. What once "was" sits in taut judgment on what has happened.

It's worth dwelling a moment on the point since appeals to 'nature' frequently amount to justification of the status quo, as Roland Barthes so dazzlingly has shown in a life-time dedicated to debunking them. Societies are replete with such justification: 'human nature being what it is,' 'in the real world,' 'common sense shows,' 'history proves.' The clichés go on and on, and in the name of what 'is,' what reputedly is 'real' or 'natural,' they turn human constructions into fixed verities beyond question or correction. Locked in an aura of eternity, 'nature' cannot change. Nor, in most of its enlistments, can it be the agent of change. It becomes so, however, in radical romanticism, particularly in poets such as Shelley, Blake, and the American poet Robert Duncan, for whom spring does not bring a Maytag vision of the world, simply the same old world slightly refreshed and recycled. Their spring is apocalyptic, profoundly rejuvenating in breaking the conservative cycle of 'nature.' (One wonders: to what extent do the circling appositional style and reflexive anaphoric structure of "Green Rain" endorse conservative myths of recurrence, cycles which "Day and Night" labours to counteract by delivering experience *into* history?)

In this light we might read Livesay's intervention, when with special standing the pastoral re-emerges in part 6. The first stanza in part 6, though syntactically mangled and therefore resistant to understanding, nevertheless seems to align the soul, a child's hands, and a leaf:

> Into thy maw I commend my body
> But the soul shines without
> A child's hands as a leaf are tender
> And draw the poison out.

Maybe the uncertainty is due simply to lost punctuation, for if we were to insert a period at the end of line two, we could make our way through the lines more confidently. In any case, the green world flows into the speaker's, healing it (drawing out the poison) and moving it into a future that, complicit with a more distant and symbolic past, will displant the present: "Green of new leaf shall deck my spirit / Laughter's roots will spread." The appeal to nature is a call to struggle and thus to attend on a future whose shape finds its origins in the past. Its promise comes into play as a projection of memory. The connection between politics and nature is so intimate that botanical terms here accompany future tense—"new leaf shall deck" and "roots will spread." And it is so sanctified it echoes in its first line the burial service for the dead, here altering it so as to express self-sacrifice rather than consignment of the dead. That intertextuality in turn confirms the persona's participation in a prophetic mode.

The residual serves to shape the emerging culture and to endow it with power and beauty. The past and the future ally themselves against the present by counteracting the wheels that have locked their victims in. In the end, their fluidity restored, the men "Pour down the hill," come out of secrecy and silence into the open or public spaces, the agora where, strategically positioned and amplified, they presumably will speak their minds and the wheel of life will be "turned" another way, against the present direction of gears and mechanisms. Freed from the wheel in which they were enmeshed (Ixion's wheel: in Greek mythology, a revolving fiery wheel on which Ixion was chained in hell), they find a new motion, a human dance. This release, curiously, is neither quite certain nor triumphant. The end is rather tenuous and is problematically related to the rest of the poem, as I suppose it must be in a radical poem that suspects authority and that anticipates a future that is not, because it can not be, guaranteed.

All the same it's remarkable that the men only sluggishly move out of their hold, out of which, dazed, like drowned bodies they drift. They escape—for me at least: I have no way of verifying this—like sleepers wakening, struggling out of dream, with the uncanny sense that the world has changed around them, the way it seems to have changed when you step out of a jet into the July sky of Saskatchewan. They themselves have returned to it, restored, but slow, almost stupefied with something they carry heavy in their heads, heavy with it—they, their world too, now, stony with strangeness, their first tentative steps. The ending, in this reading at least, is not ecstatic as we might expect it to be in apocalyptic narrative, but hesitant, as if the realization has not yet come fully upon the men. And so they walk, provisional as prisoners, somnambulist as Plato's cave man, just released, slightly stunned, into sun so new it is raw with light.

As we have seen, truth in "Green Rain" nestles in the past and becomes available through acts of re-cognition in which the real functions as what is previously known. As a result truth is extra-discursive in the lyric. In "Day and Night" where the new is not a simple recapitulation of the old (though it represents an extrusion of the past), truth, or at least certain truths, come into being in the womb of night and in the articulation of the poem. Hence the sense of uncanny ending. It more or less leaves us up in the air, without definition or resolution, the men suspended in a moment of awaited triumph. It does so partly because, like many other recent poems, it practises anti-closure and assumes that a strong resolution no longer suits our world. But that's not the only reason. The problem above all faces prophetic writers: how to name the unconstituted, how to project an unavailable (because unnamed) future with any confidence or clarity?

One could go on to explore "Day and Night" and link it to other poems of the Thirties, poems written by Livesay and by others. We could, for instance, trace how central to Livesay is the symbol of the choked and the freed voice. "The Lizard: October

1939," to name one text, laments the now silent Madrid broadcasts when in Canada at the same time "Radios blare the censored version of our living," and extends the category of language to its written versions—Vienna "blotted out" and "Letters unanswered." Against these losses she puts "the wind's message," its power and its truth of what is 'real' and what is significant (*CP* 268). A hope for language that would be commensurate with our best desire and that would carry the sanction of prophecy leads Livesay to sudden and wonderful end in "The Outrider":

> O new found land! Sudden release of lungs,
> Our own breath blows the world! Our veins, unbound
> Set free the fighting heart. We speak with tongues—
> This struggle is our miracle new found. (*CP* 120)

We find, always, a passion for the voices which are wrongfully shoved aside—unheard and unheeded—and in the Thirties a startling opening inside the conventions of poetry for a discourse that departs from what is given, beyond the prestige of lyric. There is in that new poetry no pretense of transcending history, no desire to vacate it. Perhaps the distances Livesay herself has travelled as a poet, the terrible risks she has taken in violating literary limits, were in their own way more drastic and potentially more effective than the day-to-day politics she at one time looked to. One thing is sure: Livesay has come to believe she would shape the world. That we *must* make it, that we will *make* it. After a fashion.

---

1. Frank Lentricchia, *Criticism and Social Change* (Chicago: University of Chicago, 1983), p. 119.

2. Here is a fairly complete list of criticism on Livesay:

Banting, Pamela. "Dorothy Livesay's Notations of Love and the Stance Dance of the Female Poet in Relation to Language." *CVII*, 8, No. 3 (Sept. 1984), 14-8.

Collin, W.E. "My New Found Land" in his *The White Savannahs*. "Introduction" by Germaine Warkentin. Toronto and Buffalo: University of Toronto, 1975, pp. 147-73; rpt. of 1936 edition.

Crawley, Alan. "Dorothy Livesay." *Leading Canadian Poets*. Ed. W.P. Percival. Toronto: Ryerson, 1948, pp. 117-24.

Davey, Frank. "Dorothy Livesay" in his *From There to Here: A Guide to English-Canadian Literature Since 1960*. Our Nature - Our Voices, Vol. 2. Erin, Ont.: Porcepic, 1974, pp. 168-72.

Dorney, Lindsay, Gerald Noonan, and Paul Tiessen, eds., *A Public and Private Voice: Essays on the Life and Work of Dorothy Livesay*. Waterloo, Ont.: University of Waterloo, 1986.

Foulks, Debbie. "Livesay's Two Seasons of Love." *Canadian Literature*, No. 74 (Autumn 1977), 63-73.

Kreisel, Henry. "The Poet as Radical: Dorothy Livesay in the Thirties." *CVII*, 4, No. 1 (Winter 1979), 19-21.

Leland, Doris. "Dorothy Livesay: Poet of Nature." *The Dalhousie Review*, 51, No. 3 (Autumn 1971), 404-12.

Marshall, Tom. *Harsh and Lovely Land: The Major Canadian Poets and the Making of a Canadian Tradition*. Vancouver: University of British Columbia, 1979, pp. 50-3.

Mitchell, Beverley, S.S.A. " 'How Silence Sings' in the Poetry of Dorothy Livesay 1926-1973." *The Dalhousie Review*, 54, No. 3 (Autumn 1974), 510-28.

Pacey, Desmond. "The Poetry of Dorothy Livesay" in his *Essays in Canadian Criticism 1938-1968*. Toronto: Ryerson, 1969, pp. 135-44.

Pratt, E.J. "Dorothy Livesay." *Gants du Ciel*, No. 11 (Printemps 1946), 61-5.

Stevens, Peter. "Dorothy Livesay: The Love Poetry." *Canadian Literature*, No. 47 (Winter 1971), 26-43.

_____. "Out of the Silence and Across the Distance: The Poetry of Dorothy Livesay." *Queen's Quarterly*, No. 78 (Winter 1971), 579-91.

Varma, Prem. "The Love Poetry of Dorothy Livesay." *Journal of Canadian Poetry*, 3, No. 1 (Winter 1980), 17-31.

Weaver, Robert. "The Poetry of Dorothy Livesay." *CV*, No. 26 (Fall 1948), 18-22.

Whitney, Joyce. "Death and Transfiguration: The Mature Love Poems of Dorothy Livesay." *Room of One's Own*. The Dorothy Livesay Issue, 5, Nos. 1-2 (1979), 100-12.

Woodcock, George. "Sun, Wind, and Snow: The Poems of Dorothy Livesay." *Room of One's Own*. The Dorothy Livesay Issue, 5, Nos. 1-2 (1979), 46-62.

_____. "Transmuting the Myth: Dorothy Livesay and the 1930s" in his *Northern Spring: The Flowering of Canadian Literature*. Vancouver: Douglas & McIntyre, 1987.

York, Lorraine M. " 'A Thankful Music' " Dorothy Livesay's Experiments with Feeling and Poetic Form." *Canadian Poetry*, No. 12 (Summer 1983), 13-23.

Zimmerman, Susan. "Livesay's Houses." *Canadian Literature*, No. 61 (Summer 1974), 32-45.

3. W.E. Collin, *The White Savannahs* (Toronto: University of Toronto, 1975), pp. 158-9. Originally published in 1936.

4. Many of the essays in Lindsay Dorney, Gerald Noonan, and Paul Tiessen, eds., *A Public and Private Voice: Essays on the Life and Work of Dorothy Livesay* (Waterloo, Ont.: University of Waterloo, 1986) consider the subject.

5. Paul Denham has written one of the few substantive pieces on Livesay as political poet: "Lyric and Documentary in the Poetry of Dorothy Livesay," in *A Public and Private Voice*, pp. 87-106. Peter Stevens has expressed sympathy for her political poems in "Ideas and Icons," *Canadian Literature*, No. 40 (Spring 1969), 76-7. He speaks of *The Documentaries*, which included "Day and Night," as "remarkably honest" and effective despite a tendency toward naive vision. In summary, he says, "Dorothy Livesay has never quite been given her due as a significant writer in the development of modern Canadian poetry in English" and sees the collection as "essential reading" for those who "perhaps decry the poetry of the Thirties as jejune and uninteresting" (77). Henry Kreisel's "The Poet as Radical: Dorothy Livesay in the Thirties," *CVII*, 4, No. 1 (Winter 1979), 19-21, also deals with the subject.

6. See Collin, *The White Savannahs*, pp. 159-60.

7. Beverley Mitchell, S.S.A., " 'How Silence Sings' in the Poetry of Dorothy Livesay 1926-1973," *The Dalhousie Review*, 54, No. 3 (Autumn 1974), 517.

8. Mitchell, 519.

9. R.A. York, *The Poem as Utterance* (London: Methuen, 1986), p. 9.

10. Dorothy Livesay, *Collected Poems: The Two Seasons* (Toronto: McGraw-Hill Ryerson, 1972), p. 38. Other references to *Collected Poems* will appear in the essay as *CP*.

11. I am indebted for my observations on closure to an excellent book: Barbara Herrnstein Smith, *Poetic Closure: A Study of How Poems End* (Chicago: University of Chicago, 1968).

12. Of course there can be, and often there are, references to "you" in what I am calling romantic lyrics, especially when their subject is love. But this "you" almost always is singular and is addressed in intimacy, called

only into personal relations, or mentioned in apostrophe, in recognition of its absence.

13. Bernice Lever, "An Interview with Dorothy Livesay," *The Canadian Forum*, 55, No. 654 (September 1975), 46.

14. M.H. Abrams, "Structure and Style in the Greater Romantic Lyric," in his *The Correspondent Breeze: Essays on English Romanticism*, "Foreword" by Jack Stillinger (New York: Norton, 1984), p. 93.

15. Louis L. Martz has traced the meditative poem in the seventeenth century and described it in terms that could apply to Livesay's practice: *The Poetry of Meditation: A Study in English Religious Literature of the Seventeenth Century*, rev. ed. (New Haven, Conn.: Yale, 1962), first published in 1954; and *The Paradise Within: Studies in Vaughan, Traherne, and Milton* (New Haven, Conn.: Yale, 1964).

16. Roger Fowler, *Linguistic Criticism* (Oxford: Oxford University Press, 1986), pp. 156-7.

17. Seymour Chapman, *Story and Discourse: Narrative Structure in Fiction and Film* (Ithaca, N.Y.: Cornell, 1978), p. 68.

18. Here is Livesay, well aware of similar effects in a Milton Acorn poem: "It is not a poem of action, loaded with verbs, but a 'picture' poem; therefore the nominals (modifiers and nouns) are dominant. Notice how almost every noun has a qualifier." "Search for a Style: The Poetry of Milton Acorn," *Canadian Literature*, No. 40 (Spring 1969), 35. It's interesting that in that essay she links Imagism and lyricism (33).

19. Dennis Cooley, "House / Sun / Earth: Livesay's Changing Selves," in *A Public and Private Voice*, pp. 107-25, traces spatial emphases as they change in Livesay's work.

20. Dorothy Livesay, *Right Hand Left Hand* (Erin, Ont.: Porcepic, 1977), p. 153. Other references to this book will appear as *RHLH* in the text.

21. Jonathan C. Pierce, "A Tale of Two Generations: The Public and Private Voices of Dorothy Livesay," in *A Public and Private Voice*, p. 26.

22. Roman Jakobson, "Closing Statement: Linguistics and Poetics," in Thomas A. Sebeok, ed., *Style in Language* (Cambridge, Mass.: M.I.T., 1960), pp. 353-57. I have explained the schemata in "Placing the Vernacular: The Eye and Ear in Saskatchewan Poetry," which appears earlier in *The Vernacular Muse*.

23. Dorothy Livesay, *The Documentaries* (Toronto: Ryerson, 1968), p. 17.

24. Margaret Atwood, "Amnesty International: An Address," in her *Second Words* (Toronto: Anansi, 1982), p. 394.

25. Denise Levertov, "On the Edge of Darkness: What is Political Poetry?," in her *Light up the Cave* (New York: New Directions, 1981), p. 118.

26. Levertov, p. 126. Her emphasis.

27. Hal Foster, *Recodings: Art, Spectacle, Cultural Politics* (Port Townsend, Wash.: Bay Press, 1985), p. 60.

28. Foster, p. 61.

29. Foster, pp. 62-3. My italics.

30. Dorothy Livesay, *The Documentaries*, p. 17.

31. Julian Patrick, "Going Round versus Going Straight to Meaning: The Puzzles of Auden's 'Our Bias'," in Chaviva Hosek and Patricia Parker, eds., *Lyric Poetry: Beyond New Criticism* (Ithaca, N.Y.: Cornell, 1985), p. 284.

32. As a graduate student working on the radical poet Robert Duncan I once presented to a professor, idealist to his heels, some intently written statement, only to find that my reader, a bit less enthused than I, found my comments to be "mere rhetoric!" Mere? I was dismayed, even then. What else do we have, *any* of us, but rhetoric? Trouble is, prestigious language is not often thought of as "rhetoric" by virtue of its familiarity. Being in place it is taken for granted and readily honoured—fair, judicious, free from the opinions and prejudice that colour other verbal acts: the "rhetoric" of radicals who address themselves to the baseness of history in far too committed language and far too parochial passions.

33. John Keats, letter to John Hamilton Reynolds, "Thursday 3 Feb 1818," in his *Selected Poetry and Letters*, ed. with an "Introduction" by Richard Harter Fogle (New York: Holt, Rinehart and Winston, 1959), p. 307.

34. Frank Lentricchia, *Criticism and Social Change*, p. 150.

35. William Butler Yeats, "Per Amica Silentia Lunae," in his *Mythologies* (New York: Collier Books, 1959), p. 331.

36. Lentricchia, p. 90.

37. Raymond Williams, *Marxism and Literature* (Oxford: Oxford University Press, 1977), p. 48.

38. Williams, p. 54.

39. Lentricchia, p. 76. The term originates from Antonio Gramsci.

40. Peter Stallybrass and Allon White, *The Politics and Poetics of Transgression* (Ithaca, N.Y.: Cornell, 1986), p. 87.

41. Dorothy Livesay, "Song and Dance," *Canadian Literature*, No. 41 (Summer 1969), 45. Immediately following the passage I have quoted, Livesay writes, "I suppose that all my life I have fought against obscurantism! For me, the true intellectual is a simple person who knows how to be close to nature and to ordinary people. I therefore tend to shy away from academic poets and academic critics. They miss the essence." The passage seems a little one-sided in supposing one can't be both, or that there is something inescapably wrong with being what Livesay thinks of as academic. I largely share her suspicions, but find her conclusions too easy. My point in

adding this observation is that it confirms my earlier point, namely Livesay's own participation in an aesthetic which does her political poetry disservice.

42. Walter J. Ong, *Orality and Literacy: The Technologizing of the Word* (London: Methuen, 1982), p. 161: The quest for " 'pure poetry,' sealed off from real-life concerns, derives from the feel for autonomous utterance created by writing and, even more, the feel for closure created by print."

43. The terms appear in Jakobson's "Closing Statement." See footnote #22 above.

44. Kenneth Leslie, *The Poems of Kenneth Leslie* (Ladysmith, Que.: Ladysmith, 1971).

45. One of the papers included in *A Public and Private Voice* examines the basis and practice of Livesay's dramas, from the earliest crude propaganda pieces to the more intricate later radio dramas: Rota Herzberg Lister, "From Confrontation to Conciliation: The Growth of Dorothy Livesay as a Political Dramatist," pp. 53-70. Another considers Livesay's work on the CBC: Paul Gerard Tiessen and Hildegard Froese Tiessen, "Dorothy Livesay and the Politics of Radio," pp. 71-86.

46. David Lindley, *Lyric* (London: Methuen, 1985), p. 21.

47. Dorothy Livesay, "The Documentary Poem: A Canadian Genre," in Eli Mandel, ed., *Contexts of Canadian Criticism: A Collection of Critical Essays* (Chicago: University of Chicago, 1971), p. 267.

48. "The Documentary Poem," p. 269.

49. "The Documentary Poem," p. 281.

50. "The Documentary Poem," p. 269.

51. In his book *Lyric*, p. 21, David Lindley says Donald Davie has sympathetically so argued in *Purity of Diction in English*.

52. Lentricchia, p. 69.

53. Peter Stevens, "Out of the Silence and Across the Distance: The Poetry of Dorothy Livesay," *Queen's Quarterly*, No. 78 (Winter 1971). About Livesay's social poems Stevens says "images of dream, isolation and silence recur. Sleep becomes the sleep of people trapped in the deceptions and evils of capitalist society. . . . There is always effort and struggle to break out of silence and dream" and so "the heroic figures open . . . doors" to speech and understanding (586).

54. Lentricchia, p. 15.

55. "Dorothy Livesay: Unabashed Romantic," interview by Bruce Meyer and Brian O'Riordan, in their *In Their Words: Interviews with Fourteen Canadian Writers* (Toronto: Anansi, 1984), p. 84.

56. Michel Foucault, *Discipline and Punish: The Birth of the Prison*, trans. Alan Sheridan (New York: Random, 1979).

57. Stallybrass and White, *The Politics and Poetics of Transgression*, p. 195.

58. Hal Foster, *Recodings*, p. 179.

59. The insertion of lyric is a bit problematic if we attend to Livesay's complaints about W.H. Auden's revisions or Earle Birney's revisions to their early poems when later they were reprinted. Of her own poems, reprinted in *The Documentaries*, she tells us

> most of these social histories have been reprinted from the originals, without change. When I felt it necessary to cut or revise, the fact is noted. Generally it has seemed better to leave the work untouched, as a record of the times; for, though some of the lines and patterns are not all that might be desired, I believe that the veracity of the material and mood is more important than the occasional sentimentality of expression or the lack of polish in style. I am "ornery," and I like authenticity in reportage. (*The Documentaries*, p. v)

Aside from its questionable faith in records, the declaration is further suspect: it is one Livesay was willing to forgo at some stage in reprinting "Day and Night." I have not yet turned up the first publication of the poem, its exact appearance being the cause of some confusion, but it is obvious to anyone who checks the versions now available in print that the "Day and Night" we get in Milton Wilson, ed., *Poets Between the Wars* (Toronto: McClelland and Stewart, 1967), pp. 130-34, is *not* the "Day and Night" we get in either *Collected Poems* (1972), pp. 120-4, or *Right Hand Left Hand* (1977), pp. 154-60. The later version, the one I am using as it appears in *Collected Poems* and *Right Hand Left Hand*, adds toward the end six new stanzas, including two major stanzas replete with Biblical and pastoral tones:

> Into thy maw I commend my body
> But the Soul shines without
> A child's hands as a leaf are tender
> And draw the poison out.
>
> Green of new leaf shall deck my spirit
> Laughter's roots will spread:
> Though I am overalled and silent
> Boss, I'm far from dead. (*RHLH* 159, *CP* 124)

The material appears in print at least as early as *The Documentaries* (1968), where it is not by the way acknowledged as being new, and where it shows up within a year of Wilson's anthology, *Poets Between the Wars* (1967), the one missing the lyrical passage. Where and when these changes occurred I can't say, but they *seem* to have first been made in *The Documentaries*. Whatever Livesay has said about the impropriety of this kind of activity, I myself am grateful for the interpolations. The poem is strengthened, to my mind, by smuggling back the very lyricism Livesay had at first dismantled.

60. Heather Robertson, "Dorothy Livesay: 'My aim was to merge the political and the lyrical. I'm an unabashed romantic,' " *Quill & Quire*, 49, No. 3 (March 1983), 6.

61. In his essay, "Lyric and Documentary in the Poetry of Dorothy Livesay," *A Public and Private Voice*, Paul Denham argues that "both lyric and documentary are essential aspects of her poetic genius, and that part of the power and authority of her best work derives from the coalescence of the lyric and the documentary impulses" (88).

62. Herbert F. Tucker, "Dramatic Monologue and the Overhearing of Lyric," in Chaviva Hosek and Patricia Parker, eds., *Lyric Poetry: Beyond New Criticism* (Ithaca, N.Y.: Cornell, 1985), p. 230.

63. Tucker, p. 235.

64. Lindley, p. 70.

"I AM HERE ON THE EDGE": MODERN HERO/ POSTMODERN POETICS IN *THE COLLECTED WORKS OF BILLY THE KID*

1. *Doorway*

Michael Ondaatje has always been fascinated by unorthodox poetics and characters, notably Billy the Kid in *The Collected Works of Billy the Kid*, the Australian convict in *the man with seven toes*, Buddy Bolden in *Coming Through Slaughter*, and now, most recently, his own family in *Running in the Family*. The two concerns have always gone hand in hand for Ondaatje. He's equally drawn to strange figures pressing the limits of society and writing that explodes the formal boundaries of art. His two chief protagonists, Billy and Buddy, both raise some radical questions about the worlds they know and make. Throughout *Billy the Kid* and *Slaughter* (especially in their climaxes) their tortured art orgasmically explodes "out there"—in the hot, open spaces beyond the provisional edges where they constantly find themselves.[1]

Ondaatje's Billy, sitting inside a room alongside a doorway, tells us at a crucial point in the book, "I am on the edge of the cold dark," then says, "I am here on the edge of sun / that would ignite me":

> This nightmare by this 7 foot high doorway
> waiting for friends to come
> mine or theirs
> I am 4 feet inside the room
> in the brown cold dark
> the doorway's slide of sun
> three inches from my shoes
> I am on the edge of the cold dark
> watching the white landscape in its frame
> a world that's so precise
> every nail and cobweb
> has magnified itself to my presence
>
> Waiting
> nothing breaks my vision
> but flies in their black path
> like inverted stars,
> or the shock sweep of a bird
> that's grown too hot
> and moves into the cool for an hour
>
> If I hold up my finger
> I blot out the horizon
> if I hold up my thumb
> I'd ignore the man who comes
> on a three mile trip to here
> The dog near me breathes out
> his lungs make a pattern of sound
> when he shakes
> his ears go off like whips
> he is outside the door
> mind clean, the heat
> floating his brain in fantasy
>
> I am here on the edge of sun
> that would ignite me
> looking out into pitch white

> sky and grass overdeveloped to meaninglessness
> waiting for enemies' friends or mine[2]

We find Billy, typically, staring warily at the edge, on edge. In every way an out-law, he tries, at times distends and transgresses, boundaries. More often, he fears to cross the lines, hopes to defend his hard-held borders against all trespassers. Billy's marginal situation is here represented by the doorway he sits watching, in a location he assumes throughout much of the book. That doorway provides him with a frame for the white landscape burning outside, a rigid framework which defines that outer space. Its straight vertical and horizontal lines hold the world in place, as Billy himself wants and needs to contain it. But even as Billy fastens his brackets upon that world, he sits dangerously close to it, occupying a narrow 4-foot strip between the enclosed spaces he barely controls and the wide-open nightmare territory which boils just outside the door. Billy's exquisite sense of vulnerability is heightened even more by his perception that "the doorway's slide of sun / [is] three inches from my shoes," the touch of that "slide" endowing sun with weight and motion.

The most immediate threat to Billy is physical—his chronic and justifiable fear that Pat Garrett's gang will get him. A more basic and more interesting terror rises out of his reaction to the sun. As we overhear in Billy's meditation, it is the sun, not his enemies, that would push him over the edge, "ignite" him. The sun constantly scrapes and slams against the dark inner fortifications Billy prefers to occupy (including the shelter he finds in the many private *interior* monologues where he digs in against outside intrusions). So we read about "arcs of sun . . . digging into the floor" (34), the "huge" sun that "came in and pushed out the walls . . . hitting and swirling" in his room (69), and "the bent oblong of sun / [that] hoists itself across the room" (21), the sun's shifting pressure recorded as oblique lines that transgress, or as irregular lines that arch and curve. Billy's resistance depends on predictable straight lines (verticals or horizontals) that he means to straighten up an unruly world.

The menacing violence that Billy finds in heat and light threatens to erupt within him and to blow him up. As he so fearfully knows, things can be "melted [out of shape] by getting close to fire" (51). So he goes berserk when he takes the lid off a hot biscuit tin, releasing a frantic rat:

> bang it went was hot
> under my eye
> was hot small bang did it
> almost a pop
> I didnt hear till I was red
> had a rat fyt in my head (38)

When the lid comes off, Billy loses his composure, as the pell-mell jerky rhythms, repetitions, confusions, and broken syntax indicate. The stroke Billy later suffers, when Pat Garrett lugs him unshaded across the desert, shows even more graphically the insanity he develops in light of the sun's violent assaults, which he ordinarily associates with Garrett. That sun is so savage Billy compares it to "a flashy hawk" (26) and observes its formidable power in his phrase "on the edge of sun" (74), where the absence of an article (we read simply "sun," not "a" or "the" sun) nearly transforms the sun into a verb by creating a sense of its direct force. He always becomes disoriented when phenomena shed their inertness, shake off their solidity, begin to "melt" and to run. Those connections between urgent heat and light bring us to Billy's violent death when the room where he is shot fills with packets of little suns and his perceptions fragment into a series of "lovely perfect sun balls / breaking at each other click / click click click" (95).

One of Billy's lovers, Angela D, pulls him into the galvanic frenzy he experiences in that bright world, until he takes his ultimate revenge upon her in a macabre vaudevillian song (64). Terrified that "Her throat is a kitchen / red food and old heat," and remembering that in their wild sexual encounters she nearly paralyzes him, he tries to get back at Angie with his doggerel. His horror of being broken or engulfed by Angela D is only faintly masked in his jingling verses and grotesque humour. Billy's assumption of false innocence in these verses, culminating in his baby talk ("Her toes take your ribs / her fingers your mind / her turns a gorilla / to swallow you blind") only heightens our recognition of—he is The Kid—his childish impotence. Finally, when he's disintegrating in death, Billy pictures "oranges reeling across the room" (95), an image that picks up a previous episode between himself and Angie. In that meeting she closes in on him from the door and sweeps the bright orange peels, sun parings, off the bed (21). At the same time she lets loose the sun in his room when she "jams" up the sackcloth on the window. The "slide of sun" which she admits, like her own intrusions into his retreats, threatens to ignite Billy.

In contrast, Sallie Chisum, Billy's other though less obvious lover, shuts out the searing heat and light when he, like hundreds of other broken animals, comes trailing in from the desert, seeking refuge at her ranch. Opaque. Sallie and her husband, John, empty the lamps each morning "to avoid fire." More dramatically, Sallie has "had John build shutters for every door and window, every hole in the wall. So that at eleven in the morning all she did was close and lock them all until the house was silent and dark blue with sunless quiet" (33).

When Billy comes to recuperate at this *"little world in itself"* (30) after burning his legs, Sallie shuts out the day, creating a cool dark room for him where he's safe from the sun's abrasions, where he is able to develop into the self he's nearly lost. Heat discharging into her room. The peacefulness and slowing of time conveyed by the long, easy rhythms of the "Chisum" prose counterbalances the taut, nervous speed of Billy's poems when he's under stress. (It's interesting to note the similarities between the quiet Chisum ranch and the other shelter Billy finds in a barn, where he also tries to rid himself of the heat, in this case a fever burning inside him.) Though Sallie also is erotic (and possibly in her own way an unwitting jailer), she acts as a maternal figure who nurses a defenceless Billy back to health, makes him whole, whereas Angie initiates him into a frenzied world where he goes to pieces. Derivatives of Western movies, they are both at the edge with him, but each of them offers her own response. Sallie protects Billy's precarious boundaries and maintains his sanity, Angie violates them and brings with her the sun's undoing.

2. *Photographer*

In visual terms, Sallie helps Billy to hold the lines he so badly wants in life. She strengthens the frames he tries to set on everything, so Billy can be reassured "the sun drops in perfect verticals" (72). Those upright lines embody Billy's attempts to fight off the long horizontal sky which threatens to swallow and crush him. Sallie's dim shelter seems to ensure that the sky fire won't get in. Ondaatje's terms for that protection are visual. Sallie's closed shutters and black room provide Billy with what amounts to a photographer's darkroom or, better: a camera whose shutter can be closed down to eliminate or at least reduce light.

The notion may at first seem strained, but when we remember Ondaatje's fascination with film and photography, it seems more likely.[3] Once we read through *Billy the Kid* with this hunch in mind we find much evidence to confirm it. As a matter of fact, Perry M. Nodelman, in his article "The Collected Photographs of Billy the Kid," has elaborated on the extensive and central role of "Billy's photographic objectivity" in Ondaatje's book.[4]

Photographic terms frequently emerge in Billy's mind as he sits tensely "on the edge of sun." We certainly can see his acute anxiety in the anaphoric structure of the poem I quoted earlier—the turns and returns on key expressions about his position: "I am," "If I," "watching," "looking," "waiting." On the lookout. We can also see Billy's edginess in his insistent noting of size and distance: there is "this 7 foot high doorway," "I am 4 feet inside the room," the sun is "three inches from my shoes," a man might come "on a three mile trip to here." He's trying to figure things out, to size up life, to seize it in the stability of known quantities. The importance Billy places on exact and frequent measurements marks his attempts to survey and to take hold of that room, to mark it off (doubly framed) as safely known and securely occupied, to take analgesic measures against life. But the quantitative manoeuvres are almost insignificant alongside the vast forces leaning against him, as we notice from the small and declining space he holds onto: it shrinks from a 7 foot doorway to a 4 foot buffer zone and then to a mere 3 inches, a cigarette's length, of shade.

Billy is so concerned about being caught by surprise that, like a photographer (or a director), he calculates actual lines of sight, meant to obliterate the appearance of certain images he'd rather not see:

> If I hold up my finger
> I blot out the horizon
> if I hold up my thumb
> I'd ignore a man who comes
> on a three mile trip to here (74)[5]

No wonder: Billy notices details with such intensity they become startlingly exaggerated in size:

> a world that's so precise
> every nail and cobweb
> has magnified itself to my presence (74)

To concentrate—to centre himself in this world so he can retard diffusion: ego-centric. These responses are remarkable, not only because they show extraordinary acuity in Billy's sense, but also for the photographer's eye they bring to focus.[6] First the nails and cobwebs "magnified . . . to my presence," as if in his agitated state Billy were a special close-up lens enlarging the details. In those perceptions he extracts objects from their usual sites and views the edited pieces in an expanded way, so that they take on a strange hugeness, startlingly realigned. Then the long shot, rendering the imminent figures, should they appear, small with the long look he's taking through the door, blocking and blacking them out.

The whole poem climbs out of an overwhelming visual sense (though we also find strong tactile and auditory images in other Billy poems). Billy's photographic stance shows in other parts of the "doorway" poem when, fearing exposure, he is "watching the white landscape in its frame" nightmarishly jump forward, when he notices "flies in their black path / like inverted stars," and when he is "looking out into pitch white / sky and grass overdeveloped to meaninglessness," the cool, serene, and receding greens eaten out of the image (74). What Billy notices here no unaided human eye could see. Only a camera lens can admit the simultaneous register of field and ground, particularly when foreground shade and background brilliance are so extreme, as they are here. So we read in *Coming Through Slaughter*, that under sunlight "There can be *either* the narrow dark focus of the eye *or* the crazy chaos of white."[7] Billy's human eye, adjusted to the interior dimness, couldn't sense the slugs of sunlight banging against him, but in this poem he characteristically does, using his camera eye to take on the impression. An illuminating connection: in *On Photography*, Susan Sontag mentions that early photography was called heliography, literally "sun-writing," reminiscent of the inscription Billy undergoes.[8]

Ondaatje knows exactly what he's doing. He's deliberately working with references to a camera view to show Billy's anxious and unremitting attempts to manage life and to extricate himself from it. That's why Billy speculates (longingly, I think) about blotting out the horizon and ignoring a man behind his controlled sight lines. That's also why he would prefer to find that "nothing breaks my vision" (74), and why, on the very next page, he says his every move "is planned by my eye" (75). Billy wants, more than anything, by his unblinking gaze, by transferral of purpose and intelligence to his body (his eye), to freeze action in a series of still photographs, or a series of shots approaching still photographs. In Billy's perhaps envious accusations about how "you" (we readers, I guess) might escape in "blackout" (72) there may be an expression of his own last-ditch tactics to fend off discomfitting, complex images by withdrawing into photographic darkrooms and negatives. In this book, then, photos do not figure as unmediated access to reality; rather, they serve as tactical interceptions of it.

That decided wish to hide within stills, empty screens (or, on occasion, diagrams) shows up early in the book:

> so if I had a newsman's brain I'd say
> well some morals are physical
> must be clear and open
> like diagram of watch or star
> one must eliminate much
> that is one turns when the bullet leaves you
> walk off see none of the thrashing
> the very eyes welling up like bad drains
> believing then the moral of newspapers or gun
> where bodies are mindless as paper flowers you dont feed
> or give to drink
> that is why I can watch the stomach of clocks
> shift their wheels and pins into each other
> and emerge living, for hours (11)

There's no doubt that Billy tries verbal strategies to ward off realities he'd rather not face: it's not "I" but "one" or "you" who does these things, not "I" who shoots the bullet but the "bullet [that] leaves you," responsibility grammatically foisted upon the wrong person, an anonymous person, or a mechanism. Billy dodges too behind a discursive snip—"that is"—whose explanatory power shoves open a little distance—and hides in "well" behind a ripple of . . . is it flippancy? studied weariness? irritated explanation?

It's also worth reminding ourselves about Billy's most obvious out—side-stepping behind black humour, a common defence in our time against a monstrous and brutal world. Though only partly successful, Billy's retreats into grim humour provide a spur-of-the-moment defence when he's caught off guard. Shocked, he watches Charlie Bowdre dying in agony; his words of horror come only after a long numb silence registered by a huge hole—a blank—that takes up much of the page:

> Jesus I never knew that did you
> the nerves shot out
> the liver running around there
> like a headless hen jerking
> brown all over the yard
> seen that too at my aunt's
> never eaten hen since then (12)

The verbal throw-away is not a sign of callousness. It shows Billy's struggle to mask what he's seen, just as the absence of a grammatical subject in the penultimate line reveals his transparent attempt to remove himself from the frightening knowledge of his friend's death. Similar devices work in the section where he describes Gregory's death. Billy describes how he is leaving Gregory on the street

> when this chicken paddles out to him
> and as he was falling hops on his neck
> digs the beak into his throat
> straightens legs and heaves
> a red and blue vein out
>
> Meanwhile he fell
> and the chicken walked away
>
> still tugging at the vein
> till it was 12 yards long
> as if it held that body like a kite
> Gregory's last words being
>
> get away from me yer stupid chicken (15)

The demonstrative pronouns and definite articles create a distancing, impersonalizing, and comical effect ("*this* chicken," "*the* beak," "*that* body"), but so does the ridiculous distortion of normal movement ("chicken paddles out") and normal proportion (a 12 yard vein?). So does the farcical "yer," and the impossible simile with its outrageous hints of innocence, however faint, in the comparison of the body to a kite. The last line is held up as we let the previous one sink in, as we await across the stanza for culmination of the poem, some fitting completion of the line that prepares us for what Gregory has to say. Surely a matter of some import, this, a discourse whose conventions ask of us and promise to us words of consequence— thoughtful, sober, revealing, confessional. Gregory, his life leaking into the dust, his last words being . . . what? The anticlimax, travesty of the solemn, propels our understanding into new realms, smashes any vestige of pain like an egg on a wall. Who can feel for Gregory once Billy in mockery of the Western, whose unwilling character he is, has sabotaged the genre by turning the gunfighter's ritual death into a joke? The passive voice with which Billy begins this monologue ("After shooting Gregory / this is what happened") works in a similar way to minimize his own blame and awareness. The devices form what is meant to be a verbal narcotic: 'these things just happened, rather comically, and they don't have much of anything to do with me.'

Billy's verbal sleights invite our solidarity by creating a sense that 'we're in this together.' He has worked the simple present— "paddles," "straightens," "heaves"—into the anecdote with the result of situating it outside the simple past which is customary to literary narrative. Billy's present tense helps to enroll the account within the category of joke or confidence. His keen sense of audience strengthens that impact. The demonstrative pronouns and the definite articles pointedly direct our gaze. They assume we share the same world, the same values, the same understanding: oh yeah, *this* body; sure, *this* chicken. A joke, right? The method is oral and citational. It overtly appeals to listeners and speaks of what evidently is known and agreed upon in a set of sentences already in place. As givens or common knowledge, those things Billy enumerates seem familiar and beyond dispute. Placed into the role of chum by Billy's conviviality—"when this chicken"—as though he were leaning over and taking us into his trust, we are asked to be old habitués, intimates from a way back. And as buddies, brothers-in-arms, we can easily forget what Billy has done, forgive him his good-humoured escapades.

More immediate to my argument: the newsman's mind and the newspaper photo Billy mentions earlier represent the obliviousness he so badly wants. When Billy's thrashing victims are caught in a journalist's snap-shots they become reduced to "mindless flowers" on the page of newsprint. They are shaved clean of their real-life depth and agony, which is inescapably expressed in the jerking eyes of their actual bodies—eyes that won't stand still, stricken lives that in their furnace heat flail and jump past him. Overrun by those scenes with their spectre of diffusion, Billy would like to turn life into a series of safe stills; he'd "eliminate much," "turn his back on" the excruciating suffering. He must count on the conditional—would, could—look to the future. So, when Angela D comes into his room, lets in the heavy sun, and closes in on Billy with the electricity crackling inside her, he reacts with a physical catatonia rendered in appropriately photographic words: "I am very still / I take in all the angles of the room" (21).

Above all, in his frame of mind Billy doesn't want to see things changed or de-formed because when that happens his eyes start "burning from the pain of change" (68). His ceremonies of control are meant to ensure that the future will be a predictable copy of the past. Intact. His utter terror at seeing gasping people "collapsed" in their dying (10) therefore leads him immediately into attempted denial: first of all in his abrupt statement "I told no one" (10). That numb sentence brings to an emphatic halt the rush of words that describe his vivid memory of numerous deaths:

> Sometimes a normal forehead in front of me leaked
> brain gasses. Once a nose clogged right before me, a
> lock of skin formed over the nostrils, and the shocked

face had to start breathing through mouth, but then the
mustache bound itself in the lower teeth and he began
to gasp loud the hah! hah! going strong—churned onto
the floor, collapsed out, seeming in the end to be
breathing out of his eye—tiny needle jets of air reaching
into the throat. I told no one. (10)

Billy then moves on in the following poem to the newsman's
brain and his own love of unchanging machinery, as if he were
trying to put off the frightening images swarming around him.
Barely hanging on, deeply conservative.

His love of machines figures in his admiring description of
railway yards, the train's couplings and levers removing the in-
tricacies of organic life in their abstracted shapes, their singular-
ly pure forms. Perfectly repetitive, invariably there. As always.
In all ways the same. Mechanisms to rob people of their animal
properties, animals of their animation. Creatures of their visible
pain. So Billy can distill life, still his fears:

> I have seen pictures of great stars,
> drawings which show them straining to the centre
> that would explode their white
> if temperature and the speed they moved at
> shifted one degree.
>
> Or in the East have seen
> the dark grey yards where trains are fitted
> and the clean speed of machines
> that make machines, their
> red golden pouring which when cooled
> mists out to rust or grey.
>
> The beautiful machines pivoting on themselves
> sealing and fusing to others
> and men throwing levers like coins at them.
> And there is there the same stress as with stars,
> the one altered move that will make them maniac. (41)

In the train world, all the separate parts are "fitted," speed is "clean," and "The beautiful machines [are] pivoting on themselves / sealing and fusing to others," strangely reminiscent of Billy's coupling with Angela. Billy finds some composure in these thoughts, hoping that this integrated and immobilized world, at least, will not break up, will guarantee his immunity. Bodies may be collapsing,[9] but trains are "fusing." Yet, he can't count on even this possibility. Like the stars that would explode if "shifted one degree" (in space as well as in temperature), even the trains are not exempt from "the one altered move that will make them maniac."

Here, too, in this poem about stars and trains, we find more references to photography. In what for Billy are unusually lyrical words, the molten ore (reminiscent of the angry red weather and the red "rat fyt" that boil over in his brain) "mists out to rust or grey." Out of the aggressive orange and reds, into a clockwork gray. By itself this line couldn't begin to carry my argument but, seen as one in a whole range of related words, it can be viewed as an oblique reference to the muted sepia prints common in Billy's day; and common in the grays, dark blues, faint browns, silvers, and whites blooming in Sallie Chisum's house, with its granular textures and soothing colours suggestive of pictures taken under low light with a fast film and the lens (like Huffman's) wide open. Undoubtedly Billy would find peace in transforming the hot reds into quiet darker shades that are less volatile. To put the case in photographic terms, we might consider his negotiations as turning colour into absence of colour (as in black and white photography), colour into only the semblance of its colour (as in monochromatic prints), or glaring colour into softened colour (as in sepia prints). It may be worth remembering what Ondaatje surely knows—that photography in Billy's time had developed no great capacity for accommodating colour.

Billy thinks of his visual extractions as some form of near-magical possession to control powers outside himself that keep threatening to get out of hand. He is almost primitive in his hope of appropriating, if not actually propitiating, those powers. In doing so, he is only insisting on a stance which, according to Susan Sontag, we bring to photography in the twentieth century:

> Our irrepressible feeling that the photographic process is something magical has a genuine basis. No one takes an easel painting to be in any sense co-substantial with its subject; it only represents or refers. But a photograph is not only like its subject, an homage to the subject. It is *part of, an extension of that subject; and a potent means of acquiring it, of gaining control over it.* (my emphasis)[10]

I am suggesting, therefore, Billy's photographic excisions are not cherished in any sentimental way, but they may serve him as talismans.[11]

Finally, Billy shows little capacity for denial of any kind. Wanting to black out, to become as negative as possible, he desperately struggles to get the world into alignment and to keep it there. But he can't. Even Sallie Chisum ("My picture") keeps getting out of focus, as she does in Billy's delirious view of her (trailing into that wonderful "only I didn't . . ." pinned onto the tail of the following passage):

> Sallie approaching from the far end of the room like
> some ghost. I didn't know who it was. . . . Me
> screaming stop stop STOP THERE you're going to *fall* on
> me! My picture now sliding so she with her tray and
> her lamp jerked up to the ceiling and floated down
> calm again and continued forward crushing me against
> the wall only I didnt feel anything yet. (34)

The intractability of life runs throughout *Billy the Kid* in consistently visual terms.[12]

3. Cinema

More to the point, Billy's double focusing comes right out of cinema or, as we tellingly say, the movies. In Ondaatje's book cinema provides a fitting version of a mobile world that cannot be isolated and edited into stills, that resists Billy's steps to solidify motion, to turn events into nouns. In an essay called "Rhetoric of the Image," Roland Barthes argues that "the distinction between film and photograph is not a simple difference of degree but a radical opposition. Film can no longer be seen as animated photographs: the *having-been-there* [of the photograph] gives way before a *being-there* of the thing [in film]." The photograph eludes history by presenting "the always stupefying evidence of *this is how it was*, giving us, by a precious miracle, a reality from which we are sheltered."[13] In one sense photographs exist in space, movies in time—time which Billy has tried to escape and into which he ultimately is catapulted. We return to *Billy the Kid*, then, to remember the rat "reeling" off a panic-stricken Billy and the oranges "reeling" across the room as the redness breaks up Billy in death. When the "real" world goes "reeling" past and comes "reeling" in, the photographic eye loses its freeze on life, life loosens—a nut in solvent. Billy's stills never offer much of a hold; at best they provide a temporary and tenuous stay. In his flat takes Billy wants to deny what is out there but can't because that wheeling, often brutal, existence powers in upon him. Its predominance is facilitated by Billy's susceptibility—here on the edge "with the range for everything" (72), trying to preserve an impossible situation. So savage is that world that Billy's response proves to be inadequate. It is also far too simple an answer to a complex, shifting world, no more than a cliché—the French term for a trite expression *and* a photographic negative.

It is therefore necessary to qualify my earlier statement about Billy's photographic posture. In a number of his interior monologues he actually assumes the position of a *movie* camera, but he uses it in the hope of avoiding the images erupting around him.[14] So he swivels away from Angela's frantic sexuality to take in the angles of the room, in effect panning the corners of the room as a movie camera would, though in the shooting he hopes to displace Angela's galvanic presence with the safety of geometric shapes. By the same token, as he sits near the doorway in the poem we earlier considered, he is not exactly shooting photos.

It would be more accurate to say that metaphorically he runs film footage behind his lens, filming a landscape devoid of images but on the verge of filling up with them, its very emptiness (plus the conventions of the Western) drawing our attention to presences lurking just off camera. In the "doorway" poem the vast horizon looms above Billy, ready to suck something or someone into its emptiness. Billy looks for some intrusion, sensing that something is there, mysterious and powerful, just off screen, about to press into the vacuum. Billy, in a weak position below the frame, is most afraid of what he can't see—what is out of sight but not out of mind. The minimal movement in the scene guarantees that the slightest flicker in it will become explosively magnified. So does the almost interminable waiting built into the description. The scene can be taken in within a split second by the eye, but the way Billy sets it down inexorably emphasizes time, heightening the sense of anxiety to an almost unbearable degree: "what will happen next?" "will it never end?" The prolonged absence of motion in nearly empty screens creates an eerie effect that approaches the nature of photographic prints. But not quite: we *know* the screen will *some*time be smudged by movement.

Billy has always wanted to arrest objects on a two-dimensional plane in order to remove depth of field and motion, alarming dimensions which both exist in time. Outside of time or motion there would be no suffering or experience of suffering. In movies time catches up with Billy; he must pass through it. It is this persistent cinematic pressure, including its technical depth or range, that defeats Billy's strategy of visual reduction.

As soon as the images pass through time—that is, whenever they become cinematic—Billy's already weak position collapses and he's forced out of hiding. In the following piece, where we get a critical parallel to reversed film footage (the sequence of lines exactly reverses itself between the two stanzas), we discover how shaken Billy becomes when the world impinges upon his provisional immunity:

> His stomach was warm
> remembered this when I put my hand into
> a pot of luke warm tea to wash it out
> dragging out the stomach to get the bullet
> he wanted to see when taking tea
> with Sallie Chisum in Paris Texas
>
> With Sallie Chisum in Paris Texas
> he wanted to see when taking tea
> dragging out the stomach to get the bullet
> a pot of luke warm tea to wash it out
> remembered this when I put my hand into
> his stomach was warm (27)

The chiasmic passage shows how possessed Billy has become by the memory of digging out a bullet. The inversion further heightens the sense of trauma when, the syntax thrown out to where in the penultimate line the swing stops and holds for a breath at "into," it returns the poem to its point of origin, reminding us in stark finality that "his stomach was warm." Coming in the closing and framing line, these words gain special emphasis and turn our consideration to the source of Billy's horror—his direct, visceral realization of death, and the degree to which heat can set it off. At the same time, the sequence of lines in the second stanza undermines the more normal syntax and rational discourse of the first. The broken lines derive from a growing confusion and fear that break out in Billy's mind after he has lost his customary visual distance and made a tactile association in the first place, a discovery made all the more startling by Ondaatje's juxtaposition of the brutal act with the domestic innocence of removing a tea bag.

The most obvious and sustained equivalents of cinematic action in the book occur in the broken sequence that depicts Garrett closing in on Billy. Those chunks read like directors' scripts or descriptions of movie scenes.[15] The following section

presents the verbal equivalent of a slow-motion rerun of a movie
clip (the emphatic visual vocabulary and the anomalous note on
the camera's position reveal how cinematically the scenes are
rendered; the exaggerated slowness of Garrett's approach and
the almost intolerable duration of the repeated "footage"
register Billy's oppressive sense of threat):

> Down the street was a dog. Some mut spaniel, black
> and white. One dog, Garrett and two friends, stud
> looking, came down the street to the house, to me.
>
> Again.
>
> Down the street was a dog. Some mut spaniel, black
> and white. One dog, Garrett and two friends came
> down the street to the house, to me.
>
> Garrett takes off his hat and leaves it outside the door.
> The others laugh. Garrett smiles, pokes his gun towards
> the door. The others melt and surround.
> All this I would have seen if I was on the roof looking.
> (46)

The surprising last line shows us that, though we thought
otherwise, we have not been inside Billy's head for all of this
clip. The revelation (how can Billy know what he doesn't know,
be privileged with two visions?) is there as part of Ondaatje's
brand of postmodernism, just as that same aesthetics allows him
to introduce his own contemporaries, bp Nichol and The Four
Horsemen, into a fabricated 1881 interview later in the book (84).
But there are other internal reasons for overturning our expectations: as the cinematic world moves in on Billy's world of still
photographs or stable movie shots, he begins to lose control. As
a matter of fact, Billy is able to shoot his still or empty film only
when he withdraws into his silent interior monologues, where
he himself can lop off time, depth, and sound that come to him
in the shifting images and buzzing sound track of the movie
playing around him. In the narrative and dramatic sections of
the poem, including the tight film scripts—all taking place in

time—Billy is never in charge. Those events occur outside of Billy and beyond his control. As the book goes on, the film scripts increase in frequency and intensity and they crowd Billy more out of the picture. In the 'roof-top' scene Billy records the action as if he were in a high camera tilted down onto the action and panning with it. The camera's superior position, detached above the men, suggests that Billy faces unavoidable forces, while, by following the action, it creates a sense that we are on the verge of discovery. As the overseeing camera leads us, ominously, heavily, to a Billy riveted to the spot, we realize he's closer than ever to a violent death. Once, when he had some control in his life, he operated like a low stationary camera directed at and recording an almost static world. Now the world has become animated and impinging, and the camera, no longer quite his, begins to rise and tilt and pivot after him.

The clips virtually take over the book as we move closer to Billy's death, though Billy still figures marginally in most of the scenes until the end: he is the central consciousness in the take of Garrett lying in wait for him on Maxwell's bed (90); he submerges into the third-person while an unidentified character sets up a long script (92-3); then he reemerges briefly as a silent but implied viewer in the third-person account of his own death (94). The steady erosion of Billy's verbal and visual control in the dramatic scenes indicates his approaching death, which comes, as it must, in a fragmentary world. Only in Billy's dying does his interior monologue, the place for his still photos, return, but only to record Billy's lost hold on a life broken away from him and filmed in a movie camera. The first scene about Billy finding Pat Garrett in Maxwell's bed begins with the directions of a movie script: "Sound up" (90). An intensely amplified sound then dominates the poem, including "the burning hum of flies," a frequent symbol of Billy's high tension—and reminiscent of the caged birds' "brooding whirr of noise" and "steady hum" at the Chisums (36, 37); and of Billy's own barely controlled humming (a dynamo?) as he rides under heat:

MMMMMMMM mm thinking
moving across the world on horses
body split at the edge of their necks
neck sweat eating at my jeans (11)

Now, as the cinematic world takes over, Billy responds with his *ear* (before, always, it has been his *eye*), hearing each straw blade "loud in its clear flick against another," the heat "crack at the glass," Garrett's serpentine breathing "hisssssssssss ssssssssssssssss" (90), sound track overriding the silence of Billy's customary stance. The eye, with the distance it keeps, succumbing to the ear, to the greater nearness it demands—sounds shoving the outside close to him. Sounds that break in upon his interior meditations, countering Billy's spatialization of time inside silent capsules. Impelled to speech—"saying stop jeesus jesus jesus JESUS" (73). The responsibility and the danger of it: acknowledging other, entering time. To be of and in the world, where nerves brush. Once afraid to utter a sound, Billy is forced to "outer" himself, puts himself out in the open where he is vulnerable. Driven out of his lyric intervals, he now hears and articulates at the joints, and joins (at great risk) the outside world.

Then, further signs of impinging, Billy is thrown into narrative. Until now he has hidden, consistently, in lyric. He has sought lacunae in the story, sought to enlarge them. But his attempts to shrug off the rain of time no longer work. He is forced out of inner silence into sound, into narrative. Pried out of his privileged position. There's the long narrative section (92-3) summarizing his final minutes. It opens with an emphatically visual account of the action. The passage reads much like a director's script, especially in its insistent phrase "well and buckets centre."

Then, in the last scene before Billy's own final monologue, we get six to eight different camera shots in rapid-fire succession, not one of them controlled by Billy:

OUTSIDE
the outline of houses

> Garrett running from a door
> —all seen sliding round
> the screen of a horse's eye
>
> NOW dead centre in the square is Garrett with Poe
> —hands in back pockets—argues, nodding his head
> and then ALL TURNING as the naked arm, the arm from
> the body, breaks through the window. The window—
> what remains between the splits—reflecting all the
> moving too.
>
> Guiterrez goes to hold the arm but it is manic, breaks
> her second finger. His veins that controlled triggers—
> now tearing all they touch. (94)

As Pat Garrett takes over the visual space, he in Billy's pun stands "dead centre" in it. Just before that point, we get a running Garrett as he is seen "sliding round / the screen of a horse's eye." The eye acts as a fish-eye lens, which grossly exaggerates the lines at the edge of the image. Those bulges would imply that Billy is losing his eye-hold and that Garrett is forcing his way into Billy's territory, defined as usual by the verticals of his doors and windows. The extreme wide-angle lens grotesquely warps the images where, in Billy's peripheral vision, they were at the best of times unresolved or dissolving. The very short lens speeds up the sense of Pat's movement toward the (Billy's) camera because of the effect of its focal length. The shots show how fully Garrett dominates Billy, particularly when we remember that earlier, when Billy controlled the camera, he evidently was seeing through a telephoto lens, which minimizes forward movement because of its greater depth of field.

By the time we get to Billy's death, it's clear, the use of the camera has changed radically. In the long "doorway" scene, where Billy enjoys as much security as he ever finds, there is a fixed camera, controlled by Billy, in a long-drawn scan over a large and empty space, and using a long focal length. That shooting registers Billy's attempts to inform and protect himself. As his world disintegrates, we get many shots that step up the tempo. And we get cameras, some of them moving, all of them recording movement, all of them shooting at close range, and all out of Billy's hands. Once Billy's lines distend and his frames break apart, he crashes out through the window, at once trapped by the tightly framed image of himself in the window, and driven out of his fortified position, finally out of his mind, and into a street of sharded images.

As he lies dying (95), the camera returns momentarily into his hands and we see, looking up from his position on the floor, "Garrett's jaw and stomach" filling the screen.[16] The extreme low tilt shot dramatizes Billy's impotence. When the images click and lurch past, we get the verbal equivalent of a spinning, hand-held camera shot. In its jerky turning, Billy's subjective camera records the frantic instability and vulnerability he feels now that he's blown out of his sanctuary.

In the confused release that accompanies his death Billy goes through his earlier prophetic dream where Pat Garrett figured as a "blurred" star (73), an image that connects with the great stars on the verge of exploding and that indicates a loss of the clear focus that in Billy's past has established the world as photograph or empty screen. Billy's negations have always been precisely shot, rather than softly focused, as we might have suspected they would be, because often he wants to keep his eye on things, preferring on such occasions vigilance to blindness. He is in such a nervous state and is so preoccupied with what he might find that he can't avoid seeing with a razor clarity.

In the end Billy becomes unbalanced, goes over the edge, and as his arm breaks through the window it twitches in a "manic" way (94). Radically decentered. He has taken the crucial step, "the one altered move" that would make things "maniac" (41). Eccentric. Like Tom O'Folliard (7) and Charlie Bowdre (22) before him, Billy dies violently at the very edge of the frames— that dangerous, terrifying interface where Garrett cold-bloodedly kills them. Billy fails spectacularly in his bid as door man, but there's a fine irony about the door man in *Billy the Kid*. In one short, seemingly irrelevant passage (the book parodies its own solemnities and the ceremonies of the Western) we discover Frank James, who has ended up guarding the door to a Los Angeles movie theatre:

> After the amnesty he
> was given, Frank had many jobs. When Jim's grandfather
> met him, he was the doorman at the Fresco Theatre.
> GET YOUR TICKET TORN UP BY FRANK JAMES the poster
> said, and people came for that rather than the film. Frank
> would say, 'Thanks for coming, go on in'. (24)

Frank James's pathetic alcoholism and his reduction from the status of true Western hero to movie pimp, shadow of his old self guarding the wrong doors, hints at the future Billy would have faced if, obverse of legend, he had held the door.[17]

4. Coda

We can schematize a set of binaries running through the book. These polarities represent the distance Billy is forced to travel by the time the book ends.

space (static)	time (dynamic)
eye	ear
noun	verb
private (inner)	public (outer)
lyric (meditation)	narrative (action)
photo	cinema
centered	decentered
cool	hot
dark	bright

Although by my reading Garrett enjoys no heroic stature, he does operate in the very world Billy needs to face. That Garrett moves through that world largely undisturbed by human suffering is, of course, no credit to him.

5. Moderns

In the end Garrett kills Billy, but not because Garrett is more venturesome or any more flexible. On the contrary, the law man, Garrett, "gets" Billy because he is far more successful than Billy ever could be at denying life through resorts to engineered responses. Though Billy must fight to subdue his frenzy, Garrett's imposition is so total he becomes a consummate murderer in the book. He casually shoots his old friends, then without a twinge watches them die in agony. An "academic murderer" with "the mind of a doctor," he organizes schedules, develops "the ability to kill someone on the street walk back and finish a joke," and fears flowers because "they grew so slowly that he couldnt tell what they planned to do" (28). Garrett brings the same analytical, clinical mind to his hobby of taxidermy, surgically preparing dead specimens "with a rubber glove in his right hand" (88). In every respect, as killer and collector, he acts as a right-handed, right-minded man of death, in no way bringing the kind of jangled nerves that the irrational, left-handed Billy does to their world of violence. Garrett complains, in modernist fashion, about the seductive qualities of Billy's imagination, "which was usually pointless and never in control" (43). In the end, as earlier (64-71) he broke up the idyllic life at the Chisum ranch with his serpentine presence, he takes on sinister overtones when his "precise but forced" (90) breathing reminds us of a snake lying in wait for Billy:

> And then that breathing, not Maxwell's but *the other's*.
> The breathing precise but forced into quiet but regular
> streams. Think of the dark air going up through the
> nose, down to the stomach rolling around on itself, and
> then up and out like a fountain spilling through his
> teeth hissssssssssss sssssssssssssssss (90)

Besides referring to Garrett's hissing, the last 'word' acts to stretch out his presence by insisting on Garrett's state of possessing: it spells "his" too, the dental fricative picking up an extra buzz as it is sounded.

Garrett is, above all, a hero of narrative. Billy, who has sought to survive inside lyric monologue, proves no match for Garrett once he's bounced into the story line. Supremely triumphant on the paradigmatic axis, Billy is no match for Garrett on the syntagmatic chain where time happens. There Garrett operates unreflectingly, seemingly unaffected by time, having no need to resist it: Garrett as pure story, exterior life. A man with no inner existence, without lyric, he knows motion without emotion. The perfect hero of adventure stories—always moving but never moved. Proaretic. As Billy's interior monologues begin to collapse, the once scattered and forestalled narrative moves into place, enlarges its role. Garrett, the law man and the story man, lays claim to the book, and as he takes over, makes certain kinds of claims on Billy and on the reader as well. We are thrown out of Billy's mind (he out of his mind) into exterior action and into the larger structures that Garrett authors. Garrett's story. Billy's death.[18]

Livingstone, another bizarre character, operates in much the same terms. He breeds a freak strain out of "originally beautiful" spaniels, brings the same "perverse logic" to the defilement of life: "Their eyes bulged like marbles; some were blind, their eyes had split" (61). Fencing up the dogs, he turns them into sterile monsters—the ultimate desecration of nature, shaped by a mind which, fearing and loathing process, quite deliberately and systematically seeks to dominate, even to eradicate it. In John Chisum's unnerving understatement, Livingstone "seemed a pretty sane guy" but "had been mad apparently" (60). Because, like Garrett, Livingstone acts "clinically and scientifically" (61)—he is a living stone—he ironically reminds us of a famous doctor with the same name. The two eminently rational "doctors" in the book both are monstrous killers, in contrast to the maternal Sallie Chisum who nurses Billy and other broken creatures back to life.[19]

In important ways Livingstone and Garrett only succeed in doing what Billy always wants to do: they anaesthetize themselves to life. Perfect though extreme modernists, they manage to subvert and convert life, in some overarching version of meaning, to the point of destroying it. They are so prepared to maintain overriding structures, they prove to be insane in any sense that matters. As we read in the hysterical language (probably, though not necessarily, Billy's) that finishes the long passage about Garrett's manoeuvres through life, he is "a sane assassin sane assassin sane assassin sane assassin sane assassin sane" (29). Readers have noticed that when the words run together in rapid fusion, and we suppose they could in Billy's quaver, the ends of the nouns begin to couple with the beginnings of the adjectives so that a new word, "in-sane" (and possibly, to the eye, another expression "ass in"), begins to emerge.

Garrett *is* disturbing in his utter insensitivity to life. In still more general terms Garrett is too rigid. As a result, he fails artistically as well as morally. *The Collected Works of Billy the Kid* invites us to see that the world is postmodern—fluid, unpredictable, and ultimately uncontrollable (Livingstone is eaten by his twisted creations) or wrongly controlled (Garrett gains power by becoming the greatest human casualty in the entire book). The book also presents Garrett and Livingstone to us as unforgettable examples of excessively modernist responses to life—the belief that the world is chaotic and that we'd better impose some order, some superstructure, upon it, come what may. Billy gets caught between those two positions, wanting more than anything to be a modernist, but finally not being able to because Ondaatje's world reveals itself to be essentially postmodern. When Billy opts for the snapshot or the empty or static shot, he tries to assume a modernist posture in a postmodern world which, in the basic codes of the text, asserts itself in cinematic forms. Would-be modernist, he wants to act as a still camera eye in a postmodern world that is chimerical— always out of control.

Still, it would be wrong to argue that the camera shot is necessarily an assault on life or a rejection of it. L.A. Huffman, the Western photographer whose words we read as *Billy the Kid* opens, talks about how he has used his camera:

> I send you a picture of Billy made with the Perry
> shutter *as quick as it can be worked.* . . . I am making daily
> experiments now and find I am able to take passing
> horses at a lively trot square across the line of fire—bits
> of snow in the air—spokes *well defined—some blur* on top
> of wheel but *sharp in the main*—men walking are no
> trick—I will send you proofs sometime. I shall show
> you what can be done from the saddle without ground
> glass or tripod—please notice when you get the
> specimens that they were made *with the lens wide open*
> and many of the best exposed when my horse was *in
> motion.* (5, my emphases)

Despite the scattered words of detachment or aggression in
Huffman's account ("the line of fire," "making . . . experiments,"
"proofs," and "specimens")—words that in this context
Ondaatje may have found amusing, if not innocent—Huffman
brings the essential Ondaatje virtues to his art: a shutter that he
sets "quick as it can be worked" and a lens that he runs "wide
open." It's at least as important that he takes photographs of
moving subjects and that he does so when he is himself "in motion." Open, quick, mobile—that's the kind of postmodern sensibility you bring to life and art. A touch of braggadocio—"I shall
show you what can be done"—further links Huffman to
Ondaatje who in his own act of bravado has announced in sub-
title that he is sending us "Left Handed Poems." Look ma, no
hands! Identifying with Huffman and his promise to send us a
picture of Billy, Ondaatje leaves the frame above Huffman's
statement empty (perhaps because a picture could not do Billy
justice, would in its very specificity fix him too definitively in a
shape), then sends us a parody of Billy's picture at the end of the
book (more parody), a tiny copy of Ondaatje himself as a seven-
year-old dressed in cowboy costume. Huffman brings the right
methods, then. He also comes through with the best results: "bits
of snow in the air—spokes well defined—some blur on top of
wheel but sharp in the main."

6. Postmodern World

We get a glimpse of a world in motion where nothing is settled, where things only approach clarity.

This passage in *Billy the Kid* immediately brings to mind another Ondaatje poem " 'The gate in his head' " (*RJ*, 62), which, as Sam Solecki has suggested, stands at the centre of Ondaatje's poetics.[20] In that poem, which comes out of the same period as *Billy the Kid*, Ondaatje writes of wanting "not clarity but the sense of shift / a few lines, the tracks of thought," not foreplanning but discovery. Victor Coleman, for whom the poem is written and after whom it is titled, has sent his friend, Michael Ondaatje, a letter

> with a blurred photograph of a gull.
> Caught vision. The stunning white bird
> an unclear stir.
>
> And that is all this writing should be then.
> The beautiful formed things caught at the wrong moment
> so they are shapeless, awkward
> moving to the clear. (*RJ*, 62)

Art in the blurred glimpse, the artist scanning the shifting world for flashes of beauty, traces of life, surrendering to "the immaculate moment [that] is now" (*RJ*, 55).[21] So that the rational mind succumbs to the body's knowledge, just as Billy on one rare occasion lapses out of intransigence into one of those unwilled uncapturable moments:

> and my fingers touch
> this soft blue paper notebook
> control a pencil that shifts up and sideways
> mapping my thinking going its own way
> like light wet glasses drifting on polished wood. (72)

In Solecki's words, "the ultimate poem for Ondaatje is the one which transforms reality into poetry without 'crucifying' it."[22]

The modernist, Wallace Stevens, won't give things enough room when he appears in another Ondaatje poem, "his head making his hand / move where he wanted / and he saw his hand was saying / the mind is never finished, no, never" (*RJ*, 21), whereas in Billy's poem the *fingers* do the talking. In yet another Ondaatje poem Stevens offers his own "fences" to life's "chaos" and would clean up and shave the hairiness of life in his "murderer's" pose (*RJ*, 61).[23] In "Spider Blues" a spider symbolizes the modernist artist: here the "finicky" spider with its "classic" control "thinks a path" before it crosses it (*RJ*, 63), "murderous" in its art, and defied only by fly, which says in proper (playful) postmodern fashion

> no I choose who I die with
> you spider poets are all the same
> you in your close vanity of making,
> you minor drag, your saliva stars always
> soaking up the liquid from our atmosphere.
> And the spider in his loathing
> crucifies his victims in his spit
> making them the art he cannot be. (*RJ*, 64)[24]

The fly buzzes throughout *Billy the Kid*, everywhere a sign of life:

> nothing breaks my [fixed] vision
> but flies in their black path
> like inverted stars (74)

> catching flies with my left hand
> bringing the fist to my ear
> hearing the scream grey buzz
> as their legs cramp their
> heads with no air
> so eyes split and release

> open fingers
> the air and sun hit them like pollen
> sun flood drying them red

catching flies
angry weather in my head, too (58)

Sound up. Loud and vibrating in the room. My ears
picking up all the burning hum of flies letting go across
the room. (90)

Rat that fights and fits in Billy's head, that finally becomes Billy's
head—"smaller than a rat" (104) when he dies. Rat that
Ondaatje, "thinking of you," dishes up in his own poem "Rat
Jelly"—full of all the disgusting and stinking hair the modernist
Stevens would shave from his pure poems. Rat that in true
postmodern fashion will not clean up its act, will not sweep the
slate clean of all the shit and junk; rat with his "dirt thought we
want as guest / travelling mad within the poem," unquestionably, eminently, in "A bad taste" (*RJ*, 42-3). "Rat fyt" in the
postmodern Ondaatje brain. The dirty rat that won't fit politely
into the controlled poem, with its improvements on life, its well-
kept rooms, impositions of single-minded orders on a presumed
chaos. The modern poem with its agoraphobic withdrawal from
life, its authors wanting totality and certainty in art—cut out and
cut off from open ends. An art that Ondaatje detests, hating the
manipulation of his material or audience, preferring to let us in
and out of his world. In Billy's words we get the invitation: "Find
the beginning, the slight silver key to unlock it, to dig it out. Here
then is a maze to begin, be in" (20). Simply amazing. How's that
for starters?

------

1. Frank Davey and Stephen Scobie have pointed out that Ondaatje's
Billy is in some special way an artist. See Davey's excellent essay on Ondaatje
in *From There to Here: A Guide to English-Canadian Literature Since 1960* (Erin,
Ont.: Press Porcepic, 1974), pp. 222-7. Scobie's essay "Two Authors in Search
of a Character" appeared in *Canadian Literature*, No. 54 (Autumn 1972), 37-
55.

2. *The Collected Works of Billy the Kid: Left Handed Poems* (Toronto: Anansi, 1970), p. 74. All other references to the book will appear within the essay.

3. "The first time I went to a movie I knew my vision of paradise would be a cosmic movie-theatre," Ondaatje has confessed in an interview in *Manna: A Review of Contemporary Poetry*, No. 1 (March 1972), 22. That love immediately connects with his writing of *Billy the Kid*. Ondaatje says in the crucial 1975 interview with Sam Solecki, "with *Billy the Kid* I was trying to make the film I couldn't afford to shoot, in the form of a book." "An Interview with Michael Ondaatje," *Rune*, No. 2 (Spring 1975), 46.

4. *Canadian Literature*, No. 87 (Winter 1980), 70. The whole essay covers pp. 68-79. Though I agree with most of the examples in Nodelman's paper (I use several of them myself), and with his assertion that "Billy views things photographically himself to avoid emotional involvement with them" (p. 70) in a world that keeps moving (p. 73), I don't agree with him on three points. Nodelman argues that Billy is emotionally "dead," that he actually " 'fixes' " life, and that he does so out of "disgust" for things that move and change (p. 76). I argue that Billy is extremely sensitive, that he only tries to fix life but is unsuccessful in his attempts, and that he feels terror, not revulsion, at what he confronts.

5. This image is hardly new with Ondaatje. John G. Cawelti in Jack Nachbar, ed., *Focus on the Western* (Englewood Cliffs, New Jersey: Prentice Hall, 1974), p. 59, describes "that scene, beloved of Western directors, in which a rider appears like an infinitely small dot at the far end of a great empty horizon and then rides toward us across the intervening space."

6. Billy's visual skills are so finely tuned that he shows an exceptional awareness of eyes, often others', often animals', and often damaged. Here is an incomplete list of such references: "the eyes grew all over his body" (12), "eyes will / move in head like a rat" (38), "a yellow pearl of an eye cracked with veins glowed" (36), "a frozen bird's eye" (26), "the screen of a horse's eye" (94), "planned by my eye" (75), "eyes split and release" (58), "the [bird's] eyes were small and far" (14), "the very eyes welling up like bad drains" (11), dogs' "eyes bulged like marbles; some were blind, their eyes had split" (61).

7. (Toronto: Anansi, 1976), p. 68; my emphasis.

8. (New York: Farrar, Strauss and Giroux, 1977), p. 160. Louis D. Giannetti points out that surrealist filmmaker Jean Cocteau insisted he wrote with the "ink of light." *Understanding Movies*, 2nd ed. (Englewood Cliffs, N.J.: Prentice-Hall, 1976), p. 395. I am indebted to Giannetti for part of my argument on cinematic techniques later in this paper. I have also to a lesser extent used David Bordwell and Kristen Thompson, *Film Art: An*

Introduction (Reading, Mass.: Addison-Wesley, 1979), and Ross Huss and Norman Silverstein, *The Film Experience: Elements of Motion Picture Art* (New York: Delta, 1968).

9. Billy shows a constant awareness of broken bodies. He sees his friends mutilated before his eyes, each of them blown up or blown to pieces by Pat Garrett—their jaws shot off or their guts burst open. When their bodies leak and collapse, a stunned Billy seeks comfort in the thought that in an eviscerated world *some* stability may exist in death: "In the end the only thing that never changed, never became deformed, were animals" (10).

10. *On Photography*, p. 155.

11. Michel Foucault has written a fascinating study on the powers of surveillance: *Discipline & Punish: The Birth of the Prison*, trans. Alan Sheridan (New York: Random, 1979). Foucault's account offers startling parallels to Billy's geometries of control.

12. Ironically, my argument about photography doesn't take account of the actual photographs in *The Collected Works of Billy the Kid*—twelve altogether, if you count the "absent" photographs (on pages 5 and 19). Most of them convey an age long gone—log houses, cavalry officers, people in gingham, a floosy, those sorts of thing. What's especially interesting is the total absence of caption and photograph together. In the case of the "absent" photos we do get extended descriptions. The actual photos sit alone. Uncaptioned. For good reason. Captions would too surely capture the photographs (the words—caption, capture—come from the same root: to seize, take). They would insist on overly determined readings. Ondaatje wants an uncertainty, openings in the text that will allow the icons to float inside it, unweighted by subtitles that would invest them with fixed meaning (appalling thought in this "writerly" text).

Unanchored, they are free to attach themselves where they may. More accurately: where *we* may. We are left/required to make our own connections, knowing they can be only ours. Indeterminate.

13. *Image-Music-Text*, selected and translated by Stephen Heath (London: Fontana/Collins, 1977), pp. 44, 45.

14. There is a fine line between a static movie screen and a still photograph, as Ondaatje's own remark in the Solecki interview shows. Ondaatje explains how he got into a quarrel with a camera man working on one of his films: "he kept saying that the camera should be zooming or the film would be very dull." But Ondaatje wanted "that sense throughout the film that each shot would almost be a static photograph." *Rune*, 42.

15. Davey and Blott have discussed these qualities.

16. Rudolf Arnheim's observation about the relative size of tolerable images in a field is applicable here: "In order to be comfortably visible the relevant position of a visual field must be large enough to be sufficiently discernible in its detail [Billy watching over empty space] and small enough to fit into the field [Pat Garrett looming at the window when Billy dies]." *Visual Thinking* (Berkeley: University of California, 1969), p. 26.

17. For a different reading of *Billy the Kid* see Lynette Hunter, "Form and Energy in the Poetry of Michael Ondaatje," *Journal of Canadian Poetry*, 2, No. 1 (Winter 1978), 47-70.

18. Judith Owens has written a brilliant piece on narrative in the book, showing how it registers Billy's efforts and how it affects our page-by-page reading: " 'I Send You a Picture': Ondaatje's Portrait of Billy the Kid," *Studies in Canadian Literature*, 8, No. 1 (1983), 117-39. Owens argues Billy needs and welcomes narrative, but that he needs to trace out his *own* narrative.

19. Though Livingstone cold-bloodedly destroys the dogs, they ultimately resist by eating him. I take it that life cannot be totally denied and that it will assert itself, in horrible reprisals if necessary. In "Stuart's bird," a poem in *Rat Jelly* (Toronto: Coach House, 1973), p. 37, Ondaatje comically shows that life will have its vengeance once Stuart has "trod on a bird":

it thrashed at his ankles
climbed into the air
4 feet above him
and flung a ribbon, a parabola of shit
over the creek and Stuart

References to *Rat Jelly* will be in the essay from now on.

20. "Nets and Chaos: The Poetry of Michael Ondaatje," *Studies in Canadian Literature*, 2, No. 1 (Winter 1977), 36-48. I am indebted to this piece, though I don't put as much stock as Solecki does in Ondaatje's control.

21. In *On Photography*, p. 121, Sontag describes a remarkably similar view of photography in "Robert Frank's waiting for the moment of revealing disequilibrium, to catch reality off-guard, in what he calls the 'in-between moments.' "

22. "Nets and Chaos," 44.

23. Sam Solecki reads this poem very differently, finding Stevens much more attractive than I do. See his "Making and Destroying: Michael Ondaatje's *Coming Through Slaughter* and Extremist Art," *Essays on Canadian Writing*, No. 12 (Fall 1978), 31.

24. In the Solecki interview Ondaatje criticizes the spider mentality behind "the CBC kind of documentary which knows what it's going to say before the actual filming begins" (41). Ondaatje claims "I really don't plan

anything and this is what makes me very frightened while writing" (53) "on the border where . . . craft meets the accidental and the unconscious, as close as possible to the unconscious" (49). In this same interview Ondaatje makes it clear that he revises and edits a lot, but that for him the first go at his poems comes unpremeditated.